The Northwest Cottage Garden

Andrew Schulman *Photographs by* **Jacqueline Koch**

SASQUATCH BOOKS
SEATTLE

For Betsy and Dani, and for the indomitable spirit of Garbo,
who saw this book through in her last days.

Printed in Singapore by Star Standard Industries Pte Ltd.

Published by Sasquatch Books

Distributed by Publishers Group West

10 09 08 07 06 05 04   6 5 4 3 2 1

Cover design: Kate Basart

Cover photograph: Jacqueline Koch

Interior design: Stewart Williams

Interior photographs: Jacqueline Koch, except for photographs on pages 137 and 146, taken by Andrew Schulman

Author photograph: Cheri Pearl

Copy editor: Alice Copp Smith

Library of Congress Cataloging-In-Publication Data

Schulman, Andrew, 1964—
          The Northwest cottage garden / Andrew Schulman ; photographs by Jacqueline Koch.

p. cm.

Includes index.

ISBN 1-57061-363-X

Cottage gardens—Northwest, Pacific. 2. Cottage gardening—Northwest, Pacific. I. Koch, Jacqueline. II. Title.

SB454.3.C67S38 2004

635'.09795—dc22

                                   2003058976

Sasquatch Books

119 South Main Street, Suite 400

Seattle, WA 98104

(206) 467-4300

www.sasquatchbooks.com

books@sasquatchbooks.com

CONTENTS

INTRODUCTION
Something Old, Something New: *The Northwest Cottage Garden* vi

CHAPTER 1
Casual by Design: *The Character and History of the Cottage Garden* 1

CHAPTER 2
Layout: *The Hidden Order* 19

CHAPTER 3
Structures: *Making Yourself Comfortable* 31

CHAPTER 4
Furniture and Ornaments: *Accessorize It!* 67

CHAPTER 5
Planting Design: *It's Not Just Tossed Salad* 83

CHAPTER 6
Plants: *The Raw Materials* 111

CHAPTER 7
Plants With a Purpose: *The Special Agents* 155

CHAPTER 8
Maintaining Your Garden: *Preventive Medicine* 183

APPENDIX: CULTURAL NOTES FOR NORTHWEST COTTAGE
               GARDEN PLANTS 191

INDEX: 210

ACKNOWLEDGMENTS

Thanks first to Jacqueline Koch for her exquisite photographs. My thanks as well to those outstanding landscape designers, Robin Atkinson, James Bennett, and Steve Gold, for sharing so much of their work as this book was photographed and written.

A very special thank you goes to all of the talented gardeners who opened up their gardens for this book, particularly to Valerie Easton, Virginia Hand, Terry Hershey, Peggy Hoierman, Ann LeVasseur, Deborah Liming, Louise Luthy, Betty Ravenholt, Ken and Cathy Shiovitz, Megan Smith, and Brooke Thacker.

For their advice and support I thank Betsy Maurer, Shelley O'Clair, and Brooke and Perry Thacker. Without them *The Northwest Cottage Garden* would be far less rich. I am also grateful to Alice Copp Smith for her thorough and thoughtful editorial review.

Finally, my thanks to Gary Luke and Heidi Schuessler at Sasquatch Books for making this book happen, and to Stewart Williams for making it look so good.

Something Old, Something New:
The Northwest Cottage Garden

All across the Pacific Northwest, gated gardens with exuberant and colorful mixed plantings are appearing where only turf grass grew before. The appeal of these cottage gardens is easy to fathom. As our region grows more urban and our highways more congested, the relaxed and vivacious charm of a traditional English cottage garden offers a perfect antidote to our increasingly

rushed and harried lifestyle. At the same time, a well-tended cottage garden projects an image of abundance that reflects our great American dream of prosperity and plenty. The nostalgic quality of the cottage garden also lends a sense of history and tradition to a region that is still relatively young and recently settled. Let's not forget those wet and gloomy Northwest winters, either. What could be more welcome after six months of short, dark, rainy days than the vivid scents and colors of a cottage garden?

The cottage garden style is an old one, with a rich tradition, but it is still new to many of us in this region. To make the cottage garden our own, we need to reinvent it in terms that suit our Northwest lifestyle and environment. This means coordinating the cottage garden's layout and each of its physical components with local climate conditions, topography, and architecture. Yet most books on cottage gardening are by British authors, and are geared toward British gardeners and garden conditions. Though I have often heard it said that "anything grows in the

Pacific Northwest," and that our climate is "just like England's," neither statement is the least bit accurate. The Pacific Northwest is a singular environment, one that offers unique opportunities and challenges for those of us interested in the cottage garden style. Our cool and surprisingly dry summers are quite different from the English norm, and our lowland towns and cities experience far less snow in winter than do England's. Nowhere in Great Britain will you find the dramatic variations in elevation that prevail here in the Northwest, nor the enormous range of microclimates they create. While many British gardens grow on alkaline, limestone soils, gardeners in the Pacific Northwest often work with acid soils over glacial till, basalt, and granite. We live and garden in a special place, and we must respect its remarkable climate and geography when we design our cottage gardens.

Designing a successful cottage garden anywhere means blending all of the garden's various components into a coherent whole, a landscape composition that appears casual yet integrated, exuberant but not chaotic. In order to work comfortably within the cottage garden style, you will need to recognize its hallmarks and understand its origins. To build and plant a Northwest cottage garden, you will need to be familiar with the kinds of structures, furniture, decorative objects, and plants that make up a cottage garden, and with the way they are arranged. That is where this book can help. By the time you finish it, you should understand the cottage garden style and recognize its key components. You should be able to choose appropriate plants and structures, and arrange them in an inviting and informal manner. You will also learn how to keep your cottage garden healthy and well-tended through our region's seasonal cycle. Having learned this much, I hope you will be inspired to explore the cottage garden style, and feel confident about designing, planting, and maintaining a cottage garden of your own. As you develop your cottage garden, I hope you will come back to this book for ideas and inspiration.

CHAPTER ONE

Casual by Design:
The Character and History
of the Cottage Garden

Gardeners and designers toss the term "cottage garden" around quite freely nowadays. No wonder that even some of our more accomplished Pacific Northwest gardeners have trouble describing just what a cottage garden is! The cottage garden is actually a very distinct and easily recognized garden style that originated centuries ago in the towns and villages of rural England. Its hallmarks are a relaxed and simple layout, traditional materials, a mixture of ornamental and edible plants, and dense, colorful, informal plantings. A cottage per se is not a prerequisite, but cottage gardens are first and foremost home gardens, and are invariably associated with houses rather than commercial or industrial buildings. They are unpretentious, small-scale gardens that rely on grace and charm, rather than grandeur, for their impact. Everything about the true cottage garden is casual, looking as if the plants and structures had been thrown together without care. Please notice that I say "as if." The finest cottage gardens are casual *by design*, their informal air the product of considered forethought. You might say that such calculated ease is a contradiction in terms, or even a contrivance, but it is also the cottage garden's principal attraction.

How do you achieve this kind of calculated ease, you ask? You begin with an orderly, straightforward garden layout, one based upon your own needs and preferences but respectful of the land on which you build it. You define the spaces that make up your layout with simple, functional structures, such as fences, walls, gates, and walkways. You add a personal touch with garden furniture and decor, including anything from birdhouses and fountains to dining tables, benches, or sculpture. You then clothe your garden in rich, colorful, and varied plantings set out in relaxed, but harmonious, arrangements. In order to ensure your cottage garden's ultimate success, you will need to keep each of these elements modest and unimposing in its scale.

1

COTTAGE GARDEN SCALE

The cottage garden style is just as well suited to a small urban courtyard as to the farmhouse set on acreage. No matter whether small or large, though, the cottage garden should always feel cozy, homey, and somehow familiar. It must be comfortable and unimposing in scale. To achieve this intimacy of scale, you will need to keep all of the spaces, plantings, and objects within your cottage garden proportioned modestly and in relation to the human body. No cottage garden, not even the very largest, will include vast, empty spaces. Cottage gardens have no monumental structures, long reflecting pools, or large-scale statuary. Pomposity has no place in the cottage garden, and spaces that are in any way overwhelming or forbidding will ruin your garden's effect.

COTTAGE GARDEN LAYOUT

No aspect of the Northwest cottage garden is more critical to its overall comfort and utility than the basic layout—the arrangement of the spaces, passageways, structures, and planting areas within its boundaries. The cottage garden may surprise and delight visitors, but its layout will always be simple (even formulaic) and, above all, comfortable. Walkways in the cottage garden travel from point to point by the shortest path possible, curving only to avoid obstacles. Planting areas are simple shapes, laid out to facilitate maintenance rather than challenge the eye with intricate patterns. If the garden is situated in front of the house, the ground plan likely consists of little more

The layout of a cottage garden is usually simple and straightforward.

than a straight path from the street or sidewalk to the front door, dividing the garden into two roughly rectangular planted areas. The planted areas defined by this

2

main walk may or may not be symmetrical, depending upon the shape of the lot, the placement of the home, and the preferences of the gardener.

If the garden is large enough, there may be a second walkway, perpendicular to the main path, that further divides the garden into four sections. Casual as cottage gardens are, the variations on this layout are many. The subsidiary walks may meander through the plantings or expand into open areas for play or seating. On sloping sites, the main path may consist mostly of steps or stairs, with subsidiary pathways meeting it at one or more landings. Where space allows, the main walkway may expand into a more open area with furniture, statuary, or a water feature at some point along its length. There may even be a few hidden nooks or cul-de-sacs along either the main path or the subsidiary paths. Whatever the elaborations, the basic layout of the cottage garden eschews novelty and challenge for comfort and efficiency.

In the private space behind the home, the cottage garden's layout may be more flexible and less predictable. More often than not there will be a paved area for seating or outdoor dining. For convenience, this seating or dining area will most likely be close to the rear entrance of the house. There may or may not be subsidiary seating areas or paved expanses deeper within the garden. Pathways are liable to meander more than those in the front of the house, defining planted areas

Cottage gardens are modest in scale, never grand or overwhelming.

that are less formal in their geometry. Sometimes the space beyond the main seating or dining area is a looser reflection of the front garden, with a simple axial plan of crossed pathways, with or without an open space and a central decorative feature at their intersection.

The rear garden will most likely house the more utilitarian elements—the compost heap, the cutting garden, the kitchen garden, the toolshed, and perhaps even a little nursery plot to house cuttings, seedlings, and newly acquired plants. These work areas are frequently pushed to the periphery of the rear garden, while the central space is given over to plants and decorative objects that can be

Hallmarks of the cottage garden style

- Modest, intimate scale
- An emphasis on comfort
- A simple layout
- Efficient use of space
- Dense, informal plantings
- A mixture of plant types

admired from the main seating area. Often the rear garden also accommodates play activities: It may be home to a jungle gym, a playhouse, a tire swing, or a tetherball pole. More than does the front garden, the rear garden tends to express the mixture of functions—decorative, productive, and recreational—that so characterize the traditional cottage garden.

COMPONENTS OF THE COTTAGE GARDEN

The layout of the cottage garden may be variable, but certain physical components appear in every cottage garden plan. These include boundaries, entrances, pathways, open spaces, planted spaces, furniture, and decorative elements.

Boundaries for the cottage garden may take many forms. Stone or brick walls are common in England, while American cottage gardens more often feature wooden fences. Hedges, whether clipped and formal in appearance or loose and casual, may also form the cottage garden boundary. Sometimes a boundary is nothing more than a dense arrangement of ornamental plants. Whatever form the boundary takes, it will be punctuated at some point by an entry. Gates are far and away the most common form of entry, but archways are popular as well. Sometimes the entry to the cottage garden is as simple as a gap in a hedge.

Unlike the traditional American yard, the cottage garden does not feature large expanses of open lawn that visitors wander across. Instead, traffic in the cottage garden is directed along well-defined paths or walkways. Cottage garden pathways are most often paved. Their surfaces may be of gravel, stone, brick, or concrete. In the Pacific Northwest wooden decking is also a favored option. Pathways that get little traffic may actually be planted in turf grass, and this is the closest thing to a lawn that you are liable to encounter in the cottage garden. The open spaces where paths meet or terminate invite the visitor to pause and enjoy the pleasures of the garden. These open spaces may be paved with the same materials as the pathways, or differentiated with a contrasting material. In any case they will be intimate, comfortable spaces, simple in shape and modest in size. The walkways and open spaces in the cottage garden are bounded and defined by planted areas. Any planting that spans the area between a garden boundary and a walkway is called a border, while plantings that are surrounded completely by walkways or open areas are usually called islands or island beds. Cottage garden plantings always contain a great variety of plant material, and they are usually very dense. This combination of variety and density gives cottage garden plantings their characteristically lush, exuberant appearance.

In the cottage garden, plants are not arranged in rigid geometric patterns. You won't find circles, squares, or triangles outlined in hyacinths and filled with tulips. Though planted areas may be arranged symmetrically around a central walkway, they are almost never symmetrical in their content. You will not find the same plants facing each other in mirror position along both sides of the walkway—a kind of direct symmetry that would be far too rigid and formal for the cottage garden style. Cottage garden plantings also tend to have "soft" edges, with the plants allowed to spill out over adjacent pathways and pavement. The fact that the plants literally overflow their boundaries only serves to accentuate the billowing effect of the cottage garden planting.

Planted areas help to define and separate the garden's various spaces.

Both the planted areas and the open spaces in the cottage garden play host to a variety of structures, furniture, and decorative features. Structures may include boundary structures, such as fences, walls, and gates; support structures, such as arches, pergolas, and trellises; and even small outbuildings, such as a playhouse or a toolshed. Furniture will probably include some sort of dining table and chairs, but in addition the cottage garden is likely to feature a bench or two, placed where the visitor can pause to enjoy the moment. Decor may be anything from garden lights and decorative containers to fountains, birdhouses, or boxes for mason bees.

Like its basic geometry and layout, the cottage garden's structures tend to be simple and traditional. Wood, painted or oxidized metal, terra cotta, glass, brick, and stone are easier to work into the cottage garden style than are plastic, fiberglass, or polished metal. That's not to say that these more modern materials have no place—only that they should be used with care. A bench needn't be just something to sit on.

The choice of structures, furniture, and decor allows ample opportunity for self-expression in the cottage garden. The gardener can establish moods from contemplative to nostalgic to whimsical by selecting the appropriate styles and materials. The only limitation to observe is that the structures, furniture, and decor you choose must work in combination with the overall design and plantings to maintain the modesty, comfort, and informality that are crucial to the cottage garden style. Avoid items that are heavy, monumental, or out of proportion to your home or the size of your lot. Remember when selecting structures, furniture, and decorative items that the cottage garden depends upon lightness, grace, and charm, not overwhelming dramatic impact. The objects within the garden must be inviting, not imposing.

ORIGINS OF THE COTTAGE GARDEN

The relatively unsophisticated charm, vivacious color, and casual air that characterize the modern-day cottage garden are all products of the cottage garden's history. Unlike other great traditional garden styles such as the Japanese garden, the Italian Renaissance garden, or the French formal garden, the cottage garden has never been thought of as "high art." It is truly an example of folk tradition or popular culture. It is part of what landscape historians and scholars refer to as "the vernacular landscape." Its principles were never codified or taught in academic settings. Instead, it grew haphazardly, its ideas passed down by example and oral tradition from one generation to the next.

EARLY COTTAGE GARDENS

Because the cottage garden is a product of folk tradition, we have no written records of its origin. Our ideas about the earliest cottage gardens must be based in good part on surmise, common sense, and a general knowledge of history. As townsfolk and villagers in post-medieval England acquired homes and small plots of land, it was only natural that they began to garden. The earliest cottage gardeners were in all likelihood guided by practical concerns, and their gardens were surely quite utilitarian. The two most pressing realities for early cottage gardeners would have been limited space and need for food. Fruits, vegetables, and berries were grown in abundance, as were medicinal and culinary herbs. In order to obtain the greatest yield from the small cottage plot, gardeners packed fruit trees, vegetables, and herbs as densely as possible onto every square foot of available soil.

Efficiency would have been the hallmark of the early cottage garden. Hence the simple layouts, plain geometry, and direct pathways that characterize the cottage garden to this day. No doubt cottage gardens were from the beginning enclosed by walls or hedges, both to exclude nuisance wildlife such as foxes and rabbits and to contain any domestic animals the cottager might raise. There might be a couple of hens or ducks, or perhaps a beehive. No early cottage garden would have had room for anything as wasteful as a lawn; expanses of cropped grass were strictly the preserve of the landed gentry, who could afford the unproductive space they occupied and the labor to maintain them.

For early cottage gardeners, any vertical surface would have been a potential support for espaliered fruit trees, cane fruit, or vining vegetables. The greenery of gooseberries, raspberries, peas, and beans would have clambered over walls, trellises, and arbors. Even the walls of the cottage itself would be fair game. What began as measures of thrift became the hallmarks of a style. Dense plantings, efficient use of vertical space, and lack of open lawn areas have carried down to the "overstuffed" look typical of today's ornamental cottage gardens.

Fruit-bearing plants being, of course, flowering plants, early cottage gardens would have been quite colorful despite having few, if any, purely ornamental plantings. Even the most thrifty and practical examples would have shown masses of peach, apple, and elder blossoms in the spring, or the bright yellow of cucumber and pumpkin flowers against the purples of sage and lavender in summer. All of these plants would be combined casually, with little or no concern for any preconceived rules or notions of design.

Indeed, the cottage garden was not "designed" in the sense we think of today. Rather, its layout and its plantings developed spontaneously according to the

needs and experience of the gardener. Each cottage garden developed by trial and error, according to the whims and inclinations of its owners. Over time the experience of generations accumulated and coalesced. As building materials, structures, and ideas about layout were handed down, and as plants, their potential uses, and knowledge of their cultural requirements were passed along, a cottage gardening tradition began to emerge. By the sixteenth and seventeenth centuries, this tradition was firmly established in the English countryside.

Any structure is fair game for climbing plants in the traditional cottage garden.

Meanwhile, an unprecedented wave of global exploration vastly expanded the cottage gardener's choices of edible and ornamental plant materials. From the New World came potatoes, tomatoes, squashes, asters, sunflowers, and phloxes. From East Asia came peonies, chrysanthemums, and daylilies. Yet all this wealth of plant material paled before the novelties soon to come.

COTTAGE GARDENS IN THE AGE OF EXPLORATION

By the eighteenth century, England's outstanding navy and trading fleet had transformed a small and isolated island nation into an enormous colonial power with outposts spanning several continents. With colonial power came new wealth and prosperity. The days of subsistence economics were long gone, and English townsfolk and villagers found themselves able to afford new luxuries. Newly prosperous cottage gardeners could now devote more of their limited space to ornamental gardening. Even as their newfound prosperity gave them the freedom to indulge in decorative plantings, ongoing contact with the colonies and rapid developments in plant breeding enlarged the range of plant material from which they could choose. Repeat-blooming roses, rhododendrons, and exotic, large-flowered clematis came from the Far East, while black-eyed Susans, lupines, and monkey flowers came from North America. There were impatiens, dahlias, and petunias from Central and South America; kniphophias and crocosmias from South Africa; and hebes from New Zealand. This influx of new and exotic flora allowed eighteenth- and nineteenth-century cottage gardeners to cram their gardens with an unprecedented variety of plant life in a tremendous range of color, texture, and form. The English cottage gardens of this period achieved the brimming and riotously colorful appearance familiar to us today.

NINETEENTH- AND EARLY TWENTIETH-CENTURY COTTAGE GARDENS

The nineteenth century was a period of nation building in Europe. It was a time that saw the emergence of such familiar European countries as Italy and Germany, as city-states, principalities, and small dukedoms coalesced. As nations took shape and empires grew, a new romantic nationalism took hold of European culture. Cultural nationalism expressed itself in the patriotic operas of Verdi in Italy, the folktale collections of the Brothers Grimm in Germany, and the romantic paintings of David and Delacroix in France. In England, the nineteenth century revival of national folk traditions raised the cottage garden to an entirely new level of popular and critical regard. The cottage garden came to be seen as emblematic of the nation.

As the cottage garden style matured and gained popular appeal in the mid-nineteenth century, the Industrial Revolution began to permanently alter the English landscape. Production, trade, and finance concentrated in the large

9

cities, and suburbs began to emerge as major population centers. The cottage garden was superbly adapted to the new suburbia because it required limited space and allowed for flamboyant self-expression in its cheerful informality. Perhaps as eager to capture the charm of the country village as to express their individuality amidst the sea of near-identical homes, suburban English gardeners turned in numbers to the cottage garden style. A colorful cottage garden made the ideal antidote to the gray expanses of suburbia and the sooty air that drifted out of England's industrial centers. As the Industrial Revolution bred the grim urban slums that so appalled Charles Dickens and George Bernard Shaw, the rural and suburban middle class insulated itself behind the walls of its lush cottage gardens. Even in its new industrial suburban context, the cottage garden remained within the popular folk tradition rather than the realm of "sophisticated" high design.

Indeed, only one important strain of professional English garden design did come under the strong influence of the cottage garden tradition. This was the art of country estate planning and perennial border planting as practiced by Gertrude Jekyll during the early twentieth century. Gertrude Jekyll's reputation was based on a series of English estate gardens she designed, often in conjunction with architect Edwin Lutyens. These gardens featured large, colorful borders densely planted with flowering perennials. Between the 1890s and the 1920s, Gertrude Jekyll published a series of books on plants and gardening that detailed her philosophy of garden design and gave much practical instruction on the composition and arrangement of plants in the garden. Her books quickly attained classic status, and they remain immensely popular among serious gardeners and professional garden designers to this day. In them, she espouses a method of plant arrangement that is akin to painting, with the border as her canvas and the plants as her palette. Her artistry lay in carefully crafted combinations of plant color, form, and texture that appeared to be completely casual—in other words, a sophisticated and artful adaptation of the cottage garden planting tradition.

By refining the cottage garden style and incorporating some of its character into landscape designs for substantial and prestigious homes, Gertrude Jekyll legitimized the cottage garden and brought its aesthetic to bear upon the "serious" art of garden design. With Jekyll, the influence of the cottage garden style reached past the humble vernacular and into the realm of professional design. None of which should suggest that Jekyll was designing cottage gardens. Nor does it mean that the kind of meticulously composed perennial border she popularized constitutes a cottage garden. Though borders are certainly one component of the cottage garden, no traditional cottage garden would give over space to a border composed completely of flowering perennials. Both the grand scale and the limited season of interest typical of the Gertrude Jekyll perennial border are inconsistent with the cottage garden style. Borders in the cottage garden are modest in scale and combine perennials with annuals, shrubs, and edible crops to extend their season of interest and make the most of limited space. Jekyll's designs were, after all, attached to country estates with room to spare for huge borders that looked appealing only from May to September, not to mention the kind of domestic staff required to maintain them. So, while Gertrude Jekyll's observations on color, scale, and form and her advice on arranging plants remain extremely valuable to today's cottage gardener, the kind of large-scale perennial borders she designed are ultimately impractical for both the modest traditional English cottage garden and our modern Pacific Northwest urban and suburban gardens.

THE COTTAGE GARDEN IN AMERICA

Though the United States began as a British colony, it is not surprising that the cottage garden never took hold in this country the way it had in England. The driving force that had shaped the English cottage garden was the need to maximize productivity within a limited space. The overwhelming feature of the American landscape, at least in the popular imagination, was unlimited space. No wonder the cottage garden failed to appeal!

The lawn, rather than the cottage garden, became the national landscape icon for Americans. In a land of wide-open spaces, the lawn is a miniature range or prairie. It makes every house into a model homestead and fulfills the American homeowner's nostalgic yearning for an idealized frontier life. If you can't have a ranch, you can at least have a ranch house on a Lilliputian prairie. In America, as in England, the lawn is also a status symbol. Historically, the lawn in England was the prerogative of the landed gentry, who could afford the space and labor necessary to maintain it. In America, middle-class homeowners had the space for lawns and, with the advent of rotary (and later power) lawnmowers, the ability to maintain them. For Americans, having a lawn became an emblem of material success, with every homeowner the patron of his or her own estate.

The cottage garden has only recently begun to make headway in the American landscape. Several new developments have conspired to make the cottage garden style more attractive for American gardeners. One is the growing interest in gardening as a pastime. Gardening is now more popular as a hobby than in any time in American history. As more and more Americans take up gardening, they look for new ways of expressing themselves in their home landscapes. The lawn is simply too limited, too plain, and too commonplace to keep their interest. As a result, Americans

Lawn makes only limited appearances in the cottage garden.

are experimenting more freely than ever with new, or newly rediscovered, styles of gardening. One among these is the cottage garden. With its relative simplicity and its freedom from binding rules, the cottage garden offers modern American gardeners boundless opportunities for personal expression and interpretation.

Another point against the lawn and in favor of the cottage garden has been Americans' growing awareness of ecology. Of all the common American landscape features, the lawn is perhaps the least environmentally sound, contributing nearly as heavily as asphalt to excess runoff and stream degradation. In most locations, a lawn requires several pounds of lime and fertilizers each season, and these chemicals eventually make their way into local water bodies, altering the water chemistry and damaging habitat for plants, fish, and wildlife. Lawns also require heavy irrigation, with consequent wasteful runoff. The multilayered mixed plantings of herbaceous perennials, annuals, shrubs, and trees typical of the cottage garden allow much less surface runoff than does a lawn. With proper plant selection, a mixed cottage garden planting can also be maintained with far less supplemental water than an equivalent area of lawn.

Limitations on space, environmental sensitivity and the urge for self-expression in the home landscape have combined to fuel the cottage garden's growing appeal for American gardeners. But whereas English gardeners turn to cottage gardens instinctively and plant them almost without a second thought, Americans cannot. The cottage garden does not come naturally to us. It is not part of our folk tradition here in America, and we are not sufficiently familiar with its stylistic features to incorporate them without forethought. Otherwise, there would be no need for this book! As Americans, we've come to admire and appreciate the beauties and benefits of the cottage garden, but we need to familiarize ourselves with its character and its components. We also need to adapt its fundamental style to the growing conditions, the built environment, and the lifestyle demands of the land we live in.

PACIFIC NORTHWEST COTTAGE GARDENS

The cottage garden style adapts particularly well to the climate, gardening culture, and housing styles of the Pacific Northwest. Experienced Northwest gardeners will tell you that our region is a horticultural paradise. Our relatively mild winters and comfortably cool summers allow us to grow an unusually wide variety of plants, and variety is a hallmark of cottage garden plantings. Our extended growing season also makes it relatively easy to keep our gardens colorful for much of the calendar year. All of this means that, with a little forethought, Pacific Northwest cottage gardens can be year-round gardens.

Perhaps because of the favorable climate, or because of the regional passion for outdoor living, Northwesterners appear more likely than most other Americans to favor gardens of one type or another over the traditional lawn. Heightened concern for the environment in many Pacific Northwest communities may also account for the relative popularity of alternative landscape styles. Residents of the region have long experience with water shortages, conflicts over habitat, and debate over natural resources. This legacy of environmental debate, set against the background of dramatic natural landscapes, no doubt contributes to the Pacific Northwest gardener's relative willingness to experiment with a wide range of home landscape styles.

Though the image of a thatched and half-timbered cottage swathed in climbing roses persists, the cottage garden has long outgrown the cottage. The cottage garden style is easily adaptable to many common types of Pacific Northwest home architecture. Our major cities abound in fine examples of early- and mid-twentieth century construction. The predominant traditional styles, including Craftsman, Queen Anne, Victorian, Tudor Revival, and Colonial, all marry harmoniously with the cottage garden. Many contemporary Northwest homes are built with traditional materials, especially wood, which help make them comfortable backdrops for cottage gardens as well. The boxy brick ramblers that appeared throughout the cities and suburbs of the Pacific Northwest during the 1950s and 1960s can also benefit from cottage garden settings. The color and exuberance of the cottage garden can go far to offset the plainness of these sprawling single-story homes. Today's suburban houses usually have enough traditional visual cues, including mullioned windows, wooden siding, and multipaneled doors, to blend effectively with a cottage garden. The casual cottage garden style offers ample opportunities for owners of these homes to individualize their landscapes within a largely traditional framework, one that is unlikely to clash wildly with the surrounding homes.

CLIMATE AND GROWING CONDITIONS

The cottage garden style does seem well suited to the home landscapes of the Pacific Northwest, but it can succeed only when it is executed with knowledge of, and respect for, the region's climatic quirks and growing conditions. Though it's true that our gardens can support an unusually wide variety of plant life, the notion that "everything grows here" is simply erroneous. One limit is obvious: tropical and other frost-sensitive plants will not overwinter outdoors here, even in the mildest maritime climates.

Other limitations are a bit less plain to see. Although people who live in other parts of the country find it hard to believe, our Pacific Northwest summers are routinely droughty. Even some longtime residents are surprised to learn that annual rainfall in the maritime lowlands can amount to 30 inches or less. This is less rain per year than falls on New England, the mid-Atlantic states, the Deep South, the Midwest, or even parts of Texas! The Pacific Northwest earns its soggy reputation because nearly all of the region's rainfall is concentrated between

November and April. So, while it *does* rain continually throughout the winter, in most years there is almost no rain at all from June to October. This concentration of annual rainfall means that many of our soils dry out thoroughly by the end of June. It also means that soils that might otherwise be well oxygenated can become quite waterlogged in winter. To grow in our region, plants must be able to tolerate this feast-or-famine situation where the natural water supply is concerned.

Because maritime Pacific Northwest summers are so cool, plants that require lots of heat to perform well may fail to prosper, bloom, or fruit, even though our actual growing season of 250 days is quite long. Though winters are generally no harsher in our coastal and maritime interior lowlands than in states like Georgia or South Carolina, our frosts are erratic and unpredictable. A hard frost will often strike immediately after a balmy warm spell, and any plant that has been duped out of its dormancy may be severely damaged. On the other hand, winter temperatures usually do get low enough to provide ample dormancy for any plants, such as peonies and daffodils, that require chilling in order to grow vigorously and bloom during the warmer months.

Layered upon the basic regional climate conditions are a range of elevations, exposures, and resultant microclimates whose diversity is hardly rivaled by any area of similar extent. "Microclimate" is a term used to describe any highly localized variation in climate caused by factors such as elevation, orientation, prevailing winds,

Old-fashioned comfort and new limitations on space fuel American interest in the cottage garden style.

and proximity to bodies of water. For example, a west-facing hillside in Seattle, warmed by the afternoon sun and the nearby Lake Washington and Elliott Bay, may in effect fall into USDA Zone 9, where dahlias, phormiums, and cannas can often overwinter. A garden on the slopes of Squak Mountain, just 20 miles away in suburban Issaquah and 500 feet higher in elevation, may for all practical purposes be in USDA Zone 7. Though USDA zone maps will show both of these sites as being in Zone 8, anyone planning a cottage garden in our region ought to be aware of the tremendous influence of local topography on his or her own site. Without such knowledge, gardeners are likely to make inappropriate choices of plant material.

The Pacific Northwest offers unique growing conditions and design opportunities.

Generally speaking, coastal lowland sites are warmer than those farther inland, and temperatures become more extreme at higher elevations. Sites that are close to large bodies of water are generally milder and more even in temperature than those that are not, and south- and west-facing sites are typically warmer than those facing east or north. Large, dense urban areas, especially those near the water, often exhibit especially mild conditions. Sites at the foot of hills or mountains may be subject to cold-air drainage in winter and early spring. This tendency for chilled air to travel down slopes and collect at the base can lead to pockets of persisting frost in gardens that are so situated. Valleys that run east-west, especially along the larger rivers, may be subject to blasts of cold air traveling out of the interior during the winter. The best source for detailed information on microclimate issues that may affect your particular garden site is your local state agricultural extension office.

IT'S NOT JUST LIKE ENGLAND

Years ago I recall hearing a prestigious English garden designer gush after a trip to the Pacific Northwest: "Why, it's just like England!" Having spent some time in England, I beg to differ. The climate, topography, and soils of the Pacific Northwest differ significantly from those of England.

To begin with, rainfall in most of England is not so strictly confined to the winter months, and summer drought is less regular or less extreme than here in the Northwest. Lowland areas in central and northern England receive far more snow than do the cities and towns of the Oregon and British Columbia lowlands or the basin around Puget Sound. The English summers I have experienced have been significantly warmer than the Pacific Northwest norm, and plants that require summer heat may prosper better there than here. The English terrain certainly offers its own share of microclimates, but they are less varied and extreme than those found here. The highest "mountain" in England would hardly qualify as a foothill to the Cascades or the Olympics, and nowhere in England is the landscape so intricately interlaced with large bodies of water as in the area around Puget Sound and the Strait of Juan de Fuca.

Pacific Northwest soils and geology are also very different from England's. Granted, both areas were glaciated, but their underlying geologies and the bases for their soils are quite distinct. The maritime Northwest occupies an area of recent geologic uplift and ongoing volcanic activity. Though there is a wide and haphazard assortment of glacial material lying atop it, much of the region's bedrock consists of hard igneous rocks that have had relatively little time to weather. England, on the other hand, rests mostly upon older, weathered rock, including many sedimentary materials and large expanses of limestone. (Think of the white cliffs of Dover.) As a matter of fact, English gardening books devote an awful lot of space to dealing with the "chalk" (that is, alkaline) soils encountered so often in the gardens of Great Britain. In the Pacific Northwest, soil character varies tremendously from place to place. However, much of the region's open land was, until recently, forested. Forest soils, especially those under conifer forests, tend to be acidic. So it is safe to say that dealing with acidic soils is of much greater concern to Pacific Northwest gardeners than coping with alkaline limestone-based soils.

For all of these reasons, the English cottage garden style must be adapted to some extent in order to best suit our region. Structures and building materials must complement prevailing architectural styles and reflect local resources. We must select, place, and maintain our plants with an eye to regional climate and growing conditions, as well as to the microclimate that prevails on the specific site. Only by meeting these requirements can we successfully establish a true Northwest cottage garden.

CHAPTER TWO

Layout:
The Hidden Order

Casual as it may appear, a good cottage garden will be composed according to some underlying logic. That logic rests in the layout, the hidden order that underlies the garden's informal exuberance. Even though the cottage garden may at first look like a hodgepodge, its layout is never haphazard. A random assortment of plants, garden structures, furniture, and decorative knickknacks does not make a cottage garden. It makes a mess. A cottage garden is both practical and comfortable. A mess is neither.

The comfort and utility of the Northwest cottage garden depends largely upon the basic layout of its spaces, structures, and plantings. Though cottage garden layouts are inherently simple and straightforward, laying out the cottage garden is no trivial undertaking. The more care and forethought that go into the ground plan, the more likely it is that you will be satisfied with

Let utility and comfort be the guides to your cottage garden's layout.

the end results. Whether you are starting your home landscape from scratch or adapting an existing garden, it pays to plan your cottage garden layout with a clean slate and an open mind. Even if there is a mature garden on your site, try to imagine away all of the previous design decisions and begin with the site itself.

The best cottage gardens evolve out of the land they rest upon, rather than fight with it. Whether your home stands on a large and isolated rural property or a narrow urban lot, your cottage garden will come off most successfully if your design is driven by the resources your own chunk of land has to offer. In order to tailor the layout of your cottage garden to your location, you need to know just what it is you have to work with. I find that the best way to develop a layout that effectively addresses the opportunities and limitations of a site and the needs of its owners is to undertake a systematic analysis of the site before making any design decisions.

SITE ANALYSIS

I realize that the term "site analysis" can be rather off-putting. It may sound dry and overly scientific. After all, we are talking about garden design, aren't we? Or perhaps you find the idea of site analysis intimidating, as if it requires highly specialized knowledge, or even a professional degree? Actually, site analysis is a fun and revealing exercise. And no one could be better prepared to undertake it than you. After all, who is more familiar with your own site than you are? Who better knows your preferences, needs, and habits? All you need to evaluate your garden site are paper and pencil, a measuring tape, a shovel, and a bit of time. The next few pages will walk you through this rewarding—and sometimes surprising—process.

TAKING INVENTORY

To begin with, you'll need to learn the lay of the land—your land, that is. Taking inventory of the existing physical conditions on your garden site is a good start. Find all of the slopes and banks, trees, rocks and outcroppings, and permanent structures on the lot, including your home, any outbuildings, and mechanical or utility structures. If you expect to do any deep digging (more than 18 inches), call your local utility companies; they'll be glad to come out and mark the locations of any buried lines or conduits. Record all of these elements on a rough sketch of your property or on a detailed list, whichever you find more comfortable. Add to your sketch or list any existing hard surfaces, including sidewalks, driveways, patios, and pathways.

While you're learning the lay of the land, evaluate any prevailing microclimate conditions on your site. Is your home at the foot of a slope where cold-air drainage is an issue? Do you live on a ridge or promontory that is exposed to strong winds?

Is your property near a large body of water that will moderate the temperature, or adjacent to salt water, so that salt spray is a concern? Do you live at a significant elevation, where winters are relatively harsh and snow accumulates? Or do you live in a large city, where concentrated buildings and paved areas make for a relatively sheltered and warm environment? Even if such factors do not impact the general layout of your garden, you will be able to choose and locate plants and structures more effectively if you are aware of them from the very start.

WATER

Once these solid features are located, you'll want to turn your attention to your site's liquid assets. Locate any standing water on your site, along with areas where water tends to pool after rains, or where the soil stays saturated during the growing season. At the same time, locate any existing irrigation and water sources, including outdoor spigots. Take note as well of any especially dry areas on the site. If you are recording your observations as sketches, you will probably need a separate sheet for these water-related features.

SOIL

The next aspect of your site to examine is the soil. If possible, dig a few holes 12 to 18 inches deep in various portions of your lot. Take a close look at the soil. Is it sandy and loose, or dense and heavy with clay? Is it even-textured, or are there many rocks, pebbles, and other large particles?

If you are lucky, you will already have a top layer of dark-colored organic topsoil. If so, how deep is it? Take note of any earthworms in the soil. Not only is their activity beneficial to your soil's texture, but their presence indicates that organic matter is available and that the soil is reasonably well aerated.

Fill a few of the holes you have dug with water, and observe how long it takes them to drain. Holes that take more than a couple of hours to empty indicate areas of poor drainage.

Later on, as you're deciding what plants to place in your garden and where, you'll want some idea of your soil's pH, or relative acidity. You can determine soil pH yourself by using any of the available types of soil testing kits, or you can bring samples to your local agricultural extension office. Try to test samples from at least three or four different locations on your lot. Don't be surprised if the soil pH varies considerably from place to place on your lot, especially if you live in an urban neighborhood or a relatively new suburban development. These home sites often include a good deal of imported fill, which may have come from a number of different locations. As before, record your observations as a rough drawing or on your list.

A simple soil test

To determine your soil's basic texture, perform the following simple test. Collect a handful of soil from a hole dug eight or ten inches into the ground. Without adding water, firmly squeeze the soil together in your fist. Then, open your hand, and observe the lump of soil. If the soil forms a gummy, compact mass, it has a high clay content. Clay soils also feel sticky and pasty when you rub them between your fingers. Soils rich in clay retain water and nutrients, but can be slow to drain.

If the soil crumbles into a loose heap as soon as you open your hand, it probably contains a lot of sand. Sandy soils feel coarse and gritty when rubbed between your fingers. They are usually nutrient-poor in comparison with other soils and may dry out during Pacific Northwest summers.

If the soil in your hand coheres into a single mass, but crumbles easily when tapped or jiggled, it contains a balanced mixture of fine, clay particles, coarse sand, and intermediate particles. This soil texture is referred to as "loam," and is generally preferred by Northwest gardeners, as it supports the widest variety of plants. If your soil leans heavily toward either clay or sand, you may want to improve its texture by incorporating composted organic matter before you plant your cottage garden.

LIGHT

After evaluating the soils on your site, you'll need to assess the available light. Take time over a number of days to observe when and where your lot receives sunlight. Note any areas that are thrown into deep shade cast by buildings or other solid structures. Locate areas that receive dappled sunlight through overhanging trees, and those that receive sunlight for only a portion of the day. Are any parts of your lot exposed to harsh sunlight, especially in the afternoon? Though these areas may tend to bake and dry out during the day, they can also offer special planting opportunities. Note the overall exposure of your site. Is it east-facing, with morning sun, or west-facing, receiving most of its sunlight in the afternoon? Do you have a southern exposure, with ample light throughout the day, or a northern exposure, with long periods of shade each day? As before, be sure to use a sketch or a detailed list to record the exposure and light conditions around your home and yard.

Don't forget to walk your yard at night as well. Note any areas that are forbiddingly dark. Pay special attention to any paths or walkways that are too dark to navigate safely at night, and to any steps, stones, or other obstacles that might trip you up. A cottage garden should be a comfortable place that family and visitors can traverse at night without fear or injury. If yours isn't, you may want to add lighting to your cottage garden design. With this in mind, be sure to locate all outdoor electrical outlets and other possible sources of electrical power on your sketch or your list.

EXISTING PLANTS

Now that you've evaluated the inanimate components of your landscape, you can turn your attention to its existing vegetation. Though it's hardly necessary to locate every weed or blade of grass, you'll want to locate any shrubs or hedges, established planting beds, large plant groupings, or borders. It is a good idea at this point to note any plants that are doing especially well or especially poorly on your property, as this will be a good indication of what you'll be able to plant successfully later. If any especially pernicious weeds, such as blackberry, Mexican bamboo (*Polygonum cuspidatum*), or morning glory (*Convolvulus* spp.), have gained a foothold, now is the time to find those patches and record their locations.

Taking in the view

Always remember to take careful stock of your site's visual resources. Locate the best views, and note the spots on your property from which you can best appreciate them. You won't want to obstruct these views as you compose your cottage garden layout, and your plot's best vantage points will be prime candidates for seating areas in your final design. Spend some time inside the house, looking out from the windows in your favorite rooms. Note which parts of your lot are visible from indoors; you'll want to make sure they present pleasant tableaux when viewed from the windows.

NUISANCES

Don't forget to include in your inventory any factors you find particularly bothersome about your lot—the neighbor's house that was just painted fuchsia, the vista of power lines across the street, the unsightly chain-link fence. Note the source and direction of any annoying traffic noises, any areas where the privacy of your home or garden is compromised, and any animal pests, whether they be deer that browse on your plants or the dog that persistently invades your yard to relieve itself. Locating such nuisances as part of your site analysis will help you develop a garden plan that will neutralize them to the greatest degree possible.

ASSESSING YOUR NEEDS

By this point you probably have several sketches or a rather long list of the existing conditions on your property. You are probably wondering what any of this has to do with laying out your cottage garden. In fact, you are halfway to completing your layout. Assembling a detailed profile should give you a firm sense of the raw materials you have to work with in designing your cottage garden. Now it is time to assess your own needs and preferences.

CIRCULATION

I suggest you start by considering circulation—that is, how you get around your property. For this exercise, it really does help to take notes in the form of sketches or rough drawings. (Don't worry about how your drawings look—you are the only one who has to see them!) Diagrams of circulation will be the foundation of your site plan and will determine the basic layout of your cottage garden. To begin, take a pencil and paper with you, and stroll about your yard. Think about where the bulk of the foot traffic comes from and goes. Mark down where people enter the yard. Is it from the sidewalk, from the driveway, or directly from the street? Is there more than one significant entry point? If you have a hedge, are there holes where people have pushed through time after time? These are clear indications that you need an alternative entryway, something you'll want to consider when you address the final layout of your cottage garden. Next, mark all the points where people enter and leave the house. Try to observe or recall which doors are used most frequently. It's not unusual for most people to enter by one door and exit mainly through another.

Once you have identified all of the access points to both your property and your home, try to rank them in order of use. Distinguish the most frequently used entrances and exits with an extra mark on your diagram. These will be the beginning and end points for the major walkways on your cottage garden layout. Now mark down any frequently used or often visited portions of your property. These might be existing dining or seating areas, a spot with an attractive view, or even the place where you store your trash receptacles. Any of these outdoor destinations that will remain in your cottage garden will need to be served by walkways as well.

Having located the major entrances, exits, and destinations on your property, examine the existing paths and walkways. As you trace out the existing walkways on your diagram sketch, note whether they actually lead to and from the entrances and interior destinations you have already recorded. Observe, too, whether the most-traveled pathways are wide enough. Ruts worn in the lawn or plantings alongside your walkways are a sure indication that they need to be wider. Do your family and visitors actually walk on the existing paths, or do people tend to cut corners to get from place to place more easily? Diagram any of these short-cuts. Also look for improvised pathways trodden through your lawn or your existing plantings. You will want to record these so-called desire paths; they indicate where people *really* want to walk, and they suggest that your existing walkways are not where they need to be.

GARDEN ACTIVITIES

Now that you have accounted for the way people move around your property, give some thought to how you use your yard, and how you hope to use your future garden. Consider the activities that take place in your yard right now: eating, playing, lounging, exercising, entertaining, barbecuing, vegetable gardening. Include any special outdoor activities or hobbies that you or your family routinely enjoy on your property. Write all of these down on two lists. On the first, include all of those activities that take place in

Walkways and circulation patterns will shape the basic layout of your garden.

places that you think of as appropriate. On the second, list all those activities that occur where you would prefer they didn't. The activities on this second list will probably need their own designated spaces in your cottage garden layout. Otherwise, they will continue to happen in inappropriate locations.

Take time as well to consider new ways you might want to use your cottage garden. Perhaps you want a new vegetable garden, or a cutting garden where you can gather flowers for use in the house. Do you need space for outdoor dining or entertaining? Maybe you want a play area for children, or a quiet garden nook where you can escape to read. If you plan to start composting in earnest, you'll need a place to make and store your compost. Do you find that your yard is always littered with tools, flowerpots, sports equipment, or toys? You may want to consider a shed or some other outdoor storage structure. If you have a pet or are planning to get one, you may need a kennel or a doghouse. Given our rainy Pacific Northwest winters, you might also want to include a sheltered outdoor space for humans in your cottage garden plan! Poll the members of your household for any uses they hope to get out of the cottage garden as well.

PUTTING IT ALL TOGETHER

With your existing landscape conditions inventoried and your needs for the garden accounted for, you're ready lay out your cottage garden. Putting an actual plan on paper can be intimidating to many gardeners, but with your inventory and analysis complete, most of the work involved in developing your cottage garden layout is done! All that remains is to superimpose the uses, needs, and preferences you've outlined for your garden upon your site—the raw material you have to work with. From that point, your layout will just about design itself. The results of your site analysis should indicate what kinds of spaces and structures you need *and* where they need to be.

BOUNDARIES

Locating your boundary structures is a good place to start, since these will define the overall shape of your cottage garden. Deciding where to place fences, walls, or hedges is fairly straightforward. Nevertheless, you will want to refer to your site analysis and inventory to find any physical obstacles that will affect their location, and to pinpoint any spots that require extra screening, either because of noise, unsightly vistas, or the need for enhanced privacy. Your inventory and analysis will already have indicated the best locations for your garden's entry and exit points. On your layout these are the places where gates, archways, or simple gaps will allow people to pass through the garden's boundaries.

THE MAIN WALKWAY

With the boundary structures and entryways sited, locating the main walkway is a simple matter. The front walk should connect the garden's principal entry point to your home's main entrance. In most cases, this will be the front door. Keep your main pathway as direct as possible, following the traffic patterns you observed during your site analysis. Allow the path to skirt any immovable obstacles, avoiding sharp turns or angles if at all possible. Make sure the pavement is of adequate width: 3 feet is an absolute minimum for main garden pathways, and 5 feet will be necessary if people are to traverse the path two abreast. Feel free to break up the course of the path with steps and landings if it must climb a slope. If steps are required, make sure that they are of the proper proportions. A basic rule of thumb is that the run (or front-to-back depth of each step) plus twice the rise (or height) equals 26 inches. This means that a step 5 inches high should be 16 inches deep. Any landing should be deep enough for a walker to take two full steps

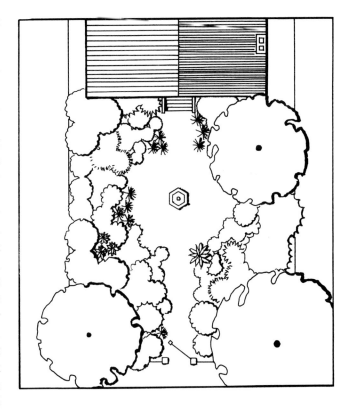

Here we see a plan view of a typical small cottage garden. Visitors enter through a gate in the fence and travel down the main walkway to the door. A fountain serves as the focus of the central open space, which is defined by dense informal plantings.

before the stairs resume. This usually means a minimum depth of 5 feet. Plan for outdoor lighting fixtures along paths and stairways that traverse any especially dark areas you may have noted in your inventory.

GARDEN SPACES

The front (and rear) walkways will usually divide the garden into two sections. It is within these sections that you will locate open areas to accommodate seating and conversation, dining and entertaining, play and relaxation, and any special

activities you and your family wish to enjoy in the garden. Let common sense and your compilation of needs and preferences guide the placement of these open areas. Dining and entertaining require relatively large spaces that are near one of the home's more private entrances and isolated from both street traffic and onlookers. Consequently, they belong in the rear of the house, with direct access from the back or side door. Play areas should be located where children's activities can be monitored from a window, and sufficiently far from the street to avoid danger from automobiles. Use the infor-

In front of the house, the main walkway normally steers a straight course from the garden entry to the door.

mation you gathered during your site inventory to place any special garden features to best advantage. Select a sunny, well-drained, level spot for your vegetable garden, an inconspicuous corner for your compost heap, and a convenient and accessible spot for a toolshed or storage structure. When locating a kennel or a water feature, consider access to outdoor water sources.

The various activity areas you define in your site plan will be the destinations for the cottage garden's secondary pathways. Like the main walkway, these should be as direct as possible and aligned to accommodate the traffic patterns revealed during your site analysis. The secondary pathways need not be as wide as the main walkway, and may be paved in a less durable material in accordance with their lighter use. The intersections of principal and secondary pathways make good locations for small open spaces that can accommodate decorative features or even modest seating areas.

PLANTED AREAS

The siting of the various pathways and activity areas will define the garden's planted areas. As you lay out your cottage garden, make sure the borders and island beds are large enough to house well-proportioned plantings. Borders composed mostly of herbaceous plants need to be, at the very least, 3 feet from front to back. If they are to contain shrubs and woody plants as well, they will need at least 6 feet of depth. As you refine your layout, try to keep both the planted areas and open spaces simple and casual in form, with gentle curves and round corners where straight lines intersect. Remember that cottage garden plantings will tend to smooth over any hard, straight edges as they spill out over adjacent pavement. Depending on how well they fit into the layout you develop, you may decide to keep, move, or eliminate the existing plantings you recorded in your inventory.

In making every layout decision for your cottage garden, let utility be your guide. Whenever possible, choose the simplest, most straightforward solution. Avoid unnecessary complication, difficult engineering feats, or complex structures. If you find your layout becoming overly elaborate, step back and simplify your plan. Don't be concerned if your layout seems insufficiently unique or distinctive. The cottage garden will reflect your individuality in other ways: through your plantings, structural details, and decor.

Loose, cascading plantings soften rigid lines and hard pavement edges.

CHAPTER THREE

Structures:
Making Yourself Comfortable

A weathered wooden gate swings open to admit the mailman. Clematis and old-fashioned roses cascade over a white picket fence. These are the images the phrase "cottage garden structures" brings to mind. But don't forget that the largest and most visually significant structure in your cottage garden is your house.

THE NORTHWEST HOME

What kind of Northwest home can make a fitting centerpiece for a cottage garden? Almost any! The cottage garden style is nothing if not pliant. Select your other garden structures—fences, paving, outbuildings, and so on—with a bit of care, and you should have no trouble adapting a cottage garden to your home, no matter what its style. All you need to do is let the proportions, details, and materials of your home be your guide.

The cities and towns, suburbs, and countryside of the Pacific Northwest are blessed with an abundance of distinct housing styles. Each affords its own challenges and opportunities for cottage garden design. I find that certain kinds of garden structures marry well with certain architectural styles, while others do not. Before we look at each of the major cottage garden structures in detail, I want to share a few basic ideas about cottage garden structures for some of the most popular Pacific Northwest housing styles.

TRADITIONAL HOMES

Much of the housing stock in the major cities of the Pacific Northwest dates from the period before World War II. The popular styles from the late nineteenth century through the 1920s included Craftsman, Queen Anne, and Victorian. During the 1930s and 1940s, Neo-Colonial and Tudor Revival homes became especially popular, and these comfortable, modestly scaled homes continue to dominate many established neighborhoods in Portland, Seattle, and Vancouver, British Columbia.

Other, less common, styles found in older Northwest neighborhoods include Spanish Colonial, Dutch Colonial, and Italian Renaissance Revival.

In small towns and rural areas throughout the Pacific Northwest, the dominant architectural style is often still the traditional farmhouse. These charming structures, with their peaked roofs, gables, and broad porches, could not be better suited to a cottage garden setting. Such gracious farmhouses occasionally appear in older urban neighborhoods as well. When they do, a well-furnished cottage garden will help establish the kind of warm and comfortable environment these homes deserve.

The traditional-style homes that dominate so many Pacific Northwest neighborhoods make fine centerpieces for cottage garden landscapes.

Most of these traditional home styles make natural partners for a Northwest cottage garden, although some pose special challenges. Queen Anne style homes, for example, are often massive and quite formal, with symmetrical façades, classically detailed pillars, and flourishes of intricately milled woodwork. While the frothy and informal plantings of a cottage garden can make your Queen Anne home especially inviting, you will want to reflect the house's form and symmetry in all of the garden's structures. In order to keep your Queen Anne home from looking underdressed in a cottage garden setting, keep your garden structures relatively simple, rectilinear, and symmetrical. Try to use paving materials such as brick or stone in relatively formal patterns, and consider replicating details of the house's trim in any fences, gates, arches, or trellis work.

The occasional Italian Renaissance Revival house found in older Northwest urban neighborhoods is also inherently formal, symmetrical, and rather large in scale. You may find that relatively spare and regular garden structures suit this style best. I think that painted wrought-iron fences, masonry walls, and paths of brick or patterned stone are some of the most pleasing structures for cottage gardens that surround Italian Renaissance Revival homes.

Spanish Colonial homes are a refreshing surprise when they appear in Pacific Northwest neighborhoods, where their pastel-painted stucco façades and tile roofs defy our dark, wet winters. In order to integrate a cottage garden with a Spanish Colonial home, try to limit the decorative details and materials for your garden structures to an appropriate palette. Stucco-faced walls or fine-textured evergreen hedges used as boundary structures are always lovely with this type of architecture. Gates and entryways that echo the barrel-arch motifs found on most Spanish Colonial houses can tie your home and garden together into a neat and tidy package. I would avoid too much wooden decking around such a home, and instead use flagstones, exposed-aggregate concrete, or compacted gravel as paving materials.

POSTWAR CONSTRUCTION

Urban and suburban developments that arose in the region during the 1950s and 1960s often feature low brick-faced or wood-sided "ramblers" with very simple façades, single-pane windows, and few other distracting architectural details. The '50s ramblers gave way during the late 1960s to the Northwest Contemporary style, usually with dark-stained wooden siding, gently sloped cedar shake roofs, clerestory windows, and generous overhangs supported by conspicuous exposed beams. Some of these Northwest contemporaries are reminiscent of Japanese or Polynesian houses in their massing and proportions. Others resemble early-twentieth-century Craftsman homes in their general outlines. At first, you might not think any of these homes from the '50s, '60s, and '70s could anchor a Northwest cottage garden.

A cottage garden dresses up the simple façade of this 1950s rambler.

But if you live in one of them, there is no reason to deprive yourself of a cottage garden. Accommodate your rambler or Northwest Contemporary with the right structural details and building materials, and it will rest happily in a cozy cottage garden setting.

In fact, a lively, colorful cottage garden is just the thing to liven up a rambler's

plain exterior. All you need to do is avoid errors of scale and incongruously fussy details in your garden structures. I find overscaled objects to be out of place in any cottage garden, but they are especially distracting against the featureless walls of a 1950s rambler. Many ramblers have little exterior detail to establish a sense of proportion, so your garden structures will bear the burden of maintaining human scale in the landscape. If you erect a tall, solid wall, hedge, or barrier fence around your rambler, you risk making it look like a frightened dwarf cowering behind a makeshift barricade. Try instead a low, trimmed hedge, a simple 3-foot fence, or a short, plain brick wall to surround your rambler's cottage garden. You are likely to find that plain garden structures, without any frilly details, will best complement a rambler. Instead of fussy structures, you can rely on the variety and exuberance of your cottage garden plantings to offset the simplicity of the house.

Northwest Contemporary homes are naturals in cottage garden settings.

Most Northwest Contemporary houses fit comfortably into a cottage garden setting. Those set on large lots in suburban or rural surroundings are especially appealing when they anchor a cottage garden that features clean-cut but rather rustic structures fashioned from the same materials as the home itself.

THE NEWEST NORTHWEST HOMES

The homes that compose the Pacific Northwest's most recent housing developments are typically updated interpretations of traditional styles, whose massing, proportions, and details can combine aspects of Colonial, Victorian, French

Provincial, and Tudor Revival architecture. They differ from the traditional urban pre-World War II homes in that they are often larger in scale and have simpler trim. With their many traditional stylistic cues, these new homes mate easily with a Northwest cottage garden.

The most aggressively modern new homes in the region often feature hard edges, sharp angles, and exteriors of industrial materials such as concrete and steel. You might be surprised to find how handily these homes accommodate simple cottage gardens. As with any other type of home, you simply need to choose garden structures that reflect the forms and materials employed in the design of the home. This is the one case where you should disregard the caution I voiced in an earlier chapter against hard, slick industrial materials. Shiny metal structures and concrete paving may be exactly what it takes to mate a cottage garden with your cutting-edge contemporary home.

TOWNHOUSES AND CONDOMINIUMS

Attached townhomes and condominiums pop up throughout the Pacific Northwest as the region's population explodes. Because cottage gardens evolved to make maximum use of limited spaces, they are one of the best and easiest options for landscaping these types of homes. By exercising a bit of restraint in choosing cottage garden structures, you can make the limited garden space most townhouses and condominiums provide into a welcoming, if small, oasis of outdoor comfort. What such pocket cottage gardens lack in size they can easily make up for in color and diversity. In order to pull off a cottage garden in so small a space, though, you'll need to plan and place each structure, furnishing, and plant with extreme care. The impact of each cottage garden structure multiplies by orders of magnitude when you set it in a small courtyard or townhouse entryway. Since the building will invariably be larger than the garden, and each object in the garden will stand quite close to the façade, you will also want to keep the style, color, and materials of every garden structure in tune with the building.

When you plan a cottage garden for a townhouse or condominium, keeping the right scale is crucial. It can be easy to forget just how small these spaces really are. That sculpture that was so appealing in the gallery may seem like a clumsy colossus near the front steps of your townhouse.

BOUNDARY STRUCTURES

Whatever the style of your home, no single component of your cottage garden design will make more of an immediate impression than the boundary structure. The boundary structure is the first part of the garden visitors encounter when approaching from the street or the sidewalk, perhaps even more conspicuous than your home itself. It will be the introduction to your cottage garden and will set the mood for all that happens once the visitor is inside it. The boundary structure will also be at least partially visible from most points within your cottage garden. For all of these reasons, the choice and design of boundary structure is one of the most critical decisions you will make in developing your cottage garden.

The structure you choose to demarcate your garden's boundaries will be more than just a visual cue for the rest of your design. It will be the backdrop against which many of your borders and garden structures are displayed. It can also be the principal source of privacy for your garden; a barrier against un-wanted visitors, both human and animal; and a means of containing pets and young children. It can screen out noise and hide eyesores, or provide support for climbing plants, espaliered fruit trees, and hanging garden decorations. You may choose from a wide and diverse range of boundary structures for your cottage garden. Hedges, whether informal or neatly clipped, evergreen or deciduous, are one popular option. Here in the Northwest, some cottage gardens are enclosed by walls of stone or brick, but by far the most common choice is a fence of wood or metal.

FENCES

Whatever fencing material you choose, certain basic design principles will affect the way your fence impacts the landscape. Open fencing, whatever the material, will always appear less heavy and imposing than a solid fence in the cottage gar-den. A light-colored finish will tend to stand out against background vegetation and make your fence more prominent among the garden's various features. An open, dark-colored fence, especially black, brown, or green, tends to blend into the surrounding landscape and can appear comparatively insubstantial. This principle does not always hold for tall, solid fences that are set along a sidewalk or roadside, where a dark color can make a big fence loom even more forbiddingly.

If your front yard is bounded by a tall, imposing fence, try painting it in a light, soft color and dressing it with climbing plants or a small border at its feet. This will break up its visual mass and make it seem less overwhelming from the street or sidewalk.

When set in the background of a cottage garden, a dark-colored fence will seem to recede into the distance and make the garden appear larger. A light-colored fence in the background can have the opposite effect, making distances seem smaller than they really are. If your property is large, you can put this effect to good use in establishing the cozy scale so typical of a cottage garden.

Visual rhythm can also impact the appearance of your fence. With a rail or picket fence, posts that are large and heavy in comparison with the rails or pickets, or that project well above the top of the fence, will seem to decrease the length of the fence. A fence whose elements are uniform in weight and height will appear comparatively long. A fence with exposed top and bottom rails will also appear to be both lower and longer than one of the same height and length but whose pickets or other vertical elements project beyond the rails. You can use a flat-topped fence to make a small property appear larger, or a fence with strong vertical rhythms to make a large cottage garden feel more comfortably human in scale. As with all cottage garden structures, coordinate both the color and texture of the fence's finish with your home's exterior.

A 3- to 4-foot-high fence should be perfectly adequate to enclose a cottage garden in front of most Pacific Northwest homes. Your fence may be taller, especially behind the house, if you are concerned about containing pets or excluding wildlife. If your fence sits atop a substantial rockery, try to keep it down to 3 feet or even less so that it doesn't completely overwhelm your cottage garden. If you must erect a tall fence at the top of a rockery, consider setting the fence back a few feet and planting a narrow border at its base. By interrupting the vertical surface in this way, you can moderate the combined scale of the two structures.

WOODEN FENCES

English cottage gardeners have always favored brick or stone walls, but here in the Pacific Northwest, as in much of the United States, the wooden fence is the favorite cottage garden boundary structure. Compared to masonry walls, wooden fences are both affordable and easy to erect. As one of the Northwest's prime economic resources, lumber has long been a source of both wealth and pride, making it a natural choice for home construction. Hence, wooden fences not only coordinate with the wooden exteriors and trim of many Northwest homes but also highlight the region's historic economic foundations. The ease with which wooden fence members can be cut and bent also means that wooden fences can take on styles to complement nearly any type of home architecture.

Wooden fences of any style have certain basic maintenance requirements. Though an unfinished split-rail fence may need no attention outside the repair of broken or fallen rails, most wooden fences will probably need repainting, resealing, or restaining every few years. Damaged rails or pickets may require replacement on occasion as well. If at all possible, try to leave a very narrow, gravel-paved walkway between the planted border and the base of the fence to allow access for maintenance and repairs.

Whatever style of wooden fence you choose, by no means set the wooden posts directly into the earth! No matter what grade of lumber you use, and no matter how it is treated, many winters' worth of exposure to soggy Pacific Northwest soils are a recipe for rot. Instead, make sure your wooden fence posts are set upon non-corroding metal pipe set into concrete footings. Be sure that all rails and pickets are also clear of contact with the soil to avoid premature rot. If

Picket fences are classic American boundary structures.

Wooden fence styles

PICKET FENCES

The classic North American picket fence is a born cottage garden enclosure that coexists happily with many Northwest home styles. Picket fences have several advantages in the cottage garden. They are effective at containing pets and children. They also make good supports for climbing plants and low espaliers. Because you can see plants and garden decor between their pickets, picket fences give a preview of the cottage garden's color and abundance before you even enter. Being relatively open, they rarely appear out of scale in a cottage garden setting—unless they are too tall.

POST-AND-RAIL FENCES

Like picket fences, post-and-rail fences allow hints of the cottage garden's pleasures to be seen from the outside, and they, too, fit right in with the unimposing cottage garden scale. On the other hand, post-and-rail fences are even more open than a picket fence, so they will do little to contain pets and children.

Depending upon their style and finish, post-and-rail fences are tremendously adaptable. If your home calls for a clean, sophisticated garden boundary, consider a post-and-rail fence with neat joints and a

The formal lines of this wooden fence contrast effectively with the bubbly cottage garden plantings inside.

A simple split-rail fence creates an air of rustic charm.

smooth finish. If your home is in a rustic setting, a simple, roughly finished post-and-rail fence makes one of the most casual of cottage garden enclosures.

PANEL FENCES

Closed-panel wooden fences, or "privacy fences," are a common sight throughout the Pacific Northwest. Panel fences offer a solid barrier to retain pets and children, while affording maximum privacy and security against uninvited guests and wildlife. They obliterate eyesores and screen out extraneous noise. You can also use a panel fence to create shade or shelter against winter winds on an especially harsh or exposed site.

Low panel fences, up to 3 or even 4 feet, make outstanding cottage garden enclosures for any traditional Northwest home, as well as most Northwest Contemporaries and 1950s ramblers. A panel fence with narrowly spaced, 2-inch slats is a popular variation that looks especially appealing with most Northwest Contemporary homes. Because a panel fence that is at or above eye level can be forbiddingly large in scale, try breaking up its mass with climbing plants or a mixed border planting at its base. A pattern of decorative cut-outs can also moderate the scale of a high panel fence, while adding a unique and personal touch to your design.

you must close the gap between your bottom rail and the soil to exclude pests or contain enterprising pets, try attaching a strip of wire mesh to the bottom rail and anchoring it securely to the ground with stakes or metal hoops.

METAL FENCES

After wood, wrought iron and cast aluminum are the most popular fencing materials for Pacific Northwest homes. Though more expensive than wooden fencing, metal fences may be more permanent and tend to require less maintenance. They are quite strong, yet at the same time open in structure, so that they seem to sit lightly upon the landscape. Metal fences are available in a wide range of colors and styles that can accommodate many types of Pacific Northwest homes. A simple wrought-iron or cast-aluminum fence can mate well with a Neo-Colonial or Tudor Revival home or even a 1950s rambler. Metal fencing also looks superb with most Spanish Colonial homes, provided the details and pattern are kept clean and simple. You can use more elaborate metal designs to complement the highly articulated and ornate exterior of the average Victorian. Wrought iron and cast aluminum are good fencing choices for Italian Renaissance Revival and Queen Anne houses, too; the neat, sophisticated air that they project is perfectly in tune with these generously scaled and highly symmetrical buildings.

Black and dark green are favorite colors for metal fences, in part because they tend to disappear into the surrounding landscape. You may find, though, that your fence benefits from a more unusual finish—perhaps slate blue to match the trim on your Victorian home, or brick red to complement the tiled roof on your Spanish Colonial. Keep in mind that metal fencing combines well with brick, stone, or stucco, so you can use any of these materials to face the pylons that support your fence, provided they coordinate with your house.

MASONRY WALLS

Masonry walls—brick, stone, or concrete—are far less popular than fences in Pacific Northwest gardens. They are, after all, much more difficult and expensive to install. On the plus side, they are more substantial and permanent than most fences, and they usually require less maintenance. Occasional repointing is often all that is necessary for a well-constructed garden wall. In many cottage garden situations, masonry walls may be the enclosure of choice.

BRICK WALLS

Brick walls complement most Neo-Colonial, Tudor Revival, Victorian, and Queen Anne architecture. They are one of the best options for Italian Renaissance Revival homes, especially when combined with wrought iron or aluminum. You may find your low-slung rambler home quite fetching behind a brick wall, too, as long as the wall is low enough to reflect the rambler's largely horizontal massing. Brick walls also make fine cottage garden enclosures for contemporary homes that feature brick in their façades.

No matter what the architectural setting, your brick wall will look most finished if capped with flat cut stone, cast terra-cotta, or high-quality molded concrete. For a slightly less formal appearance, you can cap a brick wall with an additional course of brick, preferably set on edge and perpendicular to the brickwork of the facing. You can add extra interest to a brick garden wall with any number of creative patterns. If you build a brick wall for your cottage garden, consider decorating it with patterns of colored bricks, or studding its surface with cut bricks set at angles to protrude beyond the face. You can make a brick wall appear lighter and less substantial by leaving regularly spaced openings in the face. These openings can be of any shape and size that will complement the architectural features of your home.

STONE WALLS

Stone walls are comparatively rare as boundary structures in Pacific Northwest home landscapes. Maybe this is because they are expensive. Maybe it's because wooden fences are so popular. Or, just maybe, it's because of all those rough stone retaining walls and rockeries that buttress so many slopes in our Pacific Northwest neighborhoods. Perhaps we shy away from stone walls because we see enough stone already, and we fear our yards and gardens will be overwhelmed by any more. Even if you feel this way, you should not dismiss the stone wall as an option for your cottage garden.

Stone is available in an extraordinary range of colors, shapes, sizes, and finishes. In fact, there are so many varieties and treatments of stone in garden wall construction that an inventive gardener can design a stone wall to suit nearly any home. For example, you might use limestone, shale, or sandstone cut in fairly narrow, regular horizontal blocks in front of your 1950s rambler, especially if the house has stone in its façade. Nothing could be more appropriate in front of a rustic Craftsman home with river-rock piers and exposed foundation than a garden wall of that same smooth, rounded river rock.

However, with such versatility come risks. I have found that certain stone colors, cuts, and finishes are hard to blend with the cottage garden aesthetic no matter what style of home is involved. Slick, glossy stone surfaces such as polished granite make me think of corporate office parks, not cottage gardens. Brightly colored stone may look appealing in the stoneyard, but it can clash with your home or your plantings, and you may tire of it after only a few seasons.

Of all the traditional cottage garden boundary structures, stone walls probably run the greatest risk of appearing too big for their surroundings. Even when the height of a stone wall is in proportion with the home and garden, its sheer bulk may be overwhelming. If the individual stones are too large for their context, your wall may appear awkwardly out of scale, no matter what its overall size. Be very cautious about using stones that measure more than 12 inches or 18 inches in any one dimension.

CONCRETE WALLS

For most of us, vertical concrete surfaces carry strong industrial connotations. This can make them hard to reconcile with the easy informality of a cottage garden. Nevertheless, concrete walls of various types certainly can have a place in the Northwest cottage garden.

Concrete walls can take two distinct forms: They can be poured in place, or they can be built out of precast masonry units. Poured-in-place concrete walls are just what they sound like: Wet concrete is poured into a form and allowed to harden in place. Its great advantage is that it can be formed into almost any imaginable shape. Poured concrete walls are probably most comfortable in association with aggressively modern homes that feature exposed concrete construction themselves. Faced with colored stucco, they also make an ideal enclosure for a cottage garden that surrounds a Spanish Colonial home.

Precast concrete masonry units, which can be purchased in a variety of sizes and shapes, are installed much like stones or bricks. Some are made to stack neatly into walls without the need for mortar, and many are colored and textured to resemble other building materials. Precast masonry units offer the advantages of limited expense and easy installation. You might not think that they would make a fitting cottage garden wall, but I have seen some very handsome walls built out of small, rectangular precast units, especially those with rough surfaces and subtle, natural tints. I think these walls are most appealing when finished off by flat cast concrete or stone caps in light, contrasting colors. If you are considering precast concrete masonry units for your cottage garden wall, try to borrow a few sample units and stack them in front of your home so that you can see how they will look before you commit to a major purchase.

HEDGES

Rich in traditional associations, hedges are one of the oldest forms of cottage garden enclosure. Compared with artificial structures such as walls and fences, they offer a unique combination of opportunities and challenges when used to enclose a Northwest cottage garden. Hedges, even those that are clipped into rigid geometrical forms, are inherently softer in appearance than either walls or fences. They are highly effective at muffling noise and screening out unsightly views. They can be extremely ornamental in themselves, adding interesting forms, colors, and textures to the cottage garden's plantings. Nevertheless, a hedge almost always requires more ground space than a wall or fence of similar height. Hedges also require more frequent and intensive maintenance than walls or fences, especially if they are kept clipped into formal patterns. Pets or wildlife may penetrate them; and they may also host populations of vermin, even in the most exclusive of urban neighborhoods. Finally, hedges differ from walls and fences in that they require time—often quite a bit of time—to mature. It may be years before your newly planted hedge will become solid and attain the height you want.

CLIPPED HEDGES

In form, size, and texture, hedges are tremendously flexible as design elements. They may be evergreen or deciduous, clipped or informal; and, depending upon the species you choose and the amount of pruning you give them, they may be of almost any size. The impact of a hedge upon your cottage garden design depends above all on whether or not it is clipped. As boundary structures, clipped hedges are at least as formal in appearance as most walls or fences. You may need to take special measures to reconcile their formality with the sense of casual comfort that underlies the cottage garden style. Achieving this may require no more than planting an informal mixed border along the inside of a clipped hedge so as to soften its outline and break up the unrelieved mass of greenery. If you do plant

a border to temper the mass of a formal hedge, be sure to leave enough space between the hedge and the border so that you can clip the former without squashing the latter.

Whatever profile you choose for your clipped hedge, take care to keep the top trimmed at least slightly narrower than the bottom. Otherwise, sunlight will fail to filter through to the lower branches, and the bottom of the hedge will thin out and eventually become bare. When planning a hedge that is to be clipped, keep

Hedges are perhaps the oldest form of cottage garden boundary.

in mind the ultimate width and height you prefer to maintain and select plant materials of appropriate growth habit. Don't choose a tall, columnar arborvitae for a low, broad hedge, or a spreading juniper for a tall, narrow screen. You will only wind up disappointed.

Keep the texture of the plants you choose in mind as well when you plan a hedge that is to be formally clipped. Large, coarse foliage can look shabby and tattered when subjected to frequent shearing, so you might prefer plants with dense, fine-textured foliage.

UNCLIPPED HEDGES

Unclipped, informal hedges can be any height or shape, depending upon the plants you choose for them. There are outstanding hedge plants with tall, narrow forms and with broad, spreading forms. Some have tidy, domed shapes, while others have weeping profiles or stiffly upright habits. Some are dense and tightly knit, others are more free or open.

44

Make sure the hedge is the right size for your house and your property. Those 3-foot photinias may look great when you plant them, but in five years your single-story home could be squatting behind a towering 15-foot hedge! In urban and suburban neighborhoods, I like informal hedges made from dense plants with tidy, regular habits, while in rural settings I prefer those that are more loose and irregular.

Before planting any hedge, consider the possible need for feeding and irrigation. Many popular hedging plants need little by way of supplemental water once established, but most will require irrigation for their first couple of seasons, at least until their root systems are fully established. You may also want to consider temporary boundary structures. Many hedges will take several seasons to fill out and knit together into a solid barrier. Foot traffic (human or animal) between the plants damages side branches and surface roots, and may greatly delay closure of the hedge.

BORDERS AS BOUNDARIES

A mixed border is the least formal boundary structure you can use to enclose your cottage garden. Compared with more solid and substantial boundary structures, a planted border offers little barrier against foot traffic, pets, children, or wildlife. It is at best only a visual boundary, and even in this capacity it will offer less privacy than a wall, hedge, or panel fence. A border used as a boundary extends the garden itself onto the street front or the property line, signaling the atmosphere of the cottage garden to all comers. For this reason borders are a good choice of cottage garden boundary wherever the garden's ambience has to be established quickly and decisively. They are especially effective in townhouse courtyards or on small lots in dense urban neighborhoods. If you employ a border as your cottage garden boundary, you'll want to give it a sturdy backbone of woody or evergreen plant material to make it feel substantial.

Any border with enough substance to act as a firm visual boundary will probably be wide—certainly wider than a fence or wall of comparable height. Be certain to allow enough space in your ground plan to accommodate such a wide footprint. Borders normally require more feeding and watering than hedges to remain attractive, and this makes them more labor-intensive to maintain. Getting

45

water to a boundary border with ease and regularity is a serious undertaking, so you may want to consider an automated irrigation system.

ENTRY STRUCTURES

Whether it is a weathered wooden fence or an arch festooned with flowers, the entryway is more than just a passage through your cottage garden's boundary. It is at once an invitation to enter and a means of controlling and directing traffic into and out of your garden. Entry structures for Northwest cottage gardens can be as simple as a gap in a hedge, or as complex as a gated archway, but they should always uphold the principles of scale and modesty that account for the cottage garden's comfort and charm. The styles and materials of the best cottage garden entryways reflect both the adjacent boundary structure and the home.

To work properly, an entryway needs to be obvious and clearly demarcated. After all, you wouldn't want visitors to be at all confused about where to enter your cottage garden. If you think your entryway is too inconspicuous, it may only need something as simple as a pair of urns or planted containers set at either side of it.

You will also want to locate your entryway logically in relation to both the house and the public thoroughfares, such as streets and sidewalk. Putting it in the wrong place will at best confuse visitors and, at worst, encourage them to force their way through the garden's boundaries in all sorts of awful ways. If you have undertaken the process of site analysis outlined in Chapter Two, you already know where your entrance or entrances need to be. Whenever possible, locate the entry to your cottage garden on level ground. Walking up or down a slope or stair through the garden entry is no problem, but entryways set parallel to the slant of a steeply sloping street or sidewalk are difficult to negotiate. Your entryway must be big enough to accommodate expected traffic in and out of your garden. For most situations, this means a width of at least 3 feet. If you want visitors to able to enter two abreast, plan on at least a 5-foot-wide opening.

GATES

Gates are an extremely popular choice of cottage garden entry structures in the Pacific Northwest. Their versatility is undoubtedly a reason: A gate can be set into a fence, a wall, or a hedge. Gates are also comparatively secure, and best of all, they can be made or purchased in a wide variety of styles and materials.

A wooden gate makes an especially fine canvas for decorative details and touches of design whimsy that can enliven and personalize your Northwest cottage garden. The top of a panel or picket gate may have an arched, depressed, or pointed profile. Perhaps your panel gate will have hearts, diamonds, or stars cut out of its panels. You can paint it in colors that contrast with the fence, or even with a

small mural, if that suits your garden's overall design and mood.

A metal gate can make a more refined and urbane impression in the cottage garden than a wooden one. You can purchase a ready-made metal gate in any number of styles, sizes, or finishes, or you can have one custom designed and fabricated to suit your particular garden. The range of decorative details that can be built into a metal gate is beyond limit—from simple curlicues or spirals to full-fledged metal sculptures depicting flower arrangements, wildlife, or land-

Wooden gates can be decorative as well as practical when used as cottage garden entry structures.

scapes. Metal gates can also take on many finishes, from colored powder coating to natural or chemically induced patinas.

Hardware for the cottage garden gate may be simply functional or ornamental. You will find latches and hinges in all sorts of finishes and patterns, and even some that are sculpted to resemble leaves, blossoms, or insects. Whether it's simple or elaborate, make sure all of the hardware for your garden gate can withstand wet Northwestern winters without corroding. Corroded metal fittings are not just an annoyance to replace—they can ruin the finish of your gate and fence posts as well.

ARCHWAYS

If any structure signifies the cottage garden better than an archway half engulfed in blooming clematis and roses, I cannot think of it right now. The archway just may be the quintessential cottage garden entry feature. Surely nothing has a more appealing way of framing the view into the garden, nor is any other entry structure quite so effective as a vertical accent to the garden's boundary. Used on its own or in combination with a gate, a well-placed archway can complement any fence, wall, or hedge.

This archway, woven of live plum tree branches, is a clever and inviting garden entry.

Wood and metal are the two most common building materials for archway entries into Northwest cottage gardens, and both allow for plenty of variation in style and finish. Wooden arches usually take one of three forms: the barrel arch, the peaked arch, or the flat-topped portal. You can always recognize the barrel arch by its semicircular outline. I like its clean, simple profile with many traditional Pacific Northwest home styles, including Neo-Colonial, Craftsman, Victorian, Queen Anne, Tudor Revival, and Spanish Colonials.

The peaked arch has a triangular profile, just like the rooftops of so many Pacific Northwest homes. A broad, shallow peaked arch will reflect the roofline of a Craftsman home or a traditional farmhouse, while a more acute angle will mirror the steeper roofs of Neo-Colonial, Victorian, and Tudor Revival architecture.

The flat-topped portal is the simplest of all archway designs as well as one of the most versatile. These two attributes surely help account for its great popularity as an entry structure for Pacific Northwest gardens of all styles. Flat-topped portals are often built with lintels that project out past the vertical supports on each side. You can have these projecting lintel ends carved into decorative shapes to complement the trim of the house or the finials on your fence posts.

Metal can be fabricated into barrel arches, peaked arches, and flat-topped portals, but you may also find it formed into Gothic or Tudor arches, which curve gracefully upward to a pointed top. Consider this more elaborate arch profile if you live in a Tudor Revival or Victorian home, whose rooflines, windows,

and carved trim will make an ideal backdrop for its sinuous curves. Ready-to-install metal arches in a plethora of styles and finishes are available these days in garden centers and home stores up and down the Pacific Northwest. Many are made by local artisans and will lend a unique regional flavor to the cottage garden entryway. Before purchasing a ready-made metal archway, be certain there will be sufficient headroom under it once its lower end is sunk into the necessary footings. You can assume that 7 feet will be an adequate mini-

Flat-topped arches appear in many Pacific Northwest gardens. They are simple, modest, and easy to build.

mum height, and remember that at least 1 foot of the arch's base will be below ground once installation is complete.

Besides making an inviting entry, a freestanding arch will lend structure to a mixed border or an informal hedge that is used as a boundary. If your cottage garden boundary is a hedge or a mixed border but you'd like to have a gate, a gated freestanding archway is the way to do it.

One of the most appealing properties of arched entryways in the cottage garden is their ability to support decorative climbing plants—but please do use discretion when you're choosing those plants. Big, woody, twining climbers such as

wisteria can stress the structure of your archway as they grow. In time they may break or bend the arch, or even rip it from the ground! You will also want to avoid thorny climbing roses that will tear flesh and clothing; there are plenty of lovely thornless roses that will climb a garden archway without injuring your visitors. (See Chapter Six for recommended varieties.) Ivy and other climbers that cling by holdfasts can ruin painted finishes and permanently mar stained or unfinished wood surfaces. If you plan to grow climbing plants on

This entry arch supports a wonderful display of climbing plants. Its extra width allows visitors to pass unimpeded.

your arched entryway, make sure that it is large enough to accommodate both plants and pedestrians with comfort. Visitors don't want to elbow their way through a wall of vegetation to enter your cottage garden—and you shouldn't have to leave a machete hanging by your garden gate to ease their passage.

SIMPLE GAPS AS ENTRYWAYS

Plain gaps in a fence, wall, or hedge are the simplest of all cottage garden entries. Though they offer no security and will not contain pets or children, they do possess the advantages of low cost and low maintenance. Their chief drawback is that they don't do much to signal their own presence. Without design help of some kind, a gap in a fence, wall, or hedge can be uninviting, or just plain too hard to find. A pair of large planted containers, some carefully chosen statuary, or even just some well-placed stones can often draw enough attention to highlight a plain gap as the cottage garden entrance. If all else fails, you can always make a gap more conspicuous by fitting it with a gate or archway.

WALKWAYS AND PAVED SURFACES

You can choose among a range of paving materials and styles that will mesh with the Pacific Northwest's physical environment and prevailing styles of home architecture. Traditional paving materials, such as brick, stone, and gravel, will be at home in any cottage garden. Here in the Pacific Northwest, where lumber has been a dominant resource for over a century, wooden decking is also a natural choice for cottage garden surfaces. Though it's often overlooked as industrial (or just plain ugly), concrete paving deserves neither criticism and, if well executed, has a place in the Northwest cottage garden as well. When designing pavement for a cottage garden, I prefer brick, stone, or concrete unit pavers to be set without mortar on a bed of well-compacted sharp sand. I find that mortar-set paving looks overly fussy in a cottage garden, and that the mortar joints are liable to crack or separate with time to become a messy, hazardous maintenance headache.

A free-standing gateway helps to define this gap in a hedge as a garden entry.

BRICK PAVING

Brick is the paving material of choice for many Northwest cottage gardens. It is inexpensive when compared with stone, it is readily available in a range of appealing colors, and it can be set in any number of decorative patterns. It is also consistent with any of the common Pacific Northwest home architectural styles. Because of our region's relatively mild winter temperatures, brick may be dry-set on a bed of sharp sand without danger of heaving or breakage due to heavy frosts. The warm earth tones in which brick is manufactured complement cottage garden plantings as well as most other natural building materials. Indeed, brick is just as effective as an accent to other paving materials, such as stone and concrete, as it is on its own. Brick paving may be set in the simple, traditional running pattern, or in the popular herringbone and basket weave. Other brickwork patterns may incorporate contrasting pieces of colored stone, precast concrete, or outdoor tile.

The warm tones of brick paving complement lively cottage garden plantings.

STONE PAVING

Stone paving shares many of brick's advantages, and while it may be more costly, it does offer an even wider choice of shapes and colors. There is surely a type and color of stone to suit any Pacific Northwest home. Stone pavers are available in bricklike blocks (called Belgian block if they are cut from granite), which may be set in any of the patterns commonly used with bricks. Flat stone pavers come in innumerable shapes and sizes. Irregularly shaped flat stones, referred to as flagstones, can be cut from an enormous range of different stones, including slate, bluestone, limestone, and granite. Most of these same materials are also available as regularly shaped cut-to-size pieces. When using stone for cottage garden paving, choose pavers of moderate size. I tend to worry about stones that measure more than 18 inches or 24 inches in any dimension, as they can be too large for the intimate scale of the well-planned cottage garden. Avoid choosing stones with extremely slick or polished surfaces as well. Not only may they be too suave in appearance for the unpretentious cottage garden, but, like brick, they can be hazardous to walk on during rainy Northwest winter weather.

CONCRETE PAVING

If the look of brick and stone paving appeals to you but the materials are beyond your garden budget, consider precast concrete paving units as an alternative.

Look for concrete pavers with simple shapes and natural-looking colors. Some of the very nicest precast pavers feature exposed aggregate surfaces or subtle, preweathered surface treatments that are especially well suited to the cottage garden style.

We tend to overlook poured concrete as a material for cottage garden paving. Maybe that's because of its utilitarian and commercial associations. Before dismissing concrete, though, recall that cottage gardens are utilitarian in origin, and poured concrete offers unique advantages where utility is concerned! It is strong, it is cost-effective, and it can be poured into almost any desired shape. Properly installed, it will last for decades with little or no maintenance. Poured concrete walkways can assume curved alignments that are more difficult to execute in brick or stone. Their surfaces can also be custom-tinted to suit any taste and sculpted by various means to add pattern or textural interest. Such flexibility means that you can design an attractive concrete walk for any Northwest property.

Poured concrete pavement may be washed under pressure before it is fully hardened to expose the pebbly aggregate at the surface. Such exposed aggregate finishes leave concrete looking a bit like gravel, with a lovely, soft texture that naturally suits most cottage garden plantings. You can also score, rake, or incise still-wet concrete so that the finished surface will catch light and cast shadows in any number of patterns. Parallel or wavy lines, random hatch marks, even dancing

Flagstones make a charming and informal path through this Northwest cottage garden.

footprints, can add charm or excitement to a simple concrete walkway. Take care when cutting patterns into concrete, however, for if the incisions are too wide or deep they may catch up your heels or cause visitors to trip.

For an entirely different effect, you can also inlay poured concrete with any number of materials, from stones and tiles to pieces of colored glass. You can sprinkle your contrasting inlays sparsely through the paving as occasional surprises, or cluster them densely into a veritable mosaic. Unless you limit your inlay work to the peripheries of your walkways, try to keep it flush with the concrete surface so it won't be a tripping hazard.

Don't overlook concrete as a paving material. It is not only durable, but can be treated and tinted to yield beautiful effects.

You may want to edge your poured concrete walkways and paved areas in brick or stone of contrasting color or texture. If you choose to tint the concrete for your paving, select subtle colors that will blend with, or enhance, the colors of your home and other garden structures. Bright, garish colors can quickly outwear their welcome or strike a discordant note in the cottage garden composition. Try to procure a dried sample of the tinted concrete mixture before your pavement is poured, since the final color of tinted concrete reveals itself only when completely dry.

Whether it is tinted, surface treated, or left in its natural state, concrete paving of any extent will require expansion joints to prevent cracking and heaving under Pacific Northwest climate conditions. Mercifully, expansion joints are no longer the gloppy, tar-oozing eyesores of old suburban sidewalks. You can now find non-oozing, rubberized and fiber-based expansion joint materials in a wide range of colors to blend with, or subtly highlight, your poured concrete pavement. Our relatively mild Pacific Northwest winters even let us use wooden expansion joints for concrete paths, at least on low-altitude sites where frosts tend to be moderate. These are especially attractive with softly tinted exposed aggregate concrete paving.

WOODEN WALKWAYS AND DECKING

Wood itself is the quintessential Northwestern construction material. It is not only beautiful to look at and comfortable to the touch, but relatively inexpensive and easy to work with as well. Nevertheless, wood does present significant drawbacks as a walking surface for Northwest cottage gardens. It requires much more maintenance than brick, stone, or concrete. Unless carefully treated, it is also liable to become dangerously slick during rainy winter weather. More limiting still is a certain stylistic dissonance between wooden paving and the cottage garden tradition.

Natural and common a material as it is, wood paving has never been a traditional component of cottage garden design. Unless designed with extreme care, wooden decking and walkways can seem out of place in cottage gardens built around traditional homes, even when the wood is stained or painted to match the trim of the house. I think that part of this discord stems from the relatively hard, straight edges found on most wooden decks and walkways. If you allow vegetation to sprawl over the edges of your wooden decks and walkways, you will go a long way toward reconciling them with the cottage garden setting. Natural-looking finishes help as well.

No such caveats apply when wooden walks and decking are employed for cottage gardens built around modern and Northwest Contemporary homes, especially those that feature stained or naturally finished wooden siding. If you live in one of these homes, wood may be the perfect material of choice for your cottage garden walks and surfaces. It will blend effectively with the architecture of your home and carry its style and finish out into your garden.

I prefer to keep the height of wooden walks and decks for cottage gardens at a minimum, since walks and decks set at more than a few inches above ground level leave garden occupants standing *above*, rather than *in*, the garden. This can result in a disorienting Alice-in-Wonderland perspective that is altogether at odds with the comfortable cottage garden aesthetic. High wooden decks and walkways can also tower ominously over the cottage garden landscape, ruining its vital sense of human scale.

GRAVEL PAVING

Whereas wood is a relatively novel material for cottage garden surfaces, gravel is among the oldest and most traditional. Gravel's casual, natural appearance is perfectly in tune with the cottage garden image, while its slightly yielding texture and unique crunch underfoot have a special charm all of their own. There are, however, several reasons why you may want to limit gravel paving to peripheral or secondary pathways in your Northwest cottage garden. For one thing, gravel walks can be messy, especially during winter rains, when silt and debris collect on their surfaces. In addition, they require frequent maintenance. Loose gravel walks may have to be raked several times a season to keep the gravel evenly spread, and you will have to replenish the gravel on all walks on occasion as well. Cottage gar-

den plantings tend to intrude into gravel pathways over time, requiring periodic pulling. Finally, there is the issue of weeds. By all means, set your gravel paths down over a coating of permeable landscape fabric to discourage weeds. But even if you do, weeds will inevitably sprout within the gravel itself, and you will have to take measures to control them, lest they consume your walk-

Gravel paving is soft in appearance and relatively easy on the budget.

way after only a few seasons. For secondary pathways that receive less traffic, I do like gravel paving. Sharp, angular particles one-quarter inch in diameter or smaller make the most effective gravel paving because they will compact and become solid underfoot after a little use. Smooth, rounded pea gravel will remain soft and shifty, and may well lead to twisted ankles. Likewise, larger chunks of crushed stone often fail to settle into a solid surface, making for unsure footing.

GRASS WALKWAYS

You may want to use grass walkways for your cottage garden, though they possess distinct disadvantages in comparison with solid materials such as concrete, stone, or brick. During the moist Northwest spring and fall, turf grass grows rapidly, requiring frequent mowing. Since much of the region's soil is to some extent acidic, turf walkways usually require liming as well. During the characteristically dry Pacific Northwest summer, grass becomes parched and brown without frequent irrigation. Many gardeners think the feeding, liming, and irrigation required to maintain lawn are environmentally irresponsible, and it is surely worth keeping local ecology in mind when considering grass walkways for a Northwest cottage garden.

If you do include grass pathways in your cottage garden plan, you will need to employ some kind of edging to prevent borders and beds from invading the turf or vice versa. A 2-foot-wide strip of brick or granite-block paving between the lawn and the border makes an effective boundary. A row of bricks or granite blocks set on end, either straight up or at an angle (for a sawtooth effect), is another tradi-tional cottage garden edging solution.

PLANTINGS AND EDGINGS FOR COTTAGE GARDEN PAVEMENT

When they are dry-set on a bed of sand, small pavers—whether brick, stone, or concrete—

A classic cottage garden edging

One less-permanent edging strategy is to construct a line of bent twigs along the border's edge, the ends of each twig stuck firmly into the ground. Each resulting arch should overlap its neighbors to form a scalloped pattern along the front of the border. Twigs from cherry laurels, fruit trees, and willows work especially well for such simple woven edgings. If you don't have a source for these free prunings, take heart. Tightly woven willow edging strips are available from garden stores and catalogs, as are gracious metal edging panels with Greek key patterns or elaborate Victorian scrollwork. All are easily installed using short stakes. While woven twig or willow edging is rustic and informal in the garden, metal edging adds a touch of sophisticated elegance to the cottage garden planting.

require a secure edging to hold them in place. This edging may be as simple as bricks or cut-stone blocks set on end, their exposed tops flush with the paving. For added visual interest and a very finished appearance, try using a contrasting edging material. I find that granite, sandstone, or limestone blocks in light, neutral colors make particularly lovely edgings for brick pathways. Likewise, double rows of bricks set on end are a fine, contrasting edge treatment for walkways of light-colored stone or concrete pavers. Though the edges of most cottage garden walkways are often covered by cascading plants during the growing season, decorative edge treatments will probably be visible during the winter months, when the garden will most benefit from their added ornamental quality.

Tiny plants growing in the spaces between stone, brick, or concrete pavers are a favorite cottage garden feature. Diminutive creepers, such as Irish moss *(Sagina subulata)*, baby's tears *(Soleirolia soleirolii)*, and blue star creeper *(Pratia pedunculata)*, add a certain time-worn aura that softens the appearance of any pavement. Minuscule creeping herbs, such as woolly thyme *(Thymus pseudolanuginosus)* and

Corsican mint *(Mentha requienii)*, add the pleasure of fragrance as their scented oils are released with every footfall. Once established in the spaces between pavers, all of these plants will thrive under the usual Pacific Northwest growing conditions without much extra care or watering.

Do use care introducing such creeping plants into high-traffic paved areas, though. Most will not tolerate heavy foot traffic, and even if they do survive, their wet, decomposing foliage can become hazardously slick during our sog-

A simple stone edge demarcates a cottage garden border.

gy Pacific Northwest winters. Individual stepping stones or isolated pavers set in ground cover plantings do not offer the secure footing of solid paving, so you will probably want to limit these to your less-traveled cottage garden pathways.

DESIGN PRINCIPLES FOR COTTAGE GARDEN WALKWAYS

Cottage garden walkways of any material are subject to a few essential rules of design. In keeping with the fundamental simplicity of cottage garden layout, path alignments should be as direct as possible. A site plan developed along the lines set out in Chapter Two will provide the general locations for your walkways. They need not always be straight, but they should not wander pointlessly. Wherever possible, changes in direction should be gradual, so that pedestrians do not have to turn abruptly. All cottage garden pathways should be wide enough for comfortable passage (for secondary paths, 30 inches is a safe minimum width), yet not so wide that pedestrians feel dwarfed. I believe that in most residential landscapes anything more than 6 feet wide begins to feel more like a patio than a walkway. Within these bounds, the width and alignment of the walkways will profoundly affect the way visitors experience your cottage garden.

Paths that are relatively broad and straight cause visitors to move briskly along their length, while those that are narrow or winding encourage more leisurely motion. The garden's main thoroughfares ought logically be relatively wide and straight, allowing people to move from one portion of the garden to another quickly and efficiently. You can make your subsidiary pathways more circuitous and narrow, encouraging visitors to linger among the garden's pleasures. Pathways that curve out of sight behind structures or vegetation create an inviting sense of mystery and expectation in the cottage garden. Use such curves to prepare visitors for a special visual treat, be it a set of sculptures, a fountain, or an especially colorful group of plantings.

Where two pathways intersect, make sure their surfaces are flush and level, even if they are made of different materials. An uneven junction is

Small, creeping plants soften an expanse of stone paving.

an invitation to trip, and secure footing is essential to the sense of comfort so characteristic of the cottage garden. If your pathways must negotiate slopes, avoid long grades of more than 10 percent or so, which will become uncomfortable to climb over more than a few steps. Instead, align the path so that it travels across the face of the slope in a series of S curves or switchbacks, or incorporate garden steps as necessary. For comfort and safety, also avoid any perceptible tilt across the width of a pathway.

STEPS

More than gardeners in most parts of North America, we in the Pacific Northwest must deal with the challenges of sloping sites and steep topography. This means that many of our walkways will incorporate a set of steps. In the cottage garden, steps may be made of the same material as the surrounding pavement, or they can be built of contrasting materials to add decorative value and signal the change in grade. I like steps of light-colored cut stone against a red brick path, while brick stairs can be effective accents to poured concrete walkways. You will want the steps on your primary cottage garden pathways to be smooth, level, and evenly sized. The step proportions given in Chapter Two feel natural underfoot as people traverse a stairway up or down. Try to make your cottage garden steps as low and deep as feasible, since low, deep steps require less effort to climb and descend than do steep ones. Make sure all the steps are set securely, so that they do not slip, tilt, or jiggle underfoot. The exposed front edges of stone steps may be roughly cut—a nice, informal look for a cottage garden—but be sure they are free of any large protuberances that might catch the toes.

Curved stairways, with their flowing lines, subtle angles, and gentle arcs, are exquisitely graceful in a cottage garden setting. For comfort and ease of passage, keep the curve constant, and provide a landing at any point where it becomes straight. Unless flanked by walls or buildings, any stairway that climbs more than 30 inches without a landing should have a railing on at least one side. Railings should be simple in design and neatly finished and should stand approximately 36 inches high. Avoid anything bulky, and try to coordinate the style and finish of your railings with that of your other garden structures and the trim on your house. Railings are less critical on wide, shallow flights of steps than on steep, narrow ones. Local building codes in Northwest cities, towns, and counties define the cases in which railings are strictly required and also dictate acceptable heights and design parameters.

Remember that broad stairs can do double duty as seating in the cottage garden, especially when they face important decorative elements, such as fountains, statuary, or arrangements of colorfully planted containers. Small creeping or clinging plants add a wonderfully casual touch to less heavily used cottage garden stairways. As with the plants used between pavers, try to keep these little creepers off the centers of the treads, where they may cause visitors to slip. For the same reason, you will want to avoid plants that are more than an inch or two tall.

RETAINING WALLS

The same regional topography that accounts for steps along so many garden walkways in the Northwest makes it likely that your cottage garden will need at least one retaining wall. By far the most common solution for retaining slopes in Pacific Northwest residential landscapes is the randomly stacked rockery. These are often built of native stone, and hence look fairly natural in most home landscape situations. Their sheer ubiquity in the residential neighborhoods of the major Northwest towns and cities means they rarely appear to be out of

Steps are a necessity in many Pacific Northwest landscapes. Remember that long shallow steps are easier to climb than small steep ones.

context. Brick, stone, and even concrete can make very attractive and effective retaining walls in Northwest cottage gardens, provided their proportions and style are consistent with the rest of the garden's structures, furniture, and decor. One newly popular material for retaining wall construction is broken concrete paving. Stacked with their broken edges exposed, the flat, irregular chunks of concrete that result from sidewalk or roadway demolition look surprisingly at home in the Northwest cottage garden, perhaps because of their rough surfaces and informally random proportions.

Whatever style and materials you select for your retaining walls, adequate drainage will be critical to their long-term performance and endurance. Surprising volumes of water move through most Pacific Northwest soils, especially during the winter. Unless you plan a bog garden at the foot of each retaining wall, you will need to accommodate the flow of water as it meets the back side of the wall. Otherwise it will either pool behind the wall or seep through, threatening the wall's integrity in either case. Solid retaining walls are best served by a

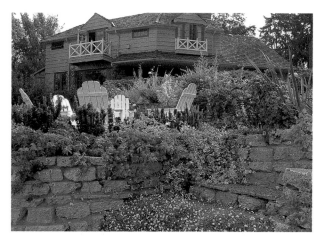

perforated drainpipe buried in a crushed rock bed set just behind the top of the wall. High retaining walls or walls that face particularly steep, wet slopes may require a number of such drains set behind them at various levels to prevent pooling along their tops. You may also need a buried drain of similar construction in front of the wall in order to prevent pooling at the base. Open stacked rockeries are often constructed without drainage and allowed to "weep" water through their faces. In such cases, a buried drain at the base of the rockery will help to prevent water from

Rockeries and rough stone retaining walls are common features of Pacific Northwest landscapes. They work well in cottage garden settings, provided the stones are not too large!

accumulating. Any stacked rockery will be more stable and durable if it is drained in the same manner as a solid retaining wall.

OUTBUILDINGS

Simplicity lies at the core of the cottage garden style, and nowhere is simplicity more vital than in the outbuildings—which, paradoxically, are potentially the most complicated of all cottage garden structures. Cottage gardens traditionally may include such elements as toolsheds, greenhouses, potting sheds, playhouses, and gazebos. Your own cottage garden layout may include one or more of these structures, depending upon your own needs and preferences. Outbuildings of any kind are subject to the same strictures of scale as any other cottage garden structure—only more so, because of their relative size and conspicuousness. Try to keep their rooflines, materials, and colors as consistent as possible with those of the house. If you live in a Craftsman home, consider a wooden shed with a shallowly sloped roof and overhanging eaves supported by exposed beams. A miniature Colonial playhouse would be ideal in the rear garden of a Neo-Colonial home. Sheds, playhouses, and gazebos are often built of wood, regardless of the materials employed on the home exterior. Stained or painted finishes should either match or complement those on the home or its trim.

No matter what their function, outbuildings in the cottage garden should be only as large or elaborate as utility and comfort require. Oversized buildings will disrupt the carefully gauged scale of your cottage garden more thoroughly than any other lapse in design. While a playhouse or a sheltered seating structure may well be the centerpiece of a given space, outbuildings that call too much attention to themselves can offer unwanted competition for your plantings and your home. That doesn't mean you have to be *too* inhibited about indulging your whimsy. The wall of a toolshed painted soft blue to accentuate the yellow-flowered climbing rose that clothes it is completely in keeping with the cottage garden style. Just remember that anything as ostentatious as a guesthouse tricked out like a medieval castle is probably not. If you keep your outbuildings modest, unobtrusive, and consistent with their surroundings, as you would any other cottage garden structure, they are certain to enhance both your home and your cottage garden's overall design.

This simple shed blends beautifully into its cottage garden setting.

GREENHOUSES AND SHEDS

Greenhouses entail their own special building materials—primarily glass, plastic, fiberglass, steel, and aluminum. Their appearance is invariably utilitarian, but not inherently unattractive. Choose the location of your greenhouse with some thought as to its construction materials and level of finish. Though an inexpensive greenhouse of inflated plastic over polyvinyl chloride (PVC) tubing would hardly be the architectural centerpiece of any Northwest cottage garden, a glass-walled greenhouse with aluminum or wood framing can be a true visual asset.

Sheds are no less utilitarian than greenhouses, but they may be built of a wider range of materials. Traditional building materials, particularly wood, are most consistent with a cottage garden setting. Vinyl-sided or aluminum-sided sheds risk looking too harsh and industrial for the cottage garden, and you might consider screening them from view if matters of budget or utility necessitate their use. Utility ought certainly to be the byword when it comes to locating a shed within your cottage garden. Tools, machinery, and gardening or recreational equipment should be stored for easy access and transport. Why drag a wheelbarrow or kayak through a border and over the vegetable patch every time you go to use it?

PLAYHOUSES AND GAZEBOS

A playhouse or gazebo is designed more for appearance and pleasure than utility, and either can function naturally as a decorative highlight in your composition. Playhouses, with their miniature details and quaint, child-friendly scale, are especially charming structures for the cottage garden. A playhouse must, above all, be safe and secure in its design and construction. This requirement being met, you are likely to find a playhouse of wood or other traditional regional building materials more in keeping with your Northwest cottage garden than one made of brightly colored plastic. Building a playhouse as a scaled-down model of your home is, of course, an aesthetically risk-free design approach.

Many sophisticated gardeners and designers sneer at gazebos, especially the popular prefabricated octagonal types. Fine and dandy, but sheltered outdoor seating certainly has its appeal in a place where it rains steadily for six months every year! The familiar Victorian gazebo earned its reputation as a landscape cliché by appearing too frequently in inappropriate garden contexts. While a

Victorian gazebo might be a respectable component of a large cottage garden set around a Victorian home, you will probably find it both out of scale and out of synch with a smaller urban cottage garden or a less ornately detailed home. I recommend a simpler wooden arbor with one or two benches as a far more appropriate structure for providing sheltered seating in most of today's Pacific Northwest cottage gardens. At least no one will snicker at it!

A quaint little playhouse like this one can be the focal point of an entire garden.

CHAPTER FOUR

Furniture and Ornaments:
Accessorize It!

A mossy stone bench, a weathered copper lantern, a fanciful birdhouse built of twigs—touches like these place a personal stamp upon your Northwest cottage garden. Cottage garden plantings are always a feast for the senses, but using garden ornaments as accents can add even further interest. Carefully chosen furniture also contributes to your garden's livability and comfort. Both furniture and decor offer you a chance to let loose and indulge your whimsy in the cottage garden. Think of furniture and ornaments as accessories to your cottage garden's "wardrobe": They complete the outfit while adding a touch of personal flair.

Elements of whimsy are always welcome in a cottage garden setting.

FURNITURE

Do you picture yourself lazing in a hammock under a bower of wisteria, or rocking gently on a porch swing while gazing at the summer stars? Perhaps your youngest child will serve tea and cookies to imaginary guests, all from a tiny garden table, while you prepare to serve the neighbors an *al fresco* dinner. Outdoor furniture sets each of these engaging scenes within the Northwest cottage garden. Cottage gardens are by nature livable, inviting places, the kind of places where you'll want to spend your leisure time. Even the tiniest of cottage gardens usually includes some furniture, if only a bench or chair from which to contemplate the plantings. You may, of course, want quite a bit more. If you plan to dine or entertain in your garden, outdoor furniture will be a significant aspect of its overall design. If you've gone through the planning process set out in Chapter Two, you probably already know just how much and what kind of furniture you'll need, and where it will go. If not, you'll want to think about the activities that will take place in your garden before you go furniture shopping.

Choose your garden furniture with scale and comfort in mind.

STYLE VERSUS COMFORT

Where furniture style is concerned, nearly anything goes in the cottage garden. Choose whatever suits your fancy, so long as it is comfortable. Outdoor furniture should satisfy your sense of style, but be sure to consult your backside, knees, elbows, and spine too! When shopping for outdoor furniture, bring a book or magazine with you, and sit down on every chair or bench you find attractive. Get comfortable, if you can, and then start reading. How do your back and tailbone feel after a few pages? If you can't spend more than a few minutes reading on it in complete comfort, that chair or bench is not worth the investment.

Looking for an outdoor dining table? Pull up a chair and spend some time at the table. Reach across, bend down as if to pick up a dropped napkin, and then get up and sit back down several times. Did you bump your head or elbows? Did your knees collide with the table's edge, its legs, or its pedestal? Does the table slide or wobble if you lean into it? Does the top tilt on the base if you rest your elbows on it? Did you almost knock the table over when you stood up? You're better off knowing all of this *before* you buy. I think you'll agree with me that the only cottage garden furniture worth owning is the cottage garden furniture you'll *use*. It makes sense to try before you buy, even if it gets you some funny looks.

SCALE AND MATERIALS

After style and comfort, the most important aspect of your cottage garden furniture will be its scale. It's relatively easy to determine whether a chair, bench, or table will fit into the space you've set aside for it, but predicting whether it will *look* right in the space is quite another matter. Given the intimate scale of most spaces in the cottage garden, the greatest risk is that the furniture that looked just perfect at the garden shop will seem too ponderous or heavy in your garden. As luck would have it, most truly comfortable outdoor furniture is built to the sort of modest, human scale that fits best into the cottage garden style. Still, the safest approach by far is to buy your outdoor furniture on approval, with the understanding that you can exchange or return it if it does not suit you on delivery.

WHERE DOES IT GO?

You may obtain the most comfortable garden furniture in the world, but put it in the wrong place, and nobody will use it! Happily, most garden furniture is easy to move, so don't be afraid to experiment and rearrange. If you try enough different configurations, you'll eventually find a layout that suits your needs. Of course, the job will go faster if you keep a few simple principles in mind.

People prefer to sit in partially enclosed private spaces with views of the garden beyond.

When you arrange an outdoor dining set, make sure you've chosen a spot close enough to the house, and preferably to the kitchen, to make serving convenient. I particularly dislike having to climb or descend garden stairs while carrying dishes laden with food and drink. It's also nice to set your outdoor dining furniture on a dry, even, level surface where guests have a commanding view of the garden. Perhaps this is why decks are so often used as outdoor dining rooms in Northwest cottage gardens.

Spots with commanding views are also great places for small groupings or lone pieces of furniture, including benches, cocktail tables, chairs, and hammocks. People love to sit in partially enclosed, private spaces that afford a view out into some larger sphere. A chair or bench set with its back against a border, building, fence, or hedge will almost always get more use than one that sits exposed out in the middle of a garden space. Perhaps it's a remnant of our animal heritage, but most of us feel most secure when seated with our backs protected against sneak attacks, unwanted visitors, or noisy surprises. People dislike sitting with their backs turned toward the entrance of a room, and outdoor seating is no different. Try to locate chairs, swings, or benches so their occupants can see the entry to the space they're in. You and your guests will all be that much more comfortable sitting in your cottage garden.

ORNAMENTS

Beyond furniture there is a whole realm of garden art and ornaments that can enliven and enrich your cottage garden. Because they are less likely to violate the fundamental scale and order of the cottage garden than are furniture or major structures, garden accessories give your imagination license to play. Containers, statuary, birdbaths, and many other garden ornaments are relatively portable, so you can also experiment freely with their placement.

Elegant, eclectic, or even capricious, the ornaments you select will help establish the overall mood of your cottage garden. Choice of decor can also be a way to enhance your garden's regional character. Certain subjects, styles, and materials in garden ornaments speak unmistakably of the Pacific Northwest and its artistic heritage. Among the surest ways to instill a distinctive Northwest ambience is to emphasize garden fixtures made by local artists in your garden design. A wooden statue by a Native American carver or a blown-glass hummingbird feeder by a student of the Pilchuck School would be a great way to add some local color to your garden. Local materials will do the trick as well: Whether driftwood gathered at the Oregon shore or river rocks from the Cascades, native materials speak eloquently of the Northwest when set out in the cottage garden.

SIGHT AND SOUND

A cast-concrete frog squats beneath a clump of irises. The wind chimes hanging from the plum tree overhead tinkle in the lazy summer breeze. Across the garden, this same breeze slowly turns the little orca whale that rests atop the weathervane. Each of these decorative accents contributes to the fabric of sights and sounds that enwrap the senses in the well-appointed cottage garden. Garden ornaments that appeal to the eyes and ears can be as simple as a few well-chosen rocks set out among your cottage garden's borders or elaborate as a group of metal sculptures on a brickwork dais. They may be as small

Garden ornaments add a personal touch to your design.

as a glass butterfly or as large as a wooden obelisk. Be careful not to select anything *too* big, of course. You'll want your ornaments to sustain the intimate scale of your cottage garden spaces!

Brightly colored flags or whimsically shaped weathervanes bring a welcome element of motion to the cottage garden. Sundials, whether newfangled or old-fashioned, set on a pedestal or flush with ground, introduce a subtle kind of motion all their own as the shadows slowly creep across their faces. Bells and wind chimes move as well, but as pretty as they may be dangling from a branch or suspended from the rafters of a porch, it is their music that endears them to us. Wind chimes and bells can be made of metal, wood, ceramics, or bamboo. Each material has its own distinctive sound, from the low, hollow chuckling of wood to

the resonant ping of metal. Listen carefully to them before you select any for your garden. In many parts of the Pacific Northwest they will sound off busily for much of the day and night, and what begins as a pleasant tinkling can become an irritant after a few hours of wind. For this reason, I suggest you hang your chimes where they are slightly sheltered from prevailing winds, so that they do not sound incessantly with the slightest breeze.

CONTAINERS

Planted containers are a long-standing tradition in cottage garden design, which aims to extract the most planting area from limited spaces. Containers can charmingly extend plantings onto decks and paved areas, but they also offer chances to juxtapose plants and decor in exciting combinations of color, form, and texture. Nearly any receptacle can play the part of cottage garden planter, provided it allows for adequate drainage and can withstand winter chills without breaking. I have seen delightful cottage garden plantings in elegant ceramic urns and in aluminum garbage cans.

Sight and sound can both add nuance to your garden's design.

For maximum impact, try grouping planted containers of various shapes, sizes, and materials into small "flotillas" here and there among your cottage garden's open areas or in-ground plantings. Whether singly or in groups, containers can also serve to divide and separate spaces within the cottage garden, or to direct traffic through your garden's open areas. You can also highlight a special plant or plant grouping by setting it in a lone, large container in the middle of a border or planted bed. Planted containers are a great way to experiment with novel plant combinations without committing to an entire border or island bed. I never tire of rearranging my many containers for a quick cottage garden makeover.

Lightweight containers mounted on brackets can add color and texture to cottage garden walls. Wall-mounted containers are also a superb means of breaking up oppressively large or featureless vertical surfaces. Window boxes, a popular variation on this theme, have been fixtures in cottage garden design for at least a century or two. Hanging containers, whether suspended from poles, porch roofs, or overhanging decks, can make a sort of "living curtain" to divide and define cottage garden spaces. Just remember that rainfall alone won't suffice for your container plantings, especially during the summer; check the soil in planted containers often for moisture, and be prepared to water them frequently throughout the warmer months.

Containers are a great way to extend your plantings onto decks or patios.

SUPPORTS

Do you swoon over lilac-flowered clematis and yellow climbing roses cascading from a Victorian wrought iron pillar? Perhaps you prefer wisteria draped across a wooden arbor? Arbors, trellises, and pillars have been part of cottage garden design for centuries. Incorporating these plant supports into your modern-day Northwest cottage garden establishes yet another link with that ancient and ongoing tradition. Like containers, they combine colors, forms, and materials for a range of decorative effects not available from plants alone. They not only create instantaneous vertical accents that highlight other plantings but also bring climbing plants up into another level of the picture, adding to the richly layered effect so typical of the cottage garden.

Custom-designed supports for climbing plants will add a unique, personal touch to your cottage garden; but these days you can also find ready-made supports in a gratifying range of sizes, styles, and materials. Whatever their material, make sure your supports are sufficiently large and steady to accommodate the plants you plan to grow on them. Heavy, twining climbers like wisteria can mangle or dismember a flimsy support after just a few seasons. Tall-growing climbers, such as *Clematis montana rubens*, will soon smother an 8-foot pillar (along with any

other nearby plant or structure). Conversely, you'll want to avoid supports that are too large or bulky for your space or that overwhelm the scale of your home and garden. Try to achieve a sense of balance between the support and the plants it will host. You may regret hiding an elaborate custom-made wrought-iron trellis underneath a mass of evergreen foliage. It would be just as sad if your most treasured climbing rose were upstaged by an ornate pillar. Think of any ornamental support and the plant or plants that climb it as a single unit in your cottage garden composition, and you will find yourself able to use it to its best advantage as a vertical accent or a focal point.

WATER FEATURES

Do you dream of a gurgling fountain, a still reflecting pool, or a basin full of water lilies to adorn a favorite corner of your garden? Water features enthrall gardeners and visitors alike, on several levels. Like flags and windmills, fountains can bring motion to the cottage garden. Like

Metal pillars can support climbing plants or stand alone as accents in a bed or border.

chimes, moving water can produce either soothing or invigorating sound effects. Pools and basins allow a Northwest cottage garden to support a selection of aquatic and marsh plants that it could not otherwise sustain. There are so many wonderful ways to introduce water into the Northwest cottage garden that the possibilities for self-expression and individual invention are beyond enumerating.

A water feature for the cottage garden can be as simple as a basin with a few aquatic plants or as elaborate as a tiled fountain, but do try to avoid anything *too* large or ostentatious. An outsized reflecting pool or an imposing fountain full of sculpted Renaissance sea gods will overwhelm the scale and balance of a well-made cottage garden. Modest water effects—ones that comfort, rather than dazzle—accord far better with the familiar domesticity that lies at the heart of the cottage garden style. Since cottage gardens are essentially domestic and obviously cultivated landscapes, I also prefer to avoid the contrived naturalism of artificial ponds and waterfalls. Unless your cottage garden actually backs up against the kind of rocky slope or forest where such things could reasonably be expected to appear, ponds, rills, and cascades that try to look "natural" will seem anything but!

Barring ostentation and incongruous naturalism, the Northwest cottage garden can accommodate water features of almost any sort. Simple birdbaths of stone, metal, or cast concrete are an easy way to bring water into the cottage garden, as are heavy-duty glazed ceramic basins. (Just be sure to empty ceramic containers before freezing weather arrives each fall, or your favorite basin may crack under the pressure of expanding ice.) A boulder or a large cut stone with a basin carved into its

Simple water features are the best bets for cottage garden accents.

upper surface makes a simple and attractive water feature when placed in a cottage garden bed or border. A small reflecting pool set into a patio or some other paved open space is exquisitely refreshing on sunny Northwest August afternoons, especially when accented by a few carefully chosen aquatic plants. I find that pools with simple geometric shapes, whether round, square, or rectangular, make the best foils for exuberant, informal cottage garden plantings.

Thanks to the advent of small submersible electric pumps, you can easily transform any of these still water features into a recirculating fountain. Try setting a tall, slender ceramic urn inside a shallow basin so that pumped water spills gently from the taller vessel's rim. Or perhaps you would prefer a trickle of water running down the side of a large, drilled stone that sits inside a small pool. Even so mundane an object as an old tin bucket with holes punched in its sides can make a charming and offbeat fountain when set astride a larger container and fitted with a pump.

Whatever the size and style of your water features, you will want to locate them where they can have their greatest possible decorative impact. Water has a hypnotic allure that makes it a natural focal point for any cottage garden composition. A basin, birdbath, pool, or fountain visible from the garden's entrance extends a refreshing welcome to your Northwest cottage garden. The sound of unseen moving water builds an expectant sense of mystery, so that a water feature deep in the garden can act as a lure for exploring visitors. Water, whether still or moving, invites quiet contemplation, so consider placing your pool or fountain near some comfortable seating. In fact, a seating area with a water feature placed in the garden's deepest interior can easily become the climax of your entire design, your cottage garden's core of comfort and repose.

LIGHTS

Whether a set of pierced copper lanterns, hidden fixtures built into a garden wall, or fanciful lamps with art glass shades, lights are at once utilitarian devices and an opportunity for decorative self-expression in the Northwest cottage garden. Outdoor lighting has come a long way since those awkward white glass globes that pocked suburban landscapes in the 1960s. Replicas of fixtures from the Victorian, Edwardian, Art Nouveau, and Art Deco periods abound, and well-made Craftsman reproductions have become extremely popular in Northwest gardens as well. Many tasteful modern outdoor fixtures with simple, geometric outlines are well suited to the cottage garden, but there is plenty of room for flights of fancy as well. With a bit of imagination, lights become another effective element in the creative cottage gardener's palette, just like furniture, containers, statuary, or plants. Lamps with posts cast as curvaceous bronze stems with copper leaves and colored blown-glass flowers for shades can blossom into welcome pools of light among clumps of coreopsis and campanula. Intricate South Asian lanterns made of brass are an exquisite accent when hung above a clump of ornamental grass or beardless irises. Colorful paper lanterns hung on strings or wires lend a festive touch to a cottage garden patio during parties or outdoor evening meals.

Garden lights differ from water features, garden art, or any of the other decorative elements discussed in this chapter in one important way: They often need to be placed with an eye to practical necessity as well as aesthetic pleasure. Paths and stairways are among the features most in need of supplemental lighting. The most effective fixtures for walks and stairs are shorter types that spread light downward over a broad expanse. These should be set well below eye level and have some kind of shade above their bulbs to prevent direct glare into the eyes. For best effect,

Lights can be important decorative features in the cottage garden.

place them close to the pavement edge, though not so close that they will trip up passersby or be damaged by the occasional wheelbarrow or trash receptacle. Patios also benefit from low fixtures placed at their periphery. Large spaces used for outdoor entertaining may require area lighting from taller fixtures; set these on posts or walls above eye level to avoid direct glare. Opaque shades that direct the output of tall lamps outward and downward will also minimize glare, as can frosted or translucent glass. Post-mounted fixtures alone may not be adequate for lighting larger outdoor entertaining areas, in which case you should consider mounting some simple, inconspicuous floodlights high overhead on your home

A pool or fountain can serve as the focal point of any garden space.

or on hidden supports among your taller plantings. These must be carefully located so as not to shine onto neighboring properties when lit.

In recent years some gardeners and designers have grown fond of highlighting trees or garden structures with powerful, upward-pointing floodlights or spotlights to outline them against the night sky. Though they are certainly dramatic, I find these up-lighting effects a little too contrived for the simple cottage garden style—besides which, they remind me of the spooky faces I once made at summer camp by shining my flashlight up from beneath my chin. You, of course, will have to come to your own conclusion.

The other recent trend, that of decking out trees and structures with strings of holiday lights, is all fine and well for special occasions, but I think that leaving these lights up all year robs the holidays of some of their festivity. I also find that trees festooned with lights all year remind me more of shopping malls than cottage gardens.

WILDLIFE

A Northwest cottage garden would hardly be its charming best without the chatter of birds among the trees and the bustling activity of bees amidst the blossoms. If the idea of attracting wildlife appeals to you, you'll find that the cottage garden style offers plenty of opportunities. The sheer variety and density of plant materials used in a cottage garden are in and of themselves a lure for wildlife. Classic cottage garden plants like buddleia, lavender, and bergamot are magnets for bees, butterflies, and hummingbirds. But why not add allure for birds and beneficial insects by providing them with extra food and shelter?

Bird feeders have always been a favorite Northwest garden feature, and many newer ones combine security from marauding cats, raccoons, and squirrels with real visual appeal. You are likely to find that bird feeders in materials such as wood, metal, and glass assort better with the rest of your cottage garden furnishings than those made of brightly colored plastic. Be sure to set your bird feeders where you can comfortably enjoy watching their patrons, and where no projecting tree limbs or structures give access to leaping squirrels.

Birdhouses have evolved well beyond the merely utilitarian and into ornamental objects of sometimes baroque intricacy. There are rustic fantasies of bark and moss, woven together atop poles or tripods of braided twigs. There are scale replicas of Victorian, Craftsman, and Colonial homes, lovingly detailed and painted by skilled regional woodworkers. There are colorfully stained bits of birdhouse whimsy built from discarded scraps of wood and metal. The birds may not opine on any of these styles, but as gardeners we have a surfeit of choice in birdhouse design. If these elaborate confections seem too studied for your tastes, a simple, traditional wooden birdhouse will be just as well-adapted to your Northwest cottage garden. Different shapes, dimensions, and openings are offered to suit various species of birds. Depending on your priorities, you may choose a birdhouse primarily for style or primarily for function, but even if it is never occupied, an attractive birdhouse will add to your cottage garden's charm and graciousness.

With their jewel-like colors and dazzling aerial acrobatics, hummingbirds could well be the Northwest cottage garden's most entertaining visitors—at least among non-humans. We are lucky beyond measure that these lovely little creatures are so at home in our region's residential neighborhoods. Today's hummingbird feeders can vie with the tiny birds themselves in brilliance. Exquisitely crafted blown-glass feeders in sparkling rainbow hues, made by Pacific Northwest artists, are exquisite garden ornaments all by themselves, and truly mesmerizing when frequented by their hovering visitors.

Cottage garden plantings invariably provide food for bees and butterflies, but insect lodgings are becoming popular as well. With the familiar honeybee endangered by parasitic mites, the orchard mason bee has gained importance as a pollinator in Pacific Northwest gardens and commercial growing fields. Orchard mason bees prefer to nest in narrow cavities, and over the past few years a range of specially constructed orchard mason bee houses have come onto the market to encourage their settlement. These mason bee houses can be as simple as a block of wood drilled with rows of uniform cylindrical holes, but of late they have begun to blossom into forms nearly elaborate and whimsical as birdhouses. Mounted on a wall, fence, post, or tree trunk, a house for orchard mason bees can serve both as a garden ornament and as a hostelry for valuable garden pollinators.

FOUND OBJECTS

Shopping for ornaments at garden centers, galleries, and nurseries can be great fun, but some of the very best decor for the cottage garden is found, not purchased. The principle of thrift that has guided cottage gardening through the centuries encourages recycling old, discarded objects into garden decor. Pieces of old farm equipment are popular as cottage garden sculpture. A rusted headboard, an old coat rack, or a metal chair can make a humorously quaint support for climbing plants. An old sign from a diner, a shop, or a gas station can add a whimsical touch of color to a border. A discarded sink or an abandoned

"Found objects" often make the best décor for cottage gardens!

clawfoot tub can be recycled as a water feature or a planter. Old pans and cutlery can be strung into wind chimes. I'm sure by now you get the picture: garage sales, antique shops, and attics are a mother lode of material for recycled cottage garden ornaments.

Increasing interest in found objects as garden art has unfortunately made the more sought-after pieces of refuse into expensive commodities. Luckily, for every old tractor wheel or headboard that retailers mark up to prohibitive prices, there are half a dozen appealing items that have not yet swept into fashion. I have no doubt that Northwest cottage gardeners will continue to find new, amusing, and attractive uses for the refuse of our disposable society. Which is as it should be, since choice of cottage garden decor, whether found or purchased, is ultimately an expression of the gardener's own personality.

THE PERFECT PLACE

Placement of your garden ornaments is just as important as your choice of garden ornaments. Where you put each piece of garden decor will determine how it impacts your overall cottage garden design. A statue or fountain set deep in a garden nook makes a pleasant surprise once visitors discover it. Set where you can see it from a distance, that same statue or fountain makes a lure to draw your visitors out into the garden. An ornament set amidst a bed or border act as a highlight to the planting, while one that stands alone out in the open is a focal point for the garden space it occupies.

Decorative objects can work much like traffic signs, marking out transitions at a slope, a stairway, or the bend in a path. The intersection of two pathways is a natural place for a garden ornament, inviting us to pause at the crossroads and decide which way we're going. The end of your main walkway is center stage for garden ornaments, the absolute focus of attention, and the place for your favorite piece of cottage garden decor. Whether it's a statue, a birdbath, a stone, or a fountain, the ornament you choose for this position should have enough size and personality to make a deep—though not overwhelming—impression. It may well set the tone for your entire cottage garden!

CHAPTER FIVE

Planting Design:
It's Not Just Tossed Salad

Abundance and exuberance are the touchstones of the cottage garden planting. Cottage garden beds and borders owe their ebullient, effervescent quality to the variety and density of their plant content. A garden can have all of the right features—a simple layout, traditional materials, comfortable structures and furnishings—but if it does not have frothy, informal plantings that overflow with color and fragrance, it will never be a cottage garden.

The typical cottage garden bed or border includes a combination of woody plants, perennials, annuals, climbers, herbs—even fruits and vegetables in many cases. The plants are closely spaced in informal arrangements that avoid any rigid, linear geometry. Successful cottage garden plantings are more than just a tossed salad of mixed greens and blossoms. Their variety is tempered by balance, their exuberance by a subtle underlying order.

COLOR

Cornflower blue and rose pink, lavender and lilac, goldenrod and primrose. Color, and lots of it: That's what we expect from cottage garden plantings! The trick is to include all of that color without causing utter chaos. Imposing some kind of order upon the garden's color schemes is one of our greatest challenges as cottage gardeners. Paradoxically, managing the apparently haphazard color combinations of a cottage garden planting calls for discipline, forethought, and a hearty measure of self-control. Remember: The cottage garden may look casual, but its effects are *calculated*. This is especially true where color is concerned.

CONTRAST AND HARMONY

The easiest and most radical form of discipline is to use only one color. After all, if your garden is planted entirely in blue, or pink, or yellow, nothing is going to clash. I am certain this was part of the appeal of those "white" gardens that came into vogue a few years ago. Keep to one color, and your cottage garden is ensured of being tastefully harmonious. And, did I forget to mention, dull? Monochromatic plantings may not clash, but they lack the element of contrast that is vital in establishing the cottage garden's fundamental verve. Cottage garden plantings depend upon contrast for their vibrant visual appeal, and for this no single color will do.

THE COLOR WHEEL

Without getting too technical, you'll need to master a few fundamentals of color theory to manage contrast and harmony effectively in your cottage garden plantings. Consider the color wheel, illustrated on this page. At equal distances around its periphery are the three primary colors: red, blue, and yellow. Between these are a series of hues that blend from one primary to the next. Moving clockwise from yellow come chartreuse, lime, true green, and then hues that become progressively bluer, until true blue appears one-third of the way around the wheel. From clear blue the spectrum shifts through violet, purple, and magenta, becoming more and more red, until, another third of the way around, true red emerges. Moving clockwise from red comes orange, blending slowly back to yellow as the wheel comes full circle.

WARM AND COOL COLORS

By convention, the colors on the wheel are grouped into two categories: "warm" and "cool." The cool colors center upon blue, becoming progressively warmer as they move away from blue in each direction on the wheel. Cool garden colors include the lavenders of *Buddleia davidii* and *Aster* x *frikartii*, the blues of scabiosa and delphinium, and the violet of *Clematis* x *jackmanii*. Cool colors are usually perceived as calming, soothing, and restful.

84

The warm colors center upon orange, directly opposite blue on the wheel. Other warm colors are the reds of cape fuchsias (*Phygelius* spp.) and 'Crimson Glory' roses, the yellow of coreopsis, and the gold of rudbeckias. Most people find that warm colors are stimulating to the eye and radiate a sense of energy and excitement. The dreary gray of our winters makes warm colors especially welcome in the Northwest cottage garden. Sunny yellows, bright tropical reds and oranges, and soft, glowing apricot are all alluring antidotes to the long, dark Pacific Northwest winter.

Broadly speaking, cool colors and warm colors contrast with one another. The farther apart on the color wheel two colors are, the greater the contrast between them. Colors that lie directly opposite one another on the wheel offer the sharpest possible contrast and are termed "complementary." The complement of a red rose lies in the green of its own foliage. A yellow goldenrod (*Solidago* spp.) is complementary to a violet salvia, and blue bachelor's buttons complement an orange Asiatic lily. Colors that are adjacent or near-adjacent to one another on the color wheel blend, or harmonize, in the garden, as do red monardas and violet geraniums, yellow Jerusalem sage (*Phlomis russeliana*) and orange geums, or blue oat grass (*Helictotrichon sempervirens*) and green junipers.

Cool colors, like blue, lilac, and lavender, are soothing to the eye.

BRIGHTNESS AND SATURATION

The colors on the rim of the color wheel are fully saturated. That is to say, they are unadulterated with black, white, or gray. Adding gray to any color mutes it and reduces its saturation. Blue mixed with gray becomes slate; yellow plus gray makes beige or tan; and magenta plus gray yields soft mauve. Shading a color with black darkens it and reduces its brightness. For instance, adding black to blue produces the navy of a dark bearded iris; adding black to yellow makes the

Warm colors, including yellow, red, and orange, excite the senses.

brown of autumn beech leaves; and adding black to magenta creates the deep burgundy of an old French moss rose.

Diluting a color with white makes it paler and softer—in other words, a pastel. The red of *Knautia macedonica* becomes the pink of a tree mallow *(Lavatera thuringiaca)*; the violet of a monkshood *(Aconitum* spp.) becomes the lavender of blooming thyme; and the orange of a trumpet vine *(Campsis radicans)* becomes the pale peach of a Noisette rose. The contrast between these diluted pastel colors is less stark than that between fully saturated colors. For example, forest green and burgundy contrast far less than kelly green and scarlet, while cream and lavender offer less contrast than violet and yellow. As you've surely noticed, dark colors contrast with light colors, even when they are derived from the same hue on the color wheel. By juxtaposing light and dark colors or warm and cool colors, you can create contrast in your cottage garden plantings. You can also moderate that contrast by choosing less-saturated colors.

THE BALANCING ACT

Contrasting color is vital in cottage garden plantings, but the cottage garden's premium on moderation and comfort means that its plantings also need to be easy on the eye. Too much contrast will amount to discord, and discord ultimately means discomfort. When we plant our Northwest cottage gardens, we want enough contrasting color to make our beds and borders sparkle, but we also want an overall sense of harmony and proportion. I feel that the true art of color in planting design lies in this balancing act between harmony and contrast.

After years of cottage gardening, I have come up with an easy way to impose discipline upon my cottage garden color schemes. Like so many basic tools, my method is simple—ridiculously so once it becomes familiar. Rather than base my plantings on two or three colors, I like to establish two contrasting palettes, from which I will then choose all the colors in a particular planting or garden space. The two palettes should contrast with one another, but the colors within each one are harmonious neighbors on the color wheel. Most of each planting contains colors from the "principal palette," while colors from the "accent palette" appear in smaller doses to provide contrast. Using two *palettes*, each of which contains a range of color, rather than two *colors*, assures an extra degree of vivacity in my plantings. By carefully adjusting the proportions between my chosen palettes, I can arrive at just the right balance between contrast and harmony in my plantings.

THE PRINCIPAL PALETTE

I like to begin each planting design by choosing my principal color palette. This main palette will account for about two-thirds to three-quarters of the foliage and flower colors that I use, and may cover a specific plant grouping, a border, or even an entire garden. Because the colors in your principal palette will dominate your

Dilute, pastel tints offer subtle contrast. Here the rose 'Lavender Pinocchio' complements a cream-colored daylily.

planting and establish its fundamental mood, you will want to choose with care. Do you want a bright, vibrant planting? Then choose warm, saturated colors for your principal palette. Would you prefer a gentle, reassuring feel? Consider a principal palette of cool pastels.

Remember, when choosing a principal palette, that a palette encompasses a *range* of colors. Red, or blue, or violet alone does not make a palette. For my principal palettes, I prefer a harmonious range of colors. For me, this means a group of colors that are neighbors on the color wheel, or that are darker and lighter variations on one or two related hues. For instance, I might choose a principal palette of fuchsia, magenta, violet, and blue for one garden, or white, pink, scarlet, and crimson for another.

My own cottage garden entryway is based upon a principal palette of white bush anemones *(Carpenteria californica)* and hellebores; cream, buff, and apricot daylilies and shrub roses; and

lemon and gold yarrow, Jerusalem sage, and Mollis azaleas. You might prefer a range of cool colors, including white Shasta daisies, lavender sage, baby-blue *Brunnera*, and deep purple clematis. Or perhaps you'll want a rich, sumptuous palette of crimson knautias, burgundy heucheras, violet irises, and a magenta rose. In any case, try to make sure your palette is wide enough to include some real variety, in either hue, saturation, or brightness. If your principal palette is too limited or uniform, your plantings will not

Two contrasting color palettes strike a balance between vivacity and order in this Northwest cottage garden planting.

have the liveliness and sparkle that we look for in a cottage garden. On the other hand, if your palette gets too broad, it's liable to be incoherent. Orange, scarlet, violet, and blue would not make a coherent principal palette because there is so much contrast among them. Generally speaking, I like to keep my principal palette limited to either the warm or the cool part of the color wheel. This ensures that the palette will have some level of coherence.

When choosing a principal color palette for your plantings, keep in mind the surrounding structures and materials. Plant colors in the cottage garden will not be seen in isolation. The colors of your home, your fence, your walls, and your walkways will all interact with your main palette of plant colors. A cool planting palette of blue, violet, and white will contrast sharply with a yellow home and brick walkways, but this same palette will blend quietly with gray-painted siding and slate pavement. Deciding from the first whether your main color palette should blend or contrast with your garden's conspicuous structures will guard against disappointing surprises when the garden starts to bloom.

THE ACCENT PALETTE

Once I have settled on a principal palette for a cottage garden planting, I develop a contrasting accent palette. The accent palette accounts for about one-quarter to

one-third of the color I will use in any given planting. If the principal palette for a planting consists of warm colors, I will use cool colors for the accent palette. If the principal palette is soft and pale, I may choose a deep, saturated accent palette for contrast. The degree of contrast between the principal palette and the accent palette determines just how vivid or subdued the entire planting will appear.

Consider a principal palette of mostly deep, cool, saturated tones: blue campanulas, violet geraniums, crimson roses, and magenta *Fuchsia magellanica*. There are several accent palettes from which to choose, each of which will impart its own flavor to the planting as a whole. Choosing an accent palette of warm, saturated colors—say, gold and orange—will make for vibrant contrast and an extremely exuberant color scheme. Warm colors of less saturation, such as buff, apricot, and pale yellow, will afford plenty of contrast as well, but the overall effect will be softer and less strident. An accent palette made up of light, paler versions of the reds, purples, and

Consider structures, as well as plants, when developing color palettes for your garden.

89

blues of the principal palette yields an entirely different outcome. If pale pink dianthus, soft lilac violas, and white bleeding hearts are used for contrast, the planting will appear more gentle and soothing. There will be contrast and sparkle, but of a much more subtle nature. Think of bubbles in champagne as opposed to fireworks.

Since the accent palette occupies by far the smaller portion of the planting, I like to keep it a bit more restricted in range than the primary palette. That way, it can remain coherent, even in the limited garden space allotted to it. The accent palette for my own small entry garden is limited to deep blues and violets from clematis, Siberian irises, and *Salvia nemorosa*, in contrast to the soft, warm principal palette of cream, yellow, white, apricot, buff, and gold.

Adjusting the proportions between the primary and accent palettes will alter the tension between the contrasting colors in your plantings. If your accent palette contrasts starkly with your principal palette, it will require only a relatively

small proportion of the planting to produce a vibrant and lively impression. Employ too much of it, and the results may be outright discordant. A tiny clump of *Viola labradorica*, with its blue flowers and dark violet leaves, is enough to shout out loud amidst a patch of golden-chartreuse *Lysimachia nummularia* 'Aurea'. Conversely, an accent palette that contrasts subtly with the principal palette may require up to one-third of the planting to make sufficient impact. The less of your accent palette you employ, the more gentle will be the impression the planting makes. Allot too much of the planting to the accent palette, and the whole planting will fall out of balance. The two palettes will clash with one another as they vie for primacy, while the eye strains to determine which is

Intense, saturated colors can create bold contrast in the garden.

dominant. For this reason, I like to make sure the principal palette accounts for at least 60 percent of the planting.

SOURCES OF COLOR

Mention color, and most gardeners' minds jump instantly to flowers. But the colors in our cottage garden planting palettes actually come from many sources. The cottage garden tradition, with its emphasis on efficiency and parsimony, demands that we wring every ounce of color from the plant materials we use. Most of any planting is made up of foliage, and foliage comes in colors besides green. Leaves may be the bronze of hybrid heucheras, the orange of New Zealand sedges *(Carex buchananii)*, the purple of purple smoke bush *(Cotinus cogyggria)*, or the silver-blue of blue fescue *(Festuca glauca)*, not to mention pink, cream, gold, and white. These foliage colors may combine with one another, or with green, in spots, stripes, blotches, veins, or washes. And that accounts only for summer colors. Autumn hues, of course, offer an entirely different palette, as do the colors of emerging foliage in spring.

Color can come from fruits as well, from the white of native snowberries *(Symphoricarpos albus)* to the purple of eggplants and *Callicarpa*, or the oranges and reds of rose hips and viburnums. Twigs and bark contribute to the cottage garden paintbox too. There are the reds of *Cornus alba* 'Sibirica' and *Acer palmatum* 'Sango Kaku', the rust and cinnamon of *Acer griseum*, and the stark white of *Perovskia* in winter. All of these plant colors can and should be part of your color calculations as you plan your Northwest cottage garden.

COLOR QUIRKS

Not all plant colors are created equal. Several common foliage and flower colors can display surprising properties when used in a mixed planting. If you are aware of these color quirks, you will be better equipped to predict the results of your chosen cottage garden color schemes. Chief among the quirky colors in the garden are white, red, and green.

Green is more than just a color in the garden. It is an inescapable fact of garden life. Wherever there are plants, there is green. Though I spoke earlier of the variety of available foliage colors, the fact is that most foliage is green. Even the blue blades of *Festuca glauca*, the silver leaves of *Artemisia* 'Powis Castle', the white-splashed foliage of pulmonarias, and the gold-striped leaves of *Carex morrowii* 'Variegata' are all to some extent infused with green. And during the growing season, foliage is most of what we see in any planting scheme. Given the ubiquity of green in any garden setting, effective color composition in the cottage garden demands that you take it into account. Any flower color in your planting palettes will appear against a background that is predominantly green.

What are the implications of this simple fact? For starters, colors that are close to green along the color wheel, such as chartreuse and blue, will always seem harmonious and subtle in a largely green environment. Hence the soothing effect of deep violet monkshoods (*Aconitum* spp.) or powder-blue forget-me-nots (*Myosotis sylvatica*) in a shady garden glen.

Ever wondered just why those bright orange crocosmias, fuchsia roses, and scarlet monardas blare so startlingly in the bed or border? Colors far from green on the color wheel will always seem at least a little loud and contrasty in any planting. Directly opposed to green on the color wheel is its complementary hue, the primary color red. Red's quirks as a garden color are directly due to its complementary relationship with green and the predominance of green in garden settings. Bright, saturated red offers stark contrast to green, and that makes red one of the most conspicuous colors in the cottage garden. The colors immediately flanking red on the

Flowers aren't the only source of color in the garden. Remember fruit and foliage as well!

color wheel also contrast boldly with the green garb of most plantings. Clear orange, in particular, becomes incendiary to the eye when set against a background of green foliage. Incorporating bright red or its neighbors into your garden color palette automatically establishes a sense of drama in your plantings. Use these colors where you want your plantings to leap fiercely into relief, or where a predominantly dark palette needs enlivening to maintain interest.

Green may be ubiquitous, and red and orange are the police sirens of garden colors, but white is a true maverick. White can glitter, even dazzle, in the cottage garden, or it can subdue and soothe. The visual effects of white in a planting scheme depend entirely upon the colors it consorts with. Use white among pastels, which already have some white in their own makeup, and it softens and blends the palette, while at once lightening it and adding a layer of visual froth. Spread within a pastel planting, white seems to throw a luminous veil over the entire arrangement.

White contrasts sharply with dark colors such as burgundy and crimson, mahogany and violet. Against dark blue it is as crisp and refreshing as an after-dinner mint. On the other hand, I have a problem mixing white with the boldest of warm colors, say bright orange, gold, or rust. A grouping of orange chrysanthemums and white snapdragons that I saw once in a public park has stayed with me for decades, and it's not a memory that I particularly cherish.

The easily forgotten dominance of green, the resulting vividness of red, and the surprising effects of white in any planting are worth keeping in mind whenever you choose a cottage garden color scheme. Ignore these color quirks when developing your planting palettes, and you'll risk some unpleasant surprises when your beds and borders come into bloom.

ARRANGING YOUR COLORS

After much thought, you've chosen the colors for your cottage garden plantings. Good work! Now you'll need to arrange your chosen colors within each planting. How you arrange the colors in each bed or border will determine whether you achieve the gay exuberance that everyone expects from cottage garden plantings.

Whether or not you use the two-palette system I employ, your final results will depend upon both the way you distribute colors and the way you group colors within each planting. Distribute your contrasting colors too thinly, in a diffuse "salt and pepper" blend, and you'll dilute the impact of your color combination. Segregate them too completely into large, discrete areas of uniform color, and you'll forfeit the effervescence that their close interaction can produce.

I prefer, instead, to arrange my principal palette into broad, blended waves, punctuated by asymmetrical drifts of accent-palette hues. The undulating tones of the principal palette establish an impression of gentle motion throughout the planting, and contrasting splashes of the accent palette bring the composition to life. My best results have come when the colors in each planting are grouped into long drifts that run diagonally across the bed or border.

White can add sparkle to dark-colored compositions or cast a soft veil over cool colors, as it does in this Pacific Northwest garden.

Rigid symmetry stultifies any cottage garden, so I try to keep my drifts of color asymmetrical and irregular in shape. To further avoid stiffness, I make sure that my masses of contrasting color are unequal in size: a small clump of accent palette here, a larger one there. Varying both the size and spacing of contrasting color groups keeps my cottage garden plantings looking loose and lively, and this strategy should work just as well for you.

FORM

We all like to discuss cottage garden plantings in painterly terms—the terms of color. After all, color is without a doubt the first thing anybody notices when entering a cottage garden: blue-flowering sage and yellow columbines, white climbing roses and ruby-red clematis. But cottage garden plantings are sculptural, too. Think of fountains of maiden grass *(Miscanthus sinensis)* erupting amidst clumps of mounding heucheras, or weeping *Leucothoe* against the shafts of a bamboo. Truth be told, cottage gardens depend nearly as much on variety of plant forms as on color for their vivacity and impact. Juxtapose a wide range of forms, and you can be certain that no eye will tire of your cottage garden plantings.

FINDING FORM

Because cottage gardens incorporate so many different kinds of plant material in close proximity, there is an enormous range of forms from which to choose. Annuals and perennials offer forms from pancake-flat to spiky and upright. In between lie a galaxy of shapes, including dense or wispy mounds, cascading fountains, squatting rosettes, and ascending spires. Shrubs and trees add columnar, weeping, contorted, pyramidal, and upwardly branching forms, while climbers make their own vertical contribution. All have their place in any well-assorted cottage garden planting.

As with colors, each basic plant form elicits certain responses when it appears in a garden setting. Spreading or creeping plants, like ajuga, vinca, or sedums, are restful, static, and comforting, as are mounded plants like geraniums and hostas. Upright plants, especially those with the sort of bold, swordlike leaves seen in yuccas or New Zealand flax (*Phormium* spp.), make an energetic, vigorous impression. Tall, pyramidal plants are always bold, stately, and dignified in the border (think of *Campanula lactiflora* or *Ligularia przewalskii* 'The Rocket'), while pendulous, or "weeping," plants whisper of serenity and ease.

To avoid stiffness in your plantings, arrange your colors in irregular drifts that run diagonally through beds and borders.

Cottage gardens are inherently relaxed, informal spaces, so to maintain their carefree, loose appearance it is important to avoid too many rigid geometric forms. For example, the precise globes and pyramids of many popular dwarf conifers are too stiff and formal to integrate easily into a fluffy

A variety of forms, from narrow and upright to rounded and squat, enliven this cottage garden planting.

cottage garden planting. Try to use such prim, starched plant forms sparingly if at all.

Variety of form is paramount in cottage garden plantings, and plant forms manifest themselves in many ways. Lombardy poplars are notable for their tall, narrow overall shape. Delphiniums and foxgloves (*Digitalis* spp.) stand out for their impressive spikes of flowers. Sweet flag (*Acorus calamus*) makes its impact with impressive, sword-shaped leaves. All are striking as vertical accent plants, yet each achieves this effect in a different manner. Interesting form can come from flowers, foliage, or growth habit—and sometimes, as in the glorious genus *Yucca*, it can come from all three.

MIXING IT UP

You can orchestrate all of these different forms within your beds and borders the same way you would arrange color. My eye never responds to form as quickly as to color, so I find I can get away with much harsher contrasts between forms than between colors within each planting. In fact, I don't just get away with it, I depend upon it.

Too much of any single form, especially the common mound or clump, gets boring very fast in any cottage garden. If my planting contains lots of clumping coreopsis, alchemilla, and geraniums, I like to include plenty of strong, upright forms, be they delphiniums, the grand spuria irises, tall, arching cascades from ornamental grasses, or bold vase-shaped shrubs such as buddleia. I prefer to juxtapose contrasting forms this way just to keep things interesting. Whereas it's easy to include too many colors in a cottage garden planting, I think it's impossible to have too many forms. A riotous assortment of form makes for a lively planting without the risk of eyestrain that can come from clashing colors.

Contrast among plant forms is a powerful effect in cottage garden plantings, but plant forms can also help to accent garden structures and decor. Try spicing up a low, horizontal wall with clumps of upright Siberian irises or columnar *Berberis thunbergii* 'Helmond Pillar'. Set off a metal obelisk with the spreading, horizontal branches of a doublefile viburnum *(V. plicatum* var. *tomentosum)*, or fill a shallow, broad container with assorted ornamental grasses, with their distinctly vertical or cascading fountain forms. This kind of play among ornaments, structures, and vegetation will fill your cottage garden compositions with engaging energy and life.

SCULPTING PLANTS

So far I have discussed plants only in their natural forms. Gardeners are an enterprising lot, however, and there is a long cottage garden tradition of training and manipulating plants, either for novelty or to save space. Casual as cottage gardens are, they usually have little place for tightly clipped and sheared plant life. The fussily trimmed junipers that adorn so many older Pacific Northwest landscapes are just too stiff and artificial in appearance for the cottage garden style. But cottage gardens do have room for the occasional whimsical topiary, and trained climbers and espaliers are both cottage garden staples.

CLIMBERS AND ESPALIERS

The age-old cottage garden emphasis on the efficient use of space puts a special value on any plant that can occupy a vertical surface. Think of the cottage garden and your mind skips instantly to fences cloaked in honeysuckles and tomato plants, to trellises of peas or clematis, a pergola engulfed by a luxuriant wisteria, or an entire home draped to the eaves in sweet-scented climbing Noisette roses.

In the Northwest cottage garden every arbor, wall, or fence is a potential home for a climbing plant of one sort or another. Whether they yield food, fragrance, or color, trained climbers increase the productive space of any cottage garden, while their own special range of forms contribute visual richness to our plantings.

Because any climber roughly takes on the form of its supporting structure, we can sculpt a climbing plant into almost any form we choose simply by selecting the desired support. The resulting combinations of plants and structures yield amalgamated forms that neither alone could achieve. Supports allow us to mold plants into pillars, arches, pyramids, and even great green walls, while foliage and flowers soften the outlines of their supports, helping to blend them into the surrounding plantings. Climbing plants trained onto pillars, obelisks, and arches are a great way to create vertical accents in a cottage garden planting without resorting to plants of stiffly upright habit. An old garden rose trained onto a wrought-iron pillar can make the same vertical impact as a columnar evergreen, but with a much softer texture and more yielding outline. Climbing plants can also alter, or at least soften, the forms of hard-edged garden structures. Any stark wall or building seems far less aggressive to the eye when clothed in vegetation.

Topiary today

After decades of disfavor, topiary has of late regained popularity. Although the old conifer topiaries that remain in many Northwest neighborhoods are usually large-scale abstract blobs, today's topiaries are often classical patterns, such as urns or medallions, or whimsical animal shapes. They are usually made from broadleaf evergreens, such as box or holly, which give them a much looser feel than the lumpy old junipers. The new topiaries tend to be more moderate in scale as well. While their artifice is out of place *within* a casual planting, topiaries are effective in a cottage garden setting if you treat them as ornaments or works of garden art. Place a topiary specimen at the focus of an outdoor space, as you would a fountain or a sculpture, and it magically changes from a stiff and awkward plant into an eye-catching garden accent.

An espalier may well be the ultimate expression of a vertically trained plant. Espaliers are woody plants that are trained absolutely flat against a wall, a fence, or any other vertical plane. Woody plants are the best subjects for espalier treatment, since they form a permanent framework of branches that retains its decorative value all year long. A plant need not have a naturally climbing habit to serve as an espalier. In fact, traditional espaliers often use nonclimbing woody plants, especially fruit trees like apples, pears, and quinces. The forms and patterns that espaliered plants assume are limited only by the gardener's imagination. Formal, linear, or gridlike patterns can make superb foils for informal cottage garden plantings, while looser, more curvaceous patterns contrast with the flat surfaces behind them. In either case, espaliered plants transform plain surfaces into striking formal accents in the cottage garden.

SCALE AND TEXTURE

Scale and texture are as much a part of cottage garden composition as color or form. The enormous range of plant materials available to Northwest gardeners means that we can choose from textures as fine and delicate as bronze fennel (*Foeniculum vulgare* 'Purpurascens') or as brash and bold as *Fatsia japonica*. There are plants as humble in their scale as creeping thyme and as monumental as a red-wood. The most exciting Northwest cottage garden plantings take full advantage of this range of scale and texture, without becoming coarse or overwhelming.

Contrast in texture—between fine and coarse textures, and between large- and small-scale plants—generates the same kind of visual excitement as contrast in form or color. The tiny fronds of *Cotula squalida* work wonders to accentuate the big, coarse foliage of *Brunnera macrophylla*. The broad leaves of hybrid heucheras make the tiny inflorescences of sweet alyssum seem all that more dainty, and the gigantic blooms of a red tree peony are rendered even more splendid by a back-drop of copper filigree from *Carex buchananii* (New Zealand sedge).

Contrasting scales and textures highlight and accentuate one another, but they also need to balance. Too many fine-textured plants in any one planting become tedious without bolder neighbors to provide some punctuation. In a cottage garden setting, where intimacy of scale is a priority, too many large-scale plants and coarse textures can be outright disruptive. Restrain yourself when using really big, coarse plants like *Acanthus*

The bold, coarse leaves of this hosta contrast effectively with the fine-textured foliage beneath them.

mollis, photinia, or cannas. Their sheer size and enormous foliage make for exciting accents, but when used too freely these giants overwhelm the cozy, comfortable scale so crucial to the cottage garden style.

99

The very largest of the woody plants—cedars of Lebanon *(Cedrus libani)*, *Sequoia sempervirens,* and *Sequoiadendron giganteum*—are nearly always out of scale in the small cottage garden. However, if one of these cyclopean specimens already adorns your property, do not despair, and by all means do not cut it down. Instead, treat the great titan as a part of the topography. Think of it as a distant, looming mountain, and frame it with more intimate plantings just as you would such far-off scenery. Use it as a backdrop for colorful plantings or for special garden ornaments, and its grandeur can actually help emphasize your cottage garden's human scale.

Of all the plant textures in the Northwest cottage garden, none is more welcome than the fine, transparent, gauzy texture found in such plants as meadow rue *(Thalictrum* spp.), purple smoke bush *(Cotinus cogyggria),* and *Perovskia*. These soft, hazy veils of blossoms or foliage smooth over rough edges, mediate harsh contrasts, and comfort the eye. Fleecy textures, whether in the foliage of *Artemisia* 'Powis Castle' or the flowers of *Tiarella*, are essential for establishing the fluffy, frothy look of cottage garden plantings. These same frothy textures work extremely well at softening transitions, especially where they spill out over hard-edged paved surfaces.

Repeating plant forms at intervals along a bed or border establishes a sense of rhythm in the planting.

RHYTHM

With so much color and so many varied forms and textures, cottage garden plantings can easily transgress the bounds between exuberance and pandemonium. Beds and borders ought to bring to mind a lively party, not a riot. Subtle patterns, or visual rhythms, built into your plantings will assert an underlying order that binds each section of the garden into a coherent whole. The easiest way to establish visual rhythms is through repetition of colors, forms, or specific plants at relatively regular intervals.

In a mixed planting our eyes tend to skim lightly over horizontal creepers like ajuga and vinca but to stop short at the stiffly upright sword-shaped foliage of Siberian irises or crocosmias. Setting clumps of such strongly vertical plants every few feet along a border of mounding or horizontal plants will encourage the eye to pause at intervals and take note of the border's contents. The visual rhythm thus established weaves the planting together into a single fabric.

Color can create a sense of rhythm just as well as form. In a border dominated by white lilies and dianthus, soft pink roses, variegated weigela, silver artemisia, and pale blue campanulas, carefully placed splashes of bright violet from *Geranium* x *magnificum* or *Salvia verticillata* 'Purple Rain' make fine rhythmic color accents. The clear whites of *Romneya coulteri* or *Anemone* x *hybrida* 'Honorine Jobert' set at intervals through plantings filled with crimson, wine, deep blue, and violet will yield a similar effect.

Placing garden ornaments within or next to plantings can also establish a unifying sense of rhythm. Try setting planted containers at intervals of a few yards along the front of a bed, or punctuate a border here and there with groupings of glass and stamped metal insects set on stakes. Repeating ornaments this way within a planting creates an underlying pattern that can unify cottage garden spaces just as effectively as rhythmic use of plant forms or colors.

MASSING

Cottage garden plantings project a special air of constant, restless activity. This is due in large part to the way plants in the cottage garden are spaced and grouped—what designers refer to as their "massing." In a cottage garden, plants are usually massed in irregular groups—clumps of *Liatris* might jostle with drifts of *Nepeta*, and asters fall over themselves to tumble after spikes of *Lobelia*, all while honeysuckle clambers on the fence behind.

Wherever space permits, try to plant annuals and herbaceous perennials in randomly shaped clumps of three, five, six, or more. Bulbs, with their comparatively thin foliage, make their best impact when planted in groups of at least five. Smaller bulbs, such as *Scilla sibirica* and grape hyacinths (*Muscari* spp.), are best used ten at a time or more. You can certainly group woody plants, especially smaller shrubs, the same way if your garden is large enough, but in most intimately scaled cottage gardens trees and shrubs are planted as single specimens. Planting a bold-textured accent plant such as *Yucca filamentosa* or *Acanthus mollis* singly helps to maximize its impact, while plants with slender, spirelike inflorescences, such as foxgloves, *Kniphofia*, and foxtail lilies (*Eremurus* spp.), benefit enormously from being grouped.

Massing plants together in irregular groups enhances their visual impact.

Cottage garden plantings are nothing if not generous, and a single row of plants always looks stingy. If possible, try to make your cottage garden beds and borders deep enough to accommodate at least three rows of plants. Otherwise, you'll have difficulty arranging your plants into irregular clumps and masses. If space is restricted, avoid single rows by using smaller plants, and intersperse a few larger, coarser plants to accentuate their jewel-like qualities and break the monotony of scale.

NO BARE EARTH

The classic cottage garden is a landscape bursting at the seams, its plantings billowing beyond their bounds with blossoms and foliage. This distinctive "over-stuffed" appearance is a legacy of the early cottage garden's preoccupation with thrift. When cottage gardeners depended on their small plots to supplement their diets, no patch of soil could go unused. This "no bare earth" policy has evolved into an essential component of the contemporary, ornamental cottage garden style. Right up to the present day, plants in the cottage garden are spaced tightly, making the most use of every inch of soil. If at the height of the growing season you can see the ground through your cottage garden plantings, they aren't full enough!

If, like me, you lack the patience to wait several seasons while your beds and borders fill to overflowing, you can space your herbaceous plants closely together when establishing a new bed or border, with the understanding that you'll move, divide, and separate the plants as they threaten to become overcrowded. This approach works well with annuals, perennials, and herbs, provided you don't mind disposing of the excess plant material in future seasons. Woody plants, of course, are less amenable to moving, so in the cottage garden trees and shrubs need to be planted with their mature size firmly in mind.

Another strategy is to use plenty of colorful annuals to build density while the slower-growing plants are filling out. Some of my favorite filler plants are bachelor's buttons *(Centaurea cyanus)*, *Nigella*, *Cosmos*, gas plant *(Dictamnus albus)*, and forget-me-nots. Annual herbs and vegetables also make great filler for newly planted cottage garden beds and borders. Swiss chard with colored stalks, red winter kale, purple basil, dill, and borage all bring wonderful scents and colors into new plantings. You can also compensate for any sparse-looking spots by using big, rapidly maturing plants like *Verbena bonariensis*, cardoons, or bronze-leafed fennel as temporary fillers. Even a few squash or tomato plants laden with late-summer fruit will help carry a cottage garden border until its shrubby denizens mature.

FRAGRANCE

Our cottage gardens would be impoverished indeed without the seductive scent of damask roses, the sweet perfume of heliotrope, or the resinous tang of rosemary. In fact, a cottage garden without fragrance is entirely unthinkable! I urge you not only to include fragrant plants throughout your cottage garden but to do so with some care and forethought.

PLACING FRAGRANT PLANTS

When choosing and siting fragrant plants in your cottage garden, consider how far their fragrance travels. Some fragrances, including those of *Daphne*, *Sarcococca*, and *Rhododendron* x *mollis* hybrids, travel far upon the breezes. Such plants are effective no matter where you place them. In order to appreciate the scent of an

103

old tea rose, on the other hand, you'll need to press your nose right into it. Other scented plants, like mint, rosemary, and eglantine *(Rosa eglanteria)*, release their scent only when you rub against them or crush their foliage. Try to place all such fragrant plants near patios, walkways, decks, or narrow passageways, where garden visitors can experience them at close quarters. Take care, however, to keep the most potent of scented plants clear of outdoor dining areas. The heavy perfume of Oriental lily hybrids can be overwhelming when you bring the blooms indoors, and it may be similarly distracting to guests about to feast at a table in your cottage garden.

Beware, too, of beautiful but malodorous plants. I grow one lovely tree peony that tempts every garden visitor to inhale from its enormous blossoms. The potently medicinal aroma that greets all who do so is as vile as the flowers are magnificent. Had I known years ago how unpleasant this beauty's scent would be, I'd certainly have planted it a good deal farther from the walkway! Certain other plants of great distinction, including crown imperial *(Fritillaria imperialis)* and certain species of *Codonopsis,* carry truly skunklike odors, and should be far from any place where you might eat or drink within the garden.

Just as some plants are fragrant at a distance and some only up close, plants vary as to *when* they release fragrance. Most culinary herbs are at their strongest early in the morning, before the volatile scented oils have departed from their foliage. The leaves of the eglantine rose release their scent after a rain shower, while the blooms of hybrid musk roses are most fragrant in the early evening. *Nicotiana,* or flowering tobacco, is fragrant primarily at night. To take best advantage of these fragrant plants, set them where you'll be most likely to encounter them at their most fragrant time of day.

Fragrance can have marvelous effects when used to emphasize the cottage garden's layout. Cleverly placed scented plants can be olfactory signposts, leading visitors from place to place about the garden. The strong, pleasant fragrances of *Daphne odora,* old garden roses, or lily-of-the-valley wafting through the garden can serve as a lure that beckons visitors to enter and explore. A scented witch hazel *(Hamamelis* x *intermedia)* can guide guests to a hidden nook deep in the winter garden, while a clump of lavender along the stoop will welcome neighbors to your door.

LIGHT AND SHADE

Let's face it, with our short winter days and six straight months of rain, we residents of the maritime Northwest crave light in our gardens. Most people think of cottage gardens as sun-filled spaces, with colorful plantings basking in the full light of day. As it happens, few of us in this once-forested region have the privilege of gardening exclusively in full sunlight—and I, for one, am not sure I would want it.

Shade is a fact of garden life, and without it our gardens would be all the poorer. Cottage gardens can and do thrive in the shade, even on sites that are heavily wooded with Douglas firs, red cedars, or spruce. Even a predominantly sunny cottage garden will be far more pleasant if it offers refuge from the heat of summer and a place for all those charming woodland plants that brighten the spring landscape with their precocious blooms and foliage.

Because the forest is the iconic Pacific Northwest landscape, a cottage garden nestled in a wooded setting may well be the paramount expression of the cottage garden genre in the Northwest. The idea of a pioneering settler carving an oasis of familiar comfort from the mighty forest landscape is still a powerful conceit here, even as highways and subdivisions proliferate throughout the region. A woodland garden also offers its own special enchantments, a certain sense of mystery and wonder that is heightened by the rustling of leaves, shifting shadows, and sight lines limited by the trunks of trees.

The range of plants available to cottage gardeners working in the shade is different from the standards of the exposed, sunny border, but no less rich and varied. It is no coincidence that many of our loveliest Northwest native plants, from bleeding hearts (*Dicentra formosa*) to deer ferns (*Blechnum spicant*), are forest dwellers that will thrive in woodland gardens. I'll discuss a number of the most rewarding woodland plants for Northwest cottage gardens in Chapter Seven.

DESIGN WITH LIGHT AND DARKNESS

The interplay of bright and dark, of light and shade, offers some special design opportunities within the cottage garden. Since even within their intimate bounds cottage gardens emphasize variety, a mixture of light and shady spaces is preferable to all-or-none. In addition to variety, light and darkness can create illusions of depth or distance that creative gardeners will use to enrich their cottage garden plantings.

When set against a backdrop of light colors in the landscape, shadows and

dark colors appear to recede into the distance. Light colors and bright patches against darker backgrounds appear, conversely, to be closer. You can take advantage of these optical illusions in your cottage garden by using dark-colored plants or shadows to enhance the apparent depth of shallow spaces. Or perhaps your cottage garden includes a long, narrow space, such as a passage between two buildings; you can make such a space seem less like a bowling lane by planting plenty of brightly colored foliage at each end. Bright plantings in the distance can also help to make a wide open space seem more intimate, in keeping with the cottage garden style.

Dark places hold a certain fascinating mystery, and few garden visitors can resist exploring a shady nook, especially if a contrasting bright planting at its entry makes it inviting. Reward visitors to these shady havens with the surprise of some quaint ornament, comfortable seat, or woodland planting, and they will quickly become favored spaces in your garden. Likewise, people love to emerge from a darkened space into the sunlight, which may account for the

Light-colored foliage or flowers like these lilies pop out dramatically against a shady background.

appeal of pergolas and hedge-bound passages in gardens everywhere. Use the openings of such tunnel-like features to frame a significant sculpture, fountain, or container in the well-lit space beyond, and you're certain to create a climax on the journey through your cottage garden.

TIME AND SEASONS

Whether flaunting the embroidered garb of their mixed plantings in full summer bloom or cloaked in hellebores and blossoms of winter hazel (*Corylopsis* spp.) in the cool damp of winter, Northwest cottage gardens are truly gardens for all seasons. The same thrifty cottage garden tradition that demands we exploit every inch of soil favors gardens that provide some benefit throughout the year. Our region's extended growing season puts such year-round planting schemes within easy reach for Pacific Northwest cottage gardeners.

The classic cottage garden mixture of annuals, perennials, woody plants, and edibles within the same space makes year-round gardening easier, since it encourages us to combine plants with differing seasons of interest. Summer-blooming polemoniums and columbines can settle in the shade of a paperbark maple (*Acer griseum*) that reveals its own true splendor in the winter, when its brightly colored bark catches the low morning light. The range of plant material available to Northwest gardeners is staggering compared to that in most other parts of North America. This enormous pool of material includes plenty of plants whose blossoms, bark, or foliage can generate some interest during any season.

This deep purple clematis effectively shares space with the shrubby dogwood *Cornus alba* 'Aurea'.

SHARING SPACE

Clever cottage gardeners will take full advantage of their space by pairing plants that occupy the same space but at different times of year. One such pairing couples daffodils with *Geranium pratense* 'Victor Reiter'. The bushy geranium will hide the withering summer daffodil leaves, while its blue flowers sparkle in the border. The glorious once-blooming old garden roses bloom only from May to July, but deck them

with a late-blooming clematis and you'll have color in the same space right through autumn. A classic cottage garden gambit is to train tall-growing climbing roses into trees so that their fragrant flowers cascade from the branches. In my garden, clumps of *Ranunculus ficaria* share space with *Brunnera macrophylla* 'Variegata'. In early spring the bright yellow ranunculus flowers mingle with the wispy blue blossoms of the brunnera. By May the bronze-veined leaves of the ranunculus have disappeared into dormancy, to be replaced by the brunnera's bold cream-margined foliage. Foxtail lilies (*Eremurus* spp.), with their stunning 6-foot spires of bloom, will vanish by late summer, but an adjacent clump of *Aster lateriflorus* 'Prince' will fill the vacancy they leave with a cloud of smoky foliage and white September blossoms. These kinds of space-sharing arrangements epitomize the cottage garden paradigm of thrift.

Autumn can be especially colorful in the Northwest cottage garden.

AUTUMN AND WINTER

Spring and summer may be the height of bloom in Northwest cottage gardens, with so many annuals, perennials, bulbs, and flowering trees showing off their wardrobes, but fall and winter have their garden pleasures too. Autumn in the Northwest cottage garden means the last yellow rose blooming against the bronze and scarlet foliage of a *Parrotia*, soft lavender pillows of *Aster* x *frikartii* 'Mönch', and turning maple leaves. Winter is all anticipation, watching for the first spring bulbs to show their faces and for early buds to swell. But winter is no barren time in Northwest cottage gardens. Witch hazels and winter viburnums

(Viburnum x *bodnantense)* adorn themselves with bloom, the candy cane maple (*Acer pensylvanicum* 'Erythrocladum') shows its peppermint-stick bark, and the glorious, honeyed scent of *Sarcococca* blankets the January garden in a sweet, sleepy mantle. By February there are daffodils, primroses, and camellias to announce the imminent advent of spring. The changing seasons do not stifle the cottage garden's beauties, but merely vary them.

Since cottage garden plantings alter with the seasons, nothing says their color schemes need to remain uniform throughout the year. Indeed, variations in color over seasons serve to make a cottage garden planting more intriguing. A carefully planned planting can flow smoothly from one color scheme to another as the months progress and the sequence of bloom unfolds. Principal and accent palettes visible in one season may give way to entirely new ones in the next. A border that in spring contains blue hyacinths and scillas, yellow daffodils and white azaleas, takes on a whole new life in summer when deep crimson roses, violet geraniums, and soft buff-colored daylilies come into bloom.

Cottage garden plantings grow and change from season to season, but the passage of years affects the cottage garden too. Cottage gardens age gracefully, as time wears down their hard edges and adds a flattering patina of use. Moss will grow on rocks and concrete furniture, wood will weather to soft silver-gray, and woody plants will take on character with age. Just like the changing seasons, age is welcome in the cottage garden. It makes the garden seem more permanent, more settled and secure, and thus, in turn, more comfortable and more familiar, just as it always should be.

CHAPTER SIX

Plants:
The Raw Materials

S ome gardens are about water; some gardens are about art; and still some others are about nature. Cottage gardens are, for the most part, about plants. They are about *lots* of plants: trees, shrubs, perennials, annuals, climbers, fruits, herbs, and vegetables, all growing together in apparent abandon. Cottage garden plantings make their impact through the sheer variety and density of their content. The Pacific Northwest accommodates the cottage garden style so exceptionally well because our climate and growing conditions support an unusually wide range of plant life. The challenge we face is making wise selections from among so many options. In this chapter and the next, I will suggest some worthy plants for Northwest cottage gardens. Some are traditional cottage garden plants, long used by English cottage gardeners, while others are less familiar plants especially adapted to our region and the cottage garden style.

Given our region's amiable climate, there are far too many outstanding Northwest cottage garden plants to possibly consider in one volume, and it's almost certain that I've overlooked somebody's favorite. In choosing which plants to discuss, I've emphasized those that have a long period of bloom or more than one season of interest, or both; that offer multiple decorative features (such as attractive flowers *and* attractive foliage); and that hold their own in crowded cottage garden plantings. I have tried to avoid plants that are overexploited in Pacific Northwest landscapes. I have included *only* plants that thrive here in the maritime Northwest without special care or coddling. Almost all are plants I grow or have grown once upon a time and with whose needs and performance I am personally familiar. Cultural notes for the ornamental plants discussed in these chapters appear in the Appendix.

PLANTS FOR FLOWER

We expect a cottage garden to be full of flowers, and flowers are often the first feature of a plant to garner our attention. Our relatively mild Pacific Northwest winters and long, cool growing season mean that our cottage gardens can remain in bloom all through the year. The array of flowering plants adapted to our soils and climate is staggering, with new introductions arriving every season. The plants that follow are among my favorites for floral display in the garden, and all are reliable performers in our region.

FLOWERING TREES

Trees and shrubs are the woody backbone of any cottage garden planting scheme. They are also the largest sources of blossom in the Northwest cottage garden. Every cottage garden, even the tiniest, will probably have room for at least one flowering tree. Those I mention are some of the most graceful and colorful available for Pacific Northwest gardens.

Among the most beloved and spectacular flowering trees to grace Pacific Northwest gardens are the spring-blooming magnolias. The many varieties of pink saucer magnolia *(Magnolia* x *soulangiana)* are by far the most popular, but the genus has much more to offer for our region. For a refreshing alternative, try planting one of the new yellow-flowered magnolia hybrids instead: 'Elizabeth', with its great, fragrant saucer flowers, and 'Butterflies', with daintier but deeper-colored blossoms, each offer a sunny April antidote to long Northwestern winters. For smaller spaces there are Loebner magnolias *(M.* x *loebneri)* and star magnolias *(M. stellata)*, with their tremendous, early yields of fluffy, fragrant, multipetaled blossoms. The sleeper of magnolias is the late-blooming *M. sieboldii*. In early summer this demure magnolia produces pure white, *downward-facing* blooms that have conspicuous, deep blood-red centers. These make a surprising and delightful display when visitors can walk beneath a specimen set high upon a bank or at the top of a retaining wall. Though they are not particular about pH, magnolias will need supplemental water for their first few summers, until their root systems are well established.

Another early-blooming genus that puts on a great show in Northwest gardens is *Amelanchier* (serviceberry). This group of small trees and large, treelike shrubs includes many similar species, all burying themselves under blankets of white blossoms during the first weeks of spring. *A. laevis, A.* x *grandiflora*, and the Northwest native *A. alnifolia* can all be found in retail nurseries and garden centers. In addition to their profuse blossoms, all offer bright orange and scarlet autumn color and a crop of decorative fruits late in the season. Amelanchiers grow happily in sun or partial shade, preferring acid soils and some water during summer droughts.

Blooming somewhat later than the amelanchiers, the silverbells (genus *Halesia*) deliver dainty white blossoms dangling beneath spreading branches in April and May. Two common species in Pacific Northwest nurseries are *H. carolina* and *H. monticola*. The latter can become a large tree (up to 60 feet under ideal conditions), while the former rarely exceeds 30 feet in cultivation. The silverbells like a rich, moist, acid, loamy soil that does not dry out too much in summer.

One flowering tree that seems to prosper on almost any Northwest soil is the goldenchain tree, *Laburnum* x *watereri*, which has long been a favorite in English cottage gardens. Laburnums are a common feature of Pacific Northwest landscapes—and in fact they are so well adapted to the region that they often crop up as unwanted seedlings along highways or in crevices in pavement. Nevertheless, when they are in bloom

Flowering trees add structure and color to cottage garden plantings. *Laburnum watereri* 'Vossii' is an old-fashioned favorite in Pacific Northwest gardens.

their long chains of bright yellow blossoms hanging from arching branches are impossible to resist. The excellent selection 'Vossii' makes a graceful, fast-growing, small tree for any Northwest cottage garden in which soil conditions are less than perfect.

An equally graceful flowering tree without any weedy tendencies is *Styrax japonicus,* the Japanese snowbell tree. *S. japonicus* bedecks its layered, horizontal branches with bell-shaped, white blossoms on slender, pendent stalks for a few weeks in the late spring. The outline of this tree is exquisite in any season, and in flower it is easily the highlight of any cottage garden space. There are at least two pink-flowered forms, 'Rosea' and 'Pink Chimes', and a slightly weeping form, 'Pendula', although this last one lacks the parent plant's uniquely gracious form. A much less well-known cousin, *S. obassia,* sometimes called the fragrant snowbell, bears its scented white flowers in 4- to 8-inch-long clusters in late spring or early summer. *S. obassia* has large oval leaves that give this small tree a distinct bold texture in the garden. Both species will grow slowly up to 30 feet (usually much less) in sun or partial shade in loamy, acid, well-drained soil.

A close ally of the styrax clan is *Pterostyrax hispida,* known by the common name of epaulette tree, no doubt because its curving panicles of scented, bell-shaped white flowers call to mind the shoulder ornaments on military dress uniforms. These appear during the early summer, when most flowering trees have finished their display. *P. hispida* will grow in any well-drained soil in full sun or partial shade, eventually reaching 20 feet or more.

Later in the season come the profuse white blooms of the evergreen *Eucryphia* x *nymansensis,* whose deep-green compound foliage is all but hidden by the flowers during August or September. The fragrant blossoms attract bees in abundance to a small, dense, shrubby tree that rarely exceeds 30 feet in Pacific Northwest gardens. *E.* x *nymansensis* grows in sun or shade on any reasonably well drained soil.

Davidia involucrata is the grand *prima donna* among Northwest cottage garden trees. While not difficult to grow under Pacific Northwest conditions, this exotic little flowering tree can take its time maturing to its blooming phase. Once it does, it makes a sight not soon forgotten: Huge, drooping white bracts, some nearly a foot in length, dangle like kerchiefs over small clusters of inconspicuous green flowers. Many who see this tree in bloom decide right then and there that it must grow somewhere in their garden. If you, too, must have *D. involucrata* in your cottage garden, site it in full sun or partial shade on moist but well-drained soil, and then bide your time until it blooms. Some new cultivars appearing in Northwest nurseries, including 'Sonoma', are supposed to bloom much younger than the species type, but only time will tell!

FLOWERING SHRUBS

Though a tree like *Davidia involucrata* or *Styrax japonicus* becomes the focal point of any planting while in bloom, flowering shrubs are the woody workhorses of the cottage garden bed or border. Providing masses of color, they sustain the cottage garden's exuberant display from season to season.

Among the first to bloom each year is our own native *Ribes sanguineum*, or red flowering currant. While the flowers of the native species rarely manage a true red, cultivars are available from deep rose pink through soft pink, blush, and white. The short, drooping flower heads light up the cottage garden just as effectively as they do the springtime woods throughout our region. *R. sanguineum* forms a rounded upright shrub to 8 feet or even 10 feet at maturity, though pruning after bloom can keep the plant much shorter if the gardener desires. It adapts to many soils, will bloom in sun or partial shade, and will also endure summer drought once established.

Few shrubs in Northwest cottage gardens are more astounding when in bloom than the tree peonies (genus *Paeonia*). Their flowers, which emerge in early May, can be 10 inches or more across, and the colors they display range from bright yellow, cream, and white through shades of pink and red or even purple. Their dramatic, deeply cut foliage emerges early in shades of bronze and red to herald the upcoming pageant of flowers. Though they are expensive and require years without disturbance before they will bloom, tree peonies are remarkably tough, long-lived plants that reward patience. For the best varieties, consult the catalogs of specialty growers, and avoid dried-up boxed plants that have spent months on the hardware store shelves. Some of the loveliest varieties I know are the lilac-flowered 'Leda', the soft lavender-and-yellow-blended 'Zephyrus', and the dazzling red-and-yellow-splashed 'Gauguin'.

One great staple of the cottage garden is the bigleaf hydrangea, *Hydrangea macrophylla*. With its enormous and long-lasting summer flower heads, this

115

hydrangea is common in Pacific Northwest gardens. And well it should be, since it grows to absolute perfection in our cool summer climate. Though the spectacular "mophead" varieties, with their spherical flower heads, are the most popular, I find that the more open and informal "lacecap" types blend more easily into cottage garden settings. 'Blue Wave' is an old favorite lacecap that blooms in clear azure blue on acid soils and in pink where soils are neutral to alkaline. 'Lanarth White' is a beautiful, clear white, while 'Quadricolor' has pale mauve blossoms and foliage marked in green, cream, gold, and white. All grow well in sun or light shade and tolerate a range of soils. Hydrangeas bloom on the previous year's growth, so prune them immediately after flowering to allow next season's flowering branches to develop.

Though slow to establish, tree peonies offer an unmatched display of gigantic blooms to highlight any Northwest garden. This is the repeat-blooming cultivar 'Hesperus'.

Another summer stalwart is the hardy fuchsia, *Fuchsia magellanica*. The most common type in Northwest gardens is the cultivar 'Riccartonii', with purple-and-magenta flowers, but there are many other hardy selections as well. *F. magellanica* var. *molinae* has softer-colored pink-and-white flowers, and its selection 'Sharpitor' adds white-margined foliage to the mix. There is even a 'Sharpitor Aurea', with gold-variegated leaves. All of these may occasionally freeze to the ground in colder winters, but will quickly resprout up to 3 feet or more in a single season. I have seen hardy fuchsias grow as tall as 6 feet or 7 feet in sheltered Seattle gardens, where they make a most impressive sight in bloom. Plant fuchsias in any well-drained soil in sun or partial shade, and don't let them dry out too much during the summer.

Far less well known than the fuchsias, but just as lovely in its special way, is the so-called bush anemone, *Carpenteria californica*. Once a great rarity, it has begun to appear in numbers in Pacific Northwest nurseries, much to our advantage. Carpenteria is a slow-growing broadleaf evergreen shrub with bark that exfoliates in cinnamon-stick curls on older branches. Its great glory, though, are its pristine white, 2-inch flowers which indeed resemble those of an anemone, except that they are also sweetly fragrant. Try growing it with blue-flowered summer perennials and purple clematis, and you'll soon understand why it has gained in popularity so rapidly. Carpenteria requires a well-drained soil and grows best in full sun and a warm exposure.

The tree mallow *(Lavatera thuringiaca)* could be classed as either a shrub or a perennial, but in most Northwest gardens it persists above ground as a shrubby mass throughout the year. Shrub or not, *L. thuringiaca* is among the longest blooming of cultivated plants. Flowering begins in May or June and persists without stop until the first hard frosts of winter. Each bloom measures 2 inches wide and has a delicate crêpe-paper texture. Hundreds of them are open on each plant at any given time, making a mass of color up to 6 feet tall and just as wide. The popular selection 'Barnsley' has pale pink flowers with deep reddish spots at their centers, while 'Rosea' blooms in medium pink and 'Burgundy Wine' in deep, rosy magenta. A new golden-leafed variety called 'Aurea' has marvelously colored, fuzzy foliage like glimmering chartreuse velvet. Lavateras grow in any soil in full sun, and once established they are very drought resistant.

In September, when many flowering trees and shrubs are winding down for the season, the unusual and lovely chaste tree *(Vitex agnus-castus)* bursts into its full glory. An upright, open shrub with grayish compound leaves and thick, heavy branches, it blooms in large spikes of lavender-to-violet flowers that never fail to grab attention in the early-autumn garden. There is a white variety too, but it does not show up as well as the more common purple. In warmer climates, *V. agnus-castus* can grow into a small tree, but here in the Northwest it rarely gets to more than 6 feet or 8 feet tall. An extra-heavy winter frost may cut the plant down to the ground, but regrowth from the base is rapid. *V. agnus-castus* needs full sun and a well-drained soil and can withstand summer drought with ease after its first few seasons.

RHODODENDRONS

It's impossible to talk about flowering shrubs for Pacific Northwest gardens without mentioning rhododendrons. They are by far the most popular flowering shrubs throughout the region, and nowhere do they grow with greater ease or vigor. I'm sure that by now you sense the word "but" coming, and in fact I have two or three "but's". To begin with, rhododendrons are simply planted too frequently, at the expense of other shrubs, in Pacific Northwest gardens. The most popular varieties have become too commonplace to generate much excitement in a cottage garden planting. On top of this, the most common types are generally dense, large-growing shrubs with coarse-textured dark green foliage, making them quite out of scale for the cottage garden. Finally, the commonly used rhododendrons are quite difficult to blend with other woody and herbaceous plants in a mixed bed or border. There is something earthbound in their rounded, heavy forms and dark green foliage that seems to squelch the effervescence of any cottage garden planting.

So large and various a genus as *Rhododendron* can't be written off as cottage garden subjects, though, especially in a region where they grow so well. Tapping their potential means looking beyond the widely planted favorites such as 'Unique', 'Nova Zembla', and 'PJM'. Among the evergreens, those with finer foliage and less stiffly formal flower clusters are much easier to work into a cottage garden planting. The pale chartreuse 'Moonstone', the dainty soft pink 'Cilpinense', with its precocious early spring blooms, and the diminutive yellow 'Patty Bcc' are all worth seeking out.

Even better suited to the mixed cottage garden planting are the deciduous azalea hybrids. Their bright gold, orange, and scarlet autumn color gives these deciduous members of the *Rhododendron* genus a longer season of interest than their plain evergreen cousins. Many also offer as a bonus a rich, sweet, far-traveling fragrance. The old Mollis, Exbury, and Knap Hill hybrids have been joined by modern types with flowers in all shades of pink, peach, apricot, orange, white, and yellow. Try to purchase these in bloom to confirm fragrance and an appealing flower color.

Perhaps the best of all plants in the genus *Rhododendron* for the cottage garden are the wild species, such as *R. schlippenbachii*, *R. periclymenoides* (both pink), *R. viscosum* (white), and *R. flammeus* (neon shades of orange and yellow). All have graceful, open growth, good fall color, and charming trumpet-shaped blossoms in springtime. They look wonderful with fritillarias, tree peonies, bleeding hearts, and pulmonarias in the late-spring border.

SPRING BULBS

Beneath the flowering trees, in front of and between the flowering shrubs, bloom the herbaceous plants. Annuals and perennials cloak the cottage garden in a mantle of colors that alters with every change of season. Some of the first herbaceous plants to flower each year are the spring-blooming bulbs, cheerful plants that ward off the last of winter's chill with their bright colors and dainty forms. Among the great heralds of the Northwest spring are the daffodils (genus *Narcissus*), whose cheerful blossoms first erupt in the early days of March. While large-flowered trumpet daffodils like 'Dutch Master' and 'King Alfred' are planted by the millions every fall, there are many other less well known narcissus whose foliage and blooms are daintier and less stiff, in keeping with the cottage garden style.

Poeticus narcissus are old standards of the English cottage garden whose broad, white outer petals, tiny orange-rimmed cups, and exquisite fragrance are just as welcome here in the Pacific Northwest. Also outstanding for its fragrance is the Triandrus narcissus 'Thalia', which bears its nodding clusters of pure white bloom late in the daffodil season. The small-flowered Tazettas bear loads of little flowers on each stem. The yellow-cupped white 'Avalanche' and the sprightly orange-cupped 'Geranium' are both reliable and beautiful in Northwest cottage gardens.

Cyclamineus narcissus are an especially graceful group, with curving, swept-back petals behind their modest cups. Outstanding members of this group are 'Jetfire', with orange cups and yellow petals, 'February Gold', all in bright yellow, and 'Jack Snipe', whose clear white petals ring a cup of butter yellow. Perhaps most delicate of all narcissus in appearance are the miniatures like the bright yellow 'Hawera' and the subtle cream-and-yellow bicolor 'Minnow'. For a complete change of pace, try planting some of the newer pink-cupped narcissus—the large-cupped 'Accent', 'Pink Charm', and 'Salome', the lovely Cyclamineus 'Foundling', and the little tiny-flowered pink Jonquilla hybrid 'Bell Song' all bring wonderful, soft, novel colors to the narcissus palette.

Though narcissus are often planted on their own, the cottage garden style demands variety, and our region comfortably hosts a wide range of early-blooming bulbs to blend with them in the spring border. One natural partner is the grape hyacinth, or *Muscari*. The common dark blue *M. armeniacum* shows up everywhere, but the genus includes several other species that are just as beautiful and easy to grow. *M. latifolium* has only one broad leaf, but its flower spikes display a marvelous two-toned effect, light blue on top and darker (nearly black) blue at the bottom. *M. botryoides* var. *album* is pure white, while *M. comosum* 'Plumosum' has feathery violet flowers that look nothing like those of the other grape hyacinths.

For taller, spiky, blue accents in spring beds and borders, there are several species of our own Northwest native camas. *Camassia quamash* is the most easily obtained, and when its 3-foot spikes of starry, 2-inch deep blue flowers open, visitors from other regions are invariably jealous of its fine performance here. *C. cusickii* has lighter blue flowers, and *C. leichtlinii alba* blooms in white. There is even a form of *C. quamash* with white-striped foliage, called 'Blue Melody', though I find it much less vigorous than the original species. All the camassias grow and bloom in sun or partial shade, eventually forming dense, compact colonies.

Crocuses can be hard to keep in Northwest cottage gardens, since squirrels, chipmunks, and other rodents prize their bulbs the way that we prize truffles or fine wine. I do know one species, *Crocus tommasinianus*, which the rodents seem to find unpalatable. *C. tommasinianus* bears dainty lavender-to-lilac flowers in great masses in the early spring, above very narrow white-striped foliage. In a sunny site with well-drained soil, it will increase rapidly from year to year to form large, colorful clumps.

Large-flowered hybrid tulips often tend to dwindle, behaving like annuals in many Northwest gardens. Since their stiff posture doesn't always seem at home in cottage gardens anyway, I prefer the relatively obscure species tulips in my plantings. These little beauties are much longer lived than their showy descendants, and many will reproduce to form expanding colonies if given well-drained soil. They display an astounding range of forms and colors, from the slender, candy-striped *Tulipa clusiana* to the starry, flat-faced white-and-yellow *T. tarda*. I adore the rose-red flowers of *T. humilis* 'Persian Pearl' and the soft pink, yellow-centered *T. bakeri* 'Lilac Wonder', which looks for all the world like an overgrown, exotically colored crocus. None of these little tulips grows much more than 8 inches tall, and all make cheerful pools of color at the front of any Northwest cottage garden planting.

PERENNIAL FAVORITES

Because all of the spring bulbs vanish into dormancy by early summer, they make great candidates for the kind of space-sharing arrangements I discussed in Chapter Five. No group of plants is more adept at masking the fading foliage of spring-flowering bulbs than the *Geraniums*, or cranesbills. These are not the tender bedding plants of the genus *Pelargonium*. No, the true geraniums (genus *Geranium*) are hardy, clump-forming perennials that provide mounds of handsome foliage and perky blue, pink, purple, or white flowers in extreme abundance. *G.* x *magnificum* is an old hybrid that forms dense, 2-foot clumps of divided foliage, topped in May and June with shimmering deep-violet 2-inch flowers. *G. himalayense* is a personal favorite of mine, with lovely, clear blue 1-inch blossoms above deep green foliage. It spreads quickly underground to form a dense mat about 18 inches tall, making a fine ground cover in sun or partial shade.

Another geranium with beautiful blue flowers is *G. pratense* 'Victor Reiter', which forms 2-foot mounds of deep, dark purple-tinted foliage. It makes a superb foil for silver-leafed artemisias, pale daylilies, or the yellow-flowered *Coreopsis verticillata* 'Moonbeam'. The several *G.* x *oxonianum* hybrids are of the same scale, but bloom mostly in shades of pink, from the deep pink of 'Claridge Druce' to the paler tint of 'A. T. Johnson'. *G. macrorrhizum* also blooms in pink, its pretty, nodding flowers held above fragrant foliage; it spreads by rhizomes to

Perennial geraniums are adaptable, reliable sources of floral color for cottage garden plantings.

form a solid ground cover up to 1-foot tall. The giant among geraniums is *G. psilostemon*, a loose, 3-foot mound of a plant that covers itself with neon-bright magenta flowers with striking black eyes in midsummer. It makes an eye-catching

The herbaceous peony 'Red Charm' blazes against a background of light-colored foliage.

grouping with purple-flowering sages or clematis in the mixed cottage garden border. Its hybrid *G.* 'Ann Folkard' adds golden-chartreuse foliage to this picture. Much more subtle, but equally beautiful, is the new hybrid *G.* 'Philippe Vapelle', whose downy, gray-green foliage is a perfect backdrop for the strongly veined violet-blue flowers. 'Philippe Vapelle' forms tidy foot-wide mounds and blooms profusely from May through July.

Late spring is time for poppies (genus *Papaver*) in the Northwest, specifically the glamorous Oriental poppy, *P. orientale*. Who could resist its huge crêpe-paper flowers in shades of scarlet, salmon, pink, and white? The hairy foliage dies back by midsummer, making *P. orientale* a fine partner for fall-blooming asters that will grow to fill the space as the season progresses.

At least as spectacular as Oriental poppies in May and June are the herbaceous peonies. Old favorites for cottage gardens are the pink 'Mrs. F. D. Roosevelt', the deep crimson 'Red Charm', and the big white 'Festiva Maxima'. Don't be afraid to try some newer peonies as well. 'Pink Hawaiian Coral' and 'Coral and Gold' in shades of bright salmon, 'Raspberry Sundae' in a blend of cream, white, and pink, and the soft, clear yellow 'Goldilocks' all bring fresh colors to the peony clan. Peonies resent crowding and thus require elbowroom, but once established they earn their space in Northwest cottage gardens with their stupendous show of flowers.

Irises have long been hailed as some of the best companion plants for peonies, the tall-growing bearded irises being the most commonly planted. Don't overlook the shorter border bearded irises, though, with similar flowers on 16- to 24-inch plants, or the little dwarf bearded types, with scads of flowers on low 6- to 12-inch stalks.

Even more valuable in Northwest cottage gardens are the beardless Siberian irises, which form attractive 2- to 3-foot clumps of narrow grasslike foliage with many large, flat, butterfly-like flowers in early summer. Colors range from the strong violet blues of 'Silver Edge' and 'Orville Fay', through lavenders like 'Dance Ballerina Dance' and 'Augury', to bright white in 'Fourfold White' and 'Harpswell Happiness'. Newer cultivars now come in soft yellow, among the best of which is 'Isabelle', which holds its color better than most others. Siberian

irises have begun to approach pink in cultivars like 'Strawberry Fair', while other recent introductions like 'Drops of Brandy' and 'Careless Sally' offer subtle blends of lavender, cream, and yellow.

The most elaborately colored irises of all are our own Pacific coast irises, hybridized from native species found in Oregon and Northern California. These low-growing irises are notoriously difficult to grow outside their native range, as they depend on mild wet winters and cool, dry summer days to thrive. Here in their home region they do well if given well-drained, acid soil and bright sun or semishade. Their colors and patterns are spectacular—matched only, I think, by some of the exotic greenhouse orchids. 'Big Wheel' is fluorescent raspberry pink, with a dramatic near-black central spot and radiating dark veins. 'Idylwild' is violet-blue splashed over white, with broad white edges and bright yellow "signal" markings on the petals. 'Baby Blanket' is soft pink with a contrasting bright metallic-blue eye, and 'Big Money' is deep yellow-gold with conspicuously darker veins.

Siberian irises are forgiving, low-maintenance plants with elegant, grassy foliage that stays attractive long after the blooms have faded.

Appearing with the irises in late spring and early summer, the columbines (*Aquilegia* spp.) bring a unique brand of grace to cottage garden plantings.

123

Their nodding, long-spurred flowers come in every conceivable color, including many pretty bicolor combinations. They vary in stature from the low-growing, short-spurred *A. flabellata* to the 2-foot tall long-spurred McKenna hybrids. When happy, they self-sow around the garden, each seedling producing a new (and invariably lovely) color combination.

Knautia macedonica is another fine perennial that tends to spread by seed in Northwest gardens. Some find it a nuisance, but I've always loved it for its superb deep crimson-red color, a shade that's hard to find among perennials. It blooms from June until September if deadheaded, and is happy on any soil in either sun or partial shade.

The daylily 'Oriental Dancer' sings out among the purple velvet blooms of *Clematis* 'Polish Spirit'.

The hybrid yarrow *Achillea* 'Moonshine' has so many virtues that I could discuss it anywhere. You could plant it for its finely cut silver-gray foliage alone, but the long-lasting flat yellow flower heads are just as lovely. *A.* 'Moonshine' is a perfect companion for deep violet Siberian irises, purple salvias, or dark blue delphiniums.

Among the most adaptable and versatile of all cottage garden perennials are daylilies (genus *Hemerocallis*). Modern hybrids come in a mind-boggling array of colors and patterns, from near-white through cream, yellow, peach, apricot, pink, orange, red, and deep purple. They may have bold, contrasting eyes, subtly blended color patterns, or elaborately fringed gold or silver edges. The best varieties are sturdy plants that grow with ease and bloom prolifically for up to a month, with some reblooming in early fall. Browse specialist mail-order catalogs for the widest selection in the colors and patterns you prefer.

Some of the best garden companions for daylilies of any color are the salvias, also known as flowering sages. *Salvia nemorosa* and its hybrid *S.* x *sylvestris* are two tough, reliable plants with long-lasting spikes of bloom through much of the summer. There are several cultivars in different colors, all sharing the same dark gray-green foliage and a neat, mounding habit. *S. nemorosa* 'Lubeca' and 'East Friesland' are violet-blue, as are *S.* x *sylvestris* 'Mainacht' and 'Blue Hill'. *S.* x *sylvestris* 'Rose Queen' blooms in lilac-pink. All grow to 18 inches in full sun on any well-drained soil. *S. verticillata* is slightly taller, at about 2 feet. The outstanding cultivar 'Purple Rain' carries loose, bright-purple spikes over fuzzy deep-green foliage.

Similar in texture to the salvias, but with less stiffly upright flower spikes, is the violet-flowered catnip *Nepeta* 'Six Hills Giant'. The flower spikes are carried loosely over 2-foot mounds of aromatic gray-green foliage from May until September, making this among the longest-blooming of summer flowers. *N.* x *faassenii* blooms in a similar color, but with somewhat shorter growth. The odd one out among the nepetas is *N. govaniana*. Whereas most members of the genus bloom in shades of lavender or violet, *N. govaniana* bears loose spikes of soft yellow, hooded flowers on wispy 3-foot stems. It makes a lovely complement to blue geraniums or violet irises.

Among the oldest and most treasured plants in English cottage gardens are the pinks and carnations of the genus *Dianthus*. These are all smaller plants, whose tufted mounds of grayish foliage are well suited to the front of cottage garden plantings. Flowers may be either double (as in carnations) or single, and their colors include white, pink, cherry red, and even yellow. Many are multicolored, with complex patterns and fringed edges. Some of my favorites are the bright-pink *D. deltoides* 'Zing Rose', the dainty reddish *D. gratianopolitanus* 'Tiny Rubies', and the highly fragrant, fringed white *D. plumarius* 'Musgrave's Pink'. Except for an intolerance of wet or acid soils, pinks

Spikes of *Salvia* x *sylvestris* 'Mainacht' punctuate a clump of hybrid yarrow *(Achillea)*.

125

and carnations grow easily in Northwest cottage gardens and often even sow themselves.

Another group of colorful, low-growing perennials for well-drained Northwest cottage plantings are the diascias, which came to our region recently from South Africa. Diascias are mostly trailing plants that bear loose, pyramidal

spikes of oddly formed half-inch flowers in varying shades of pink. *Diascia barberae* 'Blackthorn Apricot' is actually coral-peach, while *D. rigescens* and *D.* 'Strawberry Sundae' are deep rosy pink. New cultivars are appearing in lilac and lavender as well. All like a warm site in full sun and will rot if left in soggy soils over winter. With their trailing habit and their aversion to poor drainage, the diascias make superb subjects for container plantings in Pacific Northwest gardens.

As regally erect as *Dianthus* and *Diascia* are low, the lilies (genus *Lilium*) nevertheless share these shorter plants' requirements for excellent drainage. Given well-drained soils, they are some of the most dramatic and rewarding Northwest cottage garden flowers. For the foreground of a planting, there are relatively modest 3-foot Asiatic hybrid lilies such as 'Gardenia', in orange and yellow, or 'Doeskin', with nodding blooms in apricot. Oriental hybrids such as the famous pure white 'Casablanca' or the pink-stippled 'Muscadette' can reach 5 feet or more and bathe the entire garden

Trumpet lily hybrids bring tall stature and heady perfume to sunny, well-drained beds and borders.

126

in exotic, heavy perfume. Even taller, and just as well scented, are the trumpet lily hybrids, which bloom in July with flowers in pink, orange, yellow, or white. One of the loveliest of all lilies for this region is the delicately colored, fragrant *Lilium regale*, whose white blossoms show soft yellow throats and dark petal reverses. Much of the nation's lily bulb crop is grown right here in the Pacific Northwest, so local selections are broad, and many of the types available grow particularly well in Northwest gardens.

THE BLUES

Pink, purple, lilac, and white are easy to come by in flowering perennials, but clear blue is relatively rare and much sought after. Those few hardy perennials that offer pure blue flowers have been treasured by cottage gardeners for generations. Of all the blue perennials, none inspires quite the veneration we afford to the delphiniums. Perhaps it is their sheer size that so inspires us, or the purity of their blue colors. Or maybe we love them because their need for cool summer temperatures allows them to thrive here in our region as they can do nowhere else in North America. Gardeners from the South, the Midwest, or the eastern seaboard invariably grind their teeth in envy when they behold the bold 6-foot spikes of our delphiniums. The most popular ones belong to the hybrid Pacific strain, including the pale blue 'Summer Skies', the mid-blue 'Blue Bird', and the dark blue 'Blue Jay'. 'Sir Galahad', another useful Pacific hybrid, blooms in pure white. Less imposing but no less beautiful are the *Delphinium* x *belladonna* hybrids, with deeply cut foliage and more delicate flowers in shades of blue or white.

As stunning as they are, delphiniums do pose some challenges. They are a favorite food of slugs, and here in the Northwest an entire planting can disappear in one wet night. They also demand rich, well-drained soil, full sun, and an even supply of moisture during summer dry spells. Even in ideal conditions, hybrid delphiniums are not long lived, and will need to be replaced from time to time.

Less awe-inspiring than delphiniums but much more permanent in gardens are the campanulas. At up to 5 feet, *Campanula latifolia* and *C. lactiflora* have nearly the stature of delphiniums but persist for many years once planted, and can even bloom in partial shade. *C. persicifolia* is the most familiar member of the genus, with its narrow basal foliage and 18-inch spikes of blue or white blossoms in late spring. If it were any easier to grow we would consider it a weed, but its behavior is just civilized enough to make it a fine companion plant for soft-colored perennials and shrub roses in the Northwest cottage garden. The trailing *C. poscharskyana*, or Serbian bellflower, is outright rude, spreading rapidly into new territory unless it is constrained. It's still a useful plant, what with its profuse blue blossoms and tolerance for poor, dry soils. I use it at the front of dry, partially shaded mixed plantings where little else will grow.

A whole genus of blue-flowered perennials that thrive on poor, dry soils are the sea hollies (genus *Eryngium*). Eryngiums are faintly extraterrestrial in their appearance, with odd, strongly veined, spiky leaves. Their flowers are inconspicuous, resembling small thistles, but each cluster is surrounded by an elaborate ruff of spiny bracts that turn electric or metallic blue in many species. Among the most colorful are *E. alpinum*, with 3- to 4-inch steel-blue inflorescences above deep green foliage, and *E. bourgatii*, with similar blooms and finely cut gray leaves. Both stand 18 to 24 inches tall and bloom in early summer. *E.* x *tripartitum* is a long-flowering hybrid with clouds of deep blue blossoms on stems up to 3 feet tall. I count on it for its blue color from July to September. Plant eryngiums where they'll receive full sun and where their roots will not get soggy over winter.

Though *Eryngium alpinum* looks exotic, it is a long-lived, drought-tolerant perennial.

For extended bloom among the blue perennials, no plant is finer than the mounded little *Scabiosa columbaria* 'Butterfly Blue'. This 8-inch tall pincushion flower bears elaborate soft blue blossoms in great numbers starting in mid-May, and coming on and off again in flushes through late August or September. It makes a superb foil for yellow perennials like *Achillea* 'Moonshine', *Nepeta govaniana*, or *Phlomis russeliana*.

Several easy-to-grow annuals also come in appealing shades of blue, not least of which is the popular trailing annual lobelia, *Lobelia erinus*. Trays bearing selections like the deep blue 'Crystal Palace' and the paler 'Cambridge Blue' can be found by the hundreds in garden shops and nurseries around our region. In the cottage garden, they are superb trailing out of containers or at the edges of mixed plantings in full sun or partial shade. Their only requirement is even moisture through the summer when grown out in full sun.

Another clear blue trailing annual, less often seen, is the sparkling *Phacelia campanularia*. Plant its tiny seeds in early spring, and by midsummer you'll have trailing stems of half-inch bright blue flowers with glittering white centers that continue all summer long. *Nemophila menziesii*, or baby blue-eyes, is a Northwest native annual that also bears white-centered, clear blue flowers on a low mounding or trailing plant. It too grows easily from seed sown in place in the spring. For larger deep-blue flowers, try the dwarf annual morning glory *Convolvulus tricolor* 'Blue Ensign'. It displays 2-inch royal blue flowers with contrasting white-and-yellow centers on nontwining, mounded plants up to 1 foot tall.

The most unusual blue annual of all is surely *Cerinthe major* 'Purpurascens'. This peculiar-looking plant sends up 1-foot stems clothed in clasping blue-gray leaves. As they ascend each stem, the leaves take on shades of metallic blue, until they transform into closely spaced deep-blue bracts that curl downward over tiny, hidden purple flowers. The entire picture is unique and fascinating, causing garden visitors to ask "What's *that?*" at every first encounter. *Cerinthe* is more than just a curiosity, though. Its long-lasting display is marvelous with low-growing yellow floribunda roses or with black-eyed susans (*Rudbeckia* spp.) in the cottage garden.

HOT STUFF

Here in the Northwest, where the winters are so wet and gloomy, bright, warm colors are sometimes just what we need in cottage garden plantings. There's warm, and then there are the searing hot colors of *Crocosmia* (sometimes known as *Montbretia*). These familiar plants, with their narrow, sword-shaped leaves and tall, arching spikes of starry flowers, are among the most reliable perennials in Northwest cottage gardens. The popular hybrid 'Lucifer' bears 3-foot spikes of incendiary scarlet flowers above exceptionally robust foliage. Equally bright is the burnt-orange 'Emily McKenzie', whose large flowers display spots of deep brick red around their throats. For a more subtle color, I adore the apricot-to-yellow 'Solfatarre', which blooms on shorter stems and has bronze-tinted foliage.

For long-lasting warm color on a mounded, clumping plant, try *Geum chiloense*. It shows up mostly in two colors: the bright orange-red 'Mrs. Bradshaw' and the golden-yellow 'Lady Stratheden'. Both form dense mounds of hairy foliage, above which wave the flowers on wiry 2-foot stems. Each of these cultivars remains in bloom from June through September.

September is also the prime season for the black-eyed susans of the genus *Rudbeckia*. The most reliable of these is *R. fulgida* 'Goldsturm', with large, black-eyed golden flowers on a compact 2-foot plant. Rudbeckias are joined in the late summer garden by the screaming yellow goldenrods, including *Solidago rugosa* 'Fireworks' and *S. sphacelata* 'Golden Fleece'. Both bear arching plumes of golden flowers that will light up any planting, even on the poorest of dry soils.

COTTAGE GARDEN ROSES

We now come to that cottage garden flower nonpareil: the rose. I don't mean the gangly, stiff, and leggy hybrid teas, as beautiful as their blooms

Hot colors have their own special place in the Northwest cottage garden. Here the dahlia 'Bishop of Llandaff' sings a duet with the bold foliage of a hybrid canna.

are in a vase. No, the preferred cottage garden roses are the shrub roses and old garden roses, with their gently arching forms and lush, dense foliage.

OLD GARDEN ROSES THAT BLOOM ONCE

The old garden roses—comprising all of those types that originated before the mid-nineteenth century—are a diverse group that offer a wide range of growth habits, flower forms, and fragrances. The oldest of them are once-blooming types that flower in a single, pro-lific flush from May into July. Among the most important of these for the cottage gardener are the gallica, damask, alba, centifo-lia, and moss roses. The gallica roses are dense, upright, mounded shrubs, 3- to 4-feet tall and just as wide. Their 3- to 4-inch flowers vary from pale pink to deepest wine-purple, and from simple, single forms to elaborate and fluffy doubles with more than a hundred petals. Most are very fra-grant, especially the ancient semi-double *Rosa gallica officinalis*,

Roses are staples of the cottage garden repertoire.

or 'Apothecary's Rose', whose deep magenta flowers were once harvested and preserved for their scent alone. An equally well-scented white-striped version, *R. gallica versicolor*, or 'Rosa Mundi', has been a cottage garden standard for cen-turies. Other gallica varieties that are especially well suited to Pacific Northwest cottage gardens are the pale pink 'Belle Isis' and 'Duchesse d'Angoulême', the beautiful deep crimson 'Tuscany Superb', and the soft lilac-mauve and wine-red-blended 'Président de Sèze'. Plant any of these with blue delphiniums and lavender for a classic, fragrant cottage garden combination.

Equally renowned for fragrance are the grand old damask roses, whose his-tory dates back beyond the origins of cottage gardens. So potent and complex is their fragrance that they are still grown in great numbers in Europe to produce

131

rose water and supply the perfume industry. The damasks are tall roses, growing to 6 feet or more, with gently arching canes that grow into broad mounds. 'Belle Couronnée', better known as 'Celsiana', has delightful semi-double soft pink flowers with the texture of satin and a scent fit for the angels. 'Ville de Bruxelles', 'Marie Louise', and 'Ispahan' offer deeper pink, more complex double flowers with the same rich damask fragrance. The most popular and famous of the damask roses is the pure white 'Mme. Hardy', whose perfectly symmetrical pom-pom blooms are centered with a contrasting green eye. Any of these delicately colored damask roses blends easily into a pastel cottage garden color scheme.

Taller even than the damask roses are the alba roses, which clothe their vase-shaped silhouettes in distinctive dark blue-green foliage. Despite the name, the alba roses are not always white. Along with such white beauties as the semi-double *R.* x *alba* 'Semiplena' and the fluffy double 'Mme. Legras de St. Germain', there are pale pinks like 'Félicité Parmentier' and 'Maiden's Blush'. The darkest of the alba roses is the gorgeous mid-pink 'Königin von Dännemarck' (or 'Königin von Dänemark'). All are tough as nails and even bloom well in partial shade, where other roses would not prosper.

The centifolia roses are the old "cabbage roses" painted by Dutch masters in their seventeenth-century floral still lifes. So fat and full of petals are their big pink or white flowers that the whole shrub sprawls out on the ground to make a floppy 5-foot by 5-foot mound in bloom. Given their floppy habit, the centifolias benefit from training onto an upright arch or pillar. They are equally effective tied along a fence or allowed to cascade freely from the top of a retaining wall.

Perhaps due to their complex ancestry, the original centifolia roses gave rise to a number of odd sports, or mutants, the best known of which are the moss roses. These show a peculiar, mossy-looking growth of glands along their upper stems and flower buds. Besides giving the buds and flowers a charming extra layer of adornment, the glands emit a resinous secretion with a distinct scent of pine or juniper. Moss roses come in white ('Shailer's White Moss'), pink (*R.* x *centifolia* 'Muscosa'), and even deep, dark purple ('William Lobb'). Their growth habit and uses mirror those of the centifolias.

All of these once-blooming old garden roses thrive in full sun on nearly any fertile soil, even clay, provided they receive at least 1 inch per week of summer water. They are far less prone to illness than modern roses, and withstand cold that would destroy most hybrid teas or floribundas. Unlike our newer roses, these plants all bloom on the previous season's growth. This means that if you cut them back hard in winter, as is the usual practice with modern roses, all of their flowers for the coming season will be lost! If your once-blooming roses need some pruning, do it shortly after they have bloomed, leaving enough time for new flowering wood to form for the next summer.

Do not overlook these grand old-timers just because they don't repeat-bloom through to the fall. They will happily share space with the late-blooming *Clematis viticella* hybrids, *C. texensis* hybrids, and any of the repeat-blooming large-flowered clematis selections mentioned in the next chapter, any of which will clamber harmlessly through the old garden roses to provide their own glorious color when the rose flowers are finished.

REPEAT-BLOOMING ROSES

Late in the eighteenth century a revolution overtook the rose in Europe. Explorers from the East imported the first China roses *(Rosa chinensis)* into Western gardens in the 1790s, causing an immediate sensation. The China roses differed from the old European types I have just described in several aspects. They were less hardy and less robust in growth, making open, even spindly, plants with small, glossy leaves and smooth, twiggy stems. They bloomed in white and pink, but also in a clear, bright crimson, never before seen in European roses. Most important of all, though, China roses bloomed not once per year, but in flush after flush, for as long as sunlight and warm temperatures prevailed.

Some of these China roses survive in our gardens to this day. They remain valuable for their compact dimensions, airy texture, and prolonged, prolific bloom. 'Cramoisi Supérieur' has pretty little cup-shaped flowers of bright crimson on a slender, 3-foot plant, while 'Irene Watts' bears larger, flat rosettes of

> ## One dozen favorite cottage garden roses
>
> - 'Buff Beauty' (hybrid musk rose, apricot-buff flowers, grows to 5 feet)
> - 'Celsiana' (damask rose, pink flowers, grows to 6 feet)
> - 'Comte de Chambord' (Portland rose, pink flowers, grows to 3 feet)
> - 'Desprez a Fleur Jaune' (Noisette rose, peach flowers, climbs to 20 feet or more)
> - 'Mlle. Cécile Brunner' (polyantha, pink flowers, grows to 3 feet)
> - 'Mme. Hardy' (damask rose, white flowers, grows to 6 feet)
> - 'Mme. Pierre Oger' (Bourbon rose, pink and white flowers, grows to 6 feet)
> - 'Mutabilis' (China rose, yellow, orange, and pink flowers, grows to 3 or 4 feet)
> - 'Reine des Violettes' (hybrid perpetual, violet or wine-red flowers, grows to 6 feet)
> - *Rosa x alba* 'Semi-Plena' (alba rose, white flowers, grows to 6 or 7 feet)
> - *Rosa gallica officinalis* (gallica rose, magenta flowers, grows to 3 feet)
> - 'Rose de Rescht' (Portland rose, fucshia-to-magenta flowers, grows to 3 feet)

peach and pink atop its graceful stems. 'Mutabilis' has simple, single flowers that open to yellow from bright orange buds, then age to pink and finally to carmine before dropping. China roses are fine subjects for containers or small gardens, where their modest size and long season are extremely advantageous.

Soon after the China roses came to Europe, enterprising breeders began crossing them with the once-blooming roses to combine their repeat bloom with the vigor, hardiness, and fragrance of the damasks, gallicas, and albas. Among the earliest of repeat-blooming roses bred in Europe were a small group called the Portland roses. Probably the result of crosses between damask and China roses, the Portlands have the dense foliage, bushy habit, and profound scent of the old European roses, but the stature and repeating bloom of China roses. Those very few that have survived up to the present are among the most valuable of roses for the Northwest cottage garden. Portland roses like the soft pink 'Comte de Chambord' and the bright magenta 'Rose de Rescht' blend easily into mixed cottage garden or container plantings, especially when paired with salvias, campanulas, or lavender.

The old China rose 'Mutabilis' bears chameleon-colored blooms that change from orange to yellow, pink, and red as they mature.

Further crosses in the nineteenth century produced the vigorous, tall-growing Bourbon roses. Bourbon roses carry fragrant, old-fashioned-looking flowers on long canes reaching to 6 feet or more. They can be grown without support to form broad, arching shrubs, or trained onto fences, trellises, or pillars to keep them more compact. They take especially well to a traditional English style of training known as "pegging down." A rose is pegged down by bending its branches to the ground and securing their tips with short stakes or other fasteners. Pegged roses are often fanned out into wide, low mounds. Such horizontal training actually encourages prolific bloom, with flowers forming all along the branches rather than at just the very tips. Among the most robust and fragrant of the Bourbon roses are the gleaming magenta 'Mme. Isaac Pereire', the bright white 'Boule de Neige', and the clear pink 'Louise Odier'. Much shorter than the rest, and slower growing, too, is 'Souvenir de la Malmaison', a 3-foot plant that bears enormous, flat-topped buff-pink flowers of extraordinary charm. Equally lovely is the willowy, tall 'Reine Victoria', whose perfectly round, clean-pink chalice blossoms could have fallen off Grandma's Dresden teacup, though I'm certain porcelain has never smelled so sweet. 'Reine Victoria' and its paler offspring 'Mme. Pierre Oger' both make slender, vase-shaped plants up to 6 feet or more and look stupendous next to deep-blue delphiniums or behind violet spikes of *Nepeta* 'Six Hills Giant'.

While Europeans were busily crossing China roses with their own familiar hybrids, yet another brand-new type of rose arrived from the Far East. These were the tea roses, believed to have been named either for their odd, fruity fragrance or for the fact that they arrived in ships bearing cargoes of tea from China. Like the China roses, tea roses have open, twiggy growth and ample repeat bloom, though they will often grow much taller, to 5 feet or more under ideal conditions. The tea roses were even more sensitive to cold than the China roses, but they brought a novel form to European roses. While most European roses opened into cups, domes, or rosettes of petals from blunt, rounded buds, tea roses spiraled slowly open from long, pointed oval buds. So highly prized was this new form of flower that the tea rose's hybrid descendants, the hybrid teas, would eventually overwhelm all of the other rose varieties in popularity.

Important as tea roses were as breeding stock for modern roses, the surviving old varieties have special garden merits of their own. Though too tender for the Midwest and the Northeastern states, in the Northwest the old tea roses overwinter happily up through lower British Columbia, making open, graceful plants that assort well with perennials and flowering shrubs in cottage garden plantings. Their long season of bloom and subtle, often blended, colors are great assets, as is the unique, nodding posture of their flowers. Although this nodding habit frustrated nineteenth century florists, who found their blooms hopeless for arrangements, out in the garden the old tea roses have all the grace of columbines or bleeding hearts. I am particularly fond of 'Mme. Antoine Mari', whose creamy flowers have painted-on borders of lilac pink, and 'Archiduc Joseph', whose blossoms are a complex combination of copper, salmon, rose, and lilac.

As the nineteenth century wore on, rose breeders in Europe continued to cross any repeat-blooming roses they could get their hands on, the result being a mongrel class of vigorous reblooming roses in a wide range of flower forms and colors. These were the hybrid perpetual roses. A nineteenth-century collector quipped that the hybrid perpetuals were "more hybrid than perpetual," and he was not far off the mark. Most of these roses bloom in summer and then once again in autumn—much less frequently than the Portland, Bourbon, China, and tea roses from which they were bred. Nonetheless, the class includes some fragrant, large-flowered beauties, provided you can get past their leggy, upright growth. 'Baronne Prévost' has luscious clear-pink flowers with a nice strong perfume, while the lovely 'Eugène Fürst' blooms in deep crimson. Another superb dark-red member of this class is the thornless 'Souvenir du Dr. Jamain', whose flowers breathe the heady scent of damask roses.

Thornless, too, is the most magnificent of all hybrid perpetuals, 'Reine des Violettes'. Its name means "Queen of the Violets," and that's no exaggeration. Alluring, rich blooms of blended wine-purple and slate-gray open from unpromisingly tattered buds above unusual blue-green foliage. The flowers' scent is as complex and winelike as their color, and although each bloom is short-lived on the plant, this is one hybrid perpetual that earns the name: Blooms are produced wave after wave all season long. Plant 'Reine des Violettes' with the great gray cardoon, a blue-flowered clematis, and some silver artemisias, and you'll be rewarded with one of the Northwest cottage garden's finest sights!

One reliably reblooming class of old garden roses originated in North America during the nineteenth century. They are the Noisette roses, bred by crossing China roses with the beautifully scented musk rose *(R. moschata)*. The result was a group of strongly fragrant climbing roses that hold their small flowers of white or pink in big, loose, frothy clusters. The pale pink 'Blush Noisette' is a good example, climbing 8 feet to 10 feet high on any wall, trellis, or pillar. Later on, Noisettes were crossed with climbing tea roses to yield the taller-growing tea-Noisettes, with large, complex flowers in blended shades of buff, pink, apricot, and yellow. These exquisite roses have been neglected in America and Canada, since they are too cold sensitive for the Midwest or the Northeastern states and provinces. Here in the maritime Northwest, though, they endure winter readily and make some of the most reliable, floriferous, and fragrant climbing roses. An old tea-Noisette like the honey-buff 'Gloire de Dijon' or the peach-and-pink 'Desprez à Fleur Jaune' makes a stupendous sight when it cascades from the branches of a tree or clothes a cottage garden pergola.

Related to the old Noisettes is another long-neglected group known as the hybrid musks. Descended from the musk rose only through their Noisette her-itage, these versatile shrub roses bloom in clusters over elongated, glossy foliage on gently arching canes. Left to themselves, they form broad, mounded shrubs to 5 feet high and a bit more across, but their canes train easily onto fences, walls, and pillars, too. The hybrid musks are notable for their fine fragrance, most pronounced at evening, and for their tolerance of partial shade and northern exposures. A hybrid musk like the cream-white 'Penelope', the pink 'Felicia', or the soft yellow 'Francesca' would be just the rose to set against the north face of a house or fence. Perhaps the most beloved of hybrid musks is the aptly named 'Buff Beauty', whose honey-colored blossoms nestle in large clusters like so many tissue-paper flowers. It is magnificent with dark violet *Salvia* x *sylvestris* hybrids or tall blue cam-panulas.

'*Reine des Violettes*' ("Queen of the Violets") still reigns supreme in modern cottage gardens. The colored foliage belongs to *Weigela florida* 'Variegata'.

Once overlooked as well, modern shrub roses have come into their own lately, no doubt in part due to the hybridizing efforts of England's David Austin. His line of "English" roses, bred by cross-ing modern hybrid teas and floribundas with old garden roses, has done much to rekindle interest in shrub roses as garden plants. David Austin's finest introductions, including the honey-scented soft pink 'Heritage', the upright, apricot 'Jayne Austin', and the shrubby, large peach-yellow blend known as 'Abraham Darby', make superb contributions to the Northwest cottage garden. Other modern breeders have now followed David Austin's lead, introducing several trademarked series of roses with old-fashioned-looking flowers. The results are mixed, and I advise you

to observe plants in growth and bloom wherever possible before selecting from among them.

Two other groups of modern roses valuable for Northwest cottage gardens are the polyanthas and the floribundas. Polyanthas are low-growing roses that hold clusters of small flowers over dense, twiggy growth and fine-textured foliage. Soft-colored polyanthas like 'White Pet' and pale-pink 'Clotilde Soupert' blend easily into pastel color schemes, while everybody's favorite, 'Mlle. Cécile Brunner' (the "sweetheart rose"), earns its keep with marvelously formed peach flowers that resemble tiny hybrid teas.

The hybrid tea roses themselves are usually too stiff and awkward to blend well into cottage garden plantings, but their bushier, free-flowering floribunda cousins work much better. These scrappy little roses bloom and bloom, providing months of color in containers, beds, or borders. Among my favorites of the scads available these days are the gracious cream-white 'Margaret Merrill', the bright yellow 'Gold Badge', and the delicately colored 'Lavender Pinocchio'.

Among modern roses, the compact, free-blooming floribundas make great cottage garden plants. Here the subtly colored 'Lavender Pinocchio' blooms with a purple-leafed hybrid *Heuchera*.

138

If released from the monotonous old-fashioned bedding schemes where they have languished for so long, the floribunda roses adapt readily to life among perennials and other shrubs, becoming fine, upstanding citizens of the cottage garden.

PLANTS FOR COLORED FOLIAGE

Flowers might be the first aspect of a plant we notice in the garden, but plants consist mostly of foliage. Since so much of what we see in any cottage garden planting is foliage, it only makes sense to wring as much interest as possible from all those leaves! It just so happens that high temperatures dull the tones of most striped, spotted, and colored leaves, so our cool summer climate makes the Pacific Northwest a haven for variegated plants of every type. From trees to tiny creeping plants, Pacific Northwest gardens play host to a gleaming constellation of colored leaves that we can take advantage of.

WOODY PLANTS FOR FOLIAGE

Because of their comparative mass, trees and shrubs with colored foliage make a great impact upon the cottage garden. While trees and shrubs that flower are conspicuous for a few weeks at a time, colored foliage can catch the eye all season long. For both these reasons, choosing woody plants for foliage merits thought. A constantly expanding range of woody plant selections with marked or colored foliage makes choosing among them a real challenge. Here are a few that are especially rewarding in Pacific Northwest gardens.

I could have easily included the eastern redbud, *Cercis canadensis*, earlier in this chapter among the great flowering trees for Northwest cottage gardens, but its purple-leafed cultivar 'Forest Pansy' launches this small tree into a different ornamental stratum altogether. With its twigs outlined in tiny bright-pink flowers, *C. canadensis* 'Forest Pansy' is a spectacle in early spring, but when its heart-shaped, royal-purple leaves emerge a few weeks later, the effect is simply breathtaking. Place this tree carefully so that its startling color does not overwhelm your other cottage garden plantings. It blends beautifully into color schemes that feature deep rich crimsons, violets, and creamy-buff or white highlights, and makes a fine foil to a palette of pastel pinks and lavenders.

Everybody seems to grow Japanese maples (*Acer palmatum* cultivars) with colored leaves, but for a change of pace, try planting the golden fullmoon maple (*Acer shirasawanum* 'Aureum') instead. Also a native of Japan, this pretty maple forms a vase-shaped tree to 20 feet with layers of golden-chartreuse foliage draped like ribbons among the branches. It looks beautiful against a dark-colored home or in front of Douglas firs and cedars at a forest edge.

Cornus alba 'Gouchaltii' displays brilliantly variegated foliage in spring and summer and glossy red twigs all winter.

I did not mention dogwoods (genus *Cornus*) among the flowering trees earlier in this chapter, in part because the common *C. florida*, and with our West Coast native *C. nuttallii*, have been subject to a devastating anthracnose blight. Among the other dogwoods, those that offer colored foliage as well as flowers pack a double wallop. The anthracnose-resistant Asian dogwood *C. kousa* is an impressive flowering tree in any form, but its white-flowering selection 'Wolf Eyes', with cream centers on its leaves, is dazzling all summer long. As do so many dogwoods, *C. kousa* 'Wolf Eyes' assumes bright autumn colors ranging from crimson and burgundy to scarlet. *C. alternifolia* 'Argentea' is less conspicuous than most dogwoods in flower, but it makes up the difference with its stunning form and foliage. Layered, horizontal branches reach out wide to display silver-edged leaves that shimmer in the slightest breeze. 'Argentea' deserves a site where it can spread out to show off its gracious silhouette. It will grow slowly up to 15 feet or 20 feet in height and width.

Shrubs grown for foliage in Northwest cottage gardens assume all sorts of colors and a range of stature from modest to imposing. Among the larger is the well-loved purple smoke bush, *Cotinus coggygria*. Its better forms, including 'Velvet Cloak' and 'Royal Purple', hold their rich dark color through the summer before turning bright scarlet and orange in the fall. They are slow-growing, up to 15 feet in time, though careful pruning can contain them at a lower stature. Their soft, gauzy lilac heads of bloom add contrast and fine texture in the summer.

Viburnum sargentii 'Onondaga' is another purple-leafed shrub of more compact dimensions, usually content to hover at about 6 feet. It has contrasting white "lacecap" flowers in spring and bright scarlet fruits in autumn.

If it's lighter colors that you seek, you may enjoy *Weigela florida* 'Variegata'. The weigelas have fallen out of fashion as flowering shrubs, but this variety, with wide cream margins on its leaves, is one I'd welcome even if it didn't bloom. The profuse, soft pink trumpet flowers that appear in the late spring are a fine bonus on this easily grown 6-foot shrub. For tighter spaces, there is *W. florida* 'Variegata Nana', which is similar in leaf and flower but grows only 3 feet tall.

Sambucus nigra (European elderberry) is a homely, even weedy plant in its natural form, but several of its cultivars boast elegantly colored foliage. 'Madonna' is a slow-growing selection with gold-margined leaves, while 'Pulverulenta' has uniquely twisted foliage all stippled in white. The related *S. racemosa* 'Plumosa Aurea' has delicately cut, lacy foliage in bright chartreuse and gold. Each of these sambucus cultivars can reach 6 feet or more, but hard winter pruning will keep them smaller where required.

For bright golden color in a smaller shrub, few plants can outclass *Caryopteris* x *clandonensis* 'Worcester Gold'. Even without colored foliage, *C.* x *clandonensis* is a superb flowering shrub, an open 2-foot mound covered in August and September with a galaxy of tiny clear-blue flowers. 'Worcester Gold' is impressive enough out of bloom, but when it's in flower the combination of bright blue and yellow is unique and captivating.

The *Spiraea japonica* selection 'Magic Carpet' is another small-scale shrub whose colored foliage can shout across the garden. The leaves of this twiggy 2-foot plant emerge bright copper-orange and mature to golden-green. A clump of *S. japonica* 'Magic Carpet' makes a summerlong blanket of glittering flame within a cottage garden planting.

HERBACEOUS FOLIAGE PLANTS

If trees and shrubs with colored foliage are the broad brushstrokes of a cottage garden planting composition, then herbaceous plants with colored foliage are among the finishing touches. Their smaller scale allows us to embroider patterns, lively or subtle, through our beds and borders in a way that larger plants do not. Their colors may be either soft or bold, and can appear singly or in complex combinations on a single leaf. Indeed, their attributes are so diverse that there is one for every planting niche in the Northwest cottage garden.

Cool, soft-colored foliage in blue and gray is mild and soothing in most garden color schemes. It creates a platinum setting for deep jewel-like violets and purples, and glazes bright pink, fuchsia, and magenta flowers like a coat of sugar frosting. The genus *Artemisia* is a vein of silver ore for cottage garden plantings, with its members sporting shimmering, fragrant leaves in many shapes and sizes. *A. ludoviciana albula* 'Valerie Finnis' and 'Silver King' have sprawling 2- to 3-foot stems clothed in short, narrow white leaves. *A.* 'Powis Castle' is a 3-foot mound of finely cut silver foliage, and *A. schmidtiana* 'Silver Mound' is just what its name says: an 8-inch hummock of soft silver-gray. All want full sun and ample drainage and are tolerant of drought when well established.

Santolina chamaecyparissus, sometimes known as lavender cotton, makes a tidy foot-tall mound of tightly knit silver-white foliage that gleams all season long in the front of any well-drained, sunny bed or border. For bolder texture, there are lamb's ears *(Stachys byzantina)*, which cover the ground with their broad, white, fuzzy, oval leaves.

A pair of reliable grasses bring fine slate-blue foliage to Northwest cottage gardens. The taller of the two is *Helictotrichon sempervirens*, or blue oat grass, which makes neatly symmetrical mounds of slender blades to 2 feet tall, topped in late summer by 3-foot stalks with gold-brown inflorescences. A quarter-scale model is the popular blue fescue, *Festuca glauca*, similar in form and color but only 1 foot tall. Both of these evergreens (or "everblues") consort happily with pink- and purple-flowering perennials or with more brightly colored foliage.

Among the most conspicuous plants for colored foliage are those with bold white or cream markings on their green leaves. Bold in texture, too, is *Scrophularia auriculata* 'Variegata'. Its name may sound like a disease, but this plant is actually a sturdy 2-foot-tall perennial with puckered oval leaves broadly brushed along their margins in bright cream. A finer texture in these same colors comes from the cream-margined compound foliage of *Polemonium caeruleum* 'Brise d'Anjou'. While *S. auriculata* 'Variegata' bears inconspicuous brown flowers, the polemonium has showy foot-tall spikes of bright blue flowers in the early summer. Both thrive in semishade on moist, but well-drained soil. *Physostegia virginiana* 'Variegata' is a select form of the so-called obedient plant that holds spikes of bright pink flowers on 2-foot stems adorned with boldly white-striped foliage. Its leaves will hold up best if it receives some light afternoon shade.

A very different take on green and white comes from *Eryngium variifolium*, an odd little sea holly grown more for its foliage than for its flowers. The neatly formed 6-inch rosettes of this plant are composed of leathery dark green leaves whose glossy surfaces are embossed with heavy silver veins. In early summer there come foot-tall stalks supporting spiny heads of dusty gray-blue flowers. These go to seed to spread *E. variifolium* around the garden if they're not removed after they fade. Like all eryngiums, this little plant tolerates poor, dry soils and grows where many other plants would not survive.

I found the threadlike, soft tannish orange foliage of the New Zealand sedge *Carex buchananii* perplexing at my first encounter. Was it dead, or did it always look that way? Oh, perfectly alive, as it happens, and the wispy, 2-foot clumps are a useful, quiet accent for the bright flowers of *Geum chiloense*, purple irises, and blue geraniums. Far from quiet, however, is the blazing tapestry of orange, red, yellow, and green that decorates the leaves of the chameleon plant, *Houttuynia cordata* 'Variegata'. Few hardy plants exhibit so much color in a single package—but beware! This is an aggressive spreader, and its foot-high stems will

New *Heuchera* hybrids display a range of striking purple and silver-blotched foliage patterns.

propagate by rhizomes to take over a large territory if you let them. On the other hand, *H. cordata* 'Variegata' is one of the few bright-foliaged plants that will thrive on wet soils in shade.

Rich purples are the great pride of the new *Heuchera* hybrids that seem to appear by the dozens every season in the local nurseries. Though few, if any, have the colorful flowers that have earned the genus its common name of coral bells, the blotched, veined, and frosted patterns that the leaves offer in all shades of burgundy and silver more than make up for the loss. I grow them in partial shade with silver-spotted pulmonarias, in sunny containers with pale lilac roses, and in a rockery in front of the blue clumps of *Helictotrichon sempervirens*.

The sometimes-weedy genus *Lysimachia* includes some cultivars with colored foliage that's just too brilliant to ignore. *L. punctata* 'Alexander' has round, white-margined leaves on stems to 2 feet tall, adorned in spring with yellow bell-shaped flowers. The leaves emerge bright pink and green, becoming green and white just before the flowers appear. *L. ciliata* 'Firecracker' has deep bronze-to-burgundy leaves on floppy stems with contrasting bright golden flowers. I find it extremely pleasing tangled up with yellow *Coreopsis* and bright red *Monarda didyma* in the late-summer border. *L. nummularia* 'Aurea', or yellow creeping jenny, is a trailing plant with glowing chartreuse foliage that lights up the ground just like fluorescent paint. It is especially effective beneath *Salvia verticillata* 'Purple Rain' and deep burgundy daylilies.

The genus *Persicaria* offers yet another group of vigorous growers with a wide range of colored foliage. *P. virginiana* 'Painter's Palette' is a 3-foot sprawling plant whose large heart-shaped leaves are mottled cream and green with striking deep red chevrons in their centers. The brand-new *P. microcephala* clone 'Red Dragon' is one of the most exciting foliage plants to have emerged in years. Its arrowhead leaves are marked in silver, purple, burgundy, and plum, turning to blazing scarlet-orange in the fall. With new foliage plants like this appearing in the Northwest every year, we can enjoy unprecedented chances to experiment with colored leaves in our cottage garden plantings.

PLANTS FOR FRAGRANCE

Whether it originates in foliage or in flowers, fragrance is a vital part of any cottage garden planting scheme. The lilies and the old garden roses are some of the finest scented plants in all the summer garden, but fragrance in the cottage garden is a year-round priority. The all-pervasive scent of *Daphne odora* launches the Northwest growing season as early as March, flooding the garden every year with sweet perfume. Notoriously fussy about where it grows, *D. odora* requires a moist but well-drained organic soil in full sun or semishade.

If the scented daphne will not grow for you, you can get fragrance early in the season from a modest little shrub called *Fothergilla gardenii*. Soon after the spring equinox, its 2-foot branches support 3-inch bottlebrushes of white bloom that treat the nose to a strong honey fragrance. Bright orange and scarlet autumn foliage makes *F. gardenii* nearly as welcome in fall as in spring. The cultivar 'Blue Mist' has less fall color, but its foliage is a pretty bluish green when new. A larger species, *F. major*, grows up to 6 feet, with similar fragrance and foliage. Not long after the fothergillas bloom comes the Korean spice viburnum, *Viburnum carlesii*. This 6-foot shrub, with its familiar globe-shaped heads of cream-white flowers, has been loved for generations for its fragrance. Plant it or its hybrid *V.* x *carlcephalum* near a cottage garden patio or seating area where you can best enjoy its fresh spring scent.

Ten favorite plants for fragrance

- Damask roses
- Fothergillas (*Fothergilla* spp.)
- Heliotrope (*Heliotropium arborescens*)
- Hyacinths (*Hyacinthus* spp.)
- Lavender (*Lavandula* spp.)
- Lilacs (*Syringa* spp.)
- Oriental hybrid lilies
- Rosemary (*Rosmarinus officinalis*)
- *Sarcococca* spp.
- Sweet alyssum (*Lobularia maritima*)

Beneath any of these fragrant shrubs you can plant lily-of-the-valley (*Convallaria majalis*), which will tolerate the dry shade at their feet, spreading over time to form a sweetly scented ground cover. One of the few plants that will thrive under tall conifers, *C. majalis* also works in those dark spaces at the base of Douglas firs, cedars, and spruce trees.

In sunnier locations, good old-fashioned hyacinths still yield some of the finest springtime floral fragrance. The popular Dutch forcing varieties are a bit rigid for the cottage garden, with their dense spikes and military posture, but a host of looser, multistemmed types now found in fall bulb catalogs are just as fragrant. The *Hyacinthus orientalis* cultivars 'Festival Pink' and 'Festival White' are only two examples of these graceful new selections. Even the conventional Dutch hybrids like 'Delft Blue' and 'Gypsy Queen' become more loose and open if allowed to remain in the garden over several seasons.

What would springtime in the cottage garden be without the scent of lilacs? Yet, for all their fragrance and beauty when in flower, lilacs use a lot of real estate. If you'd rather not give so much space to shrubs that hold no interest beyond a few short weeks in spring, consider the compact Korean lilac *Syringa patula* 'Miss Kim'. It's alleged to grow to 6 feet in time, but I've found that 'Miss Kim' remains down at 3 feet or less with just a bit of summer pruning when the flowers fade.

Lavender 'Goodwin Creek Gray' produces fragrant blooms all summer long. It is paired here with the daylily hybrid 'Betty Warren Woods'.

The pale lavender flowers offer all the fragrance of a full-blown common lilac, but in a fraction of the space.

The mock oranges of genus *Philadelphus* bridge the boundary between spring and summer fragrance, and are as much a part of cottage gardening tradition as lilacs. They, too, can have a short season of interest, so I recommend those with colored foliage for added value in a cottage garden setting. *P.* x *lemoinei* 'Innocence' has both an outstanding fragrance *and* leaves that are variegated in cream or white. *P. coronaria* 'Aurea' has bright golden foliage that holds its color through our cool Northwest summers.

The foliage of southernwood, or *Artemisia abrotanum*, is a source of fragrance and of beauty. Not so silvery as many of its *Artemisia* cousins, *A. abrotanum* nonetheless does make a pretty 2- to 3-foot mound of fine, feathery leaves. These have a strong scent of sweet fruit, pine resin, and spice that is at once intriguing and peculiar. Plant it near a path or a frequently used paved area, where visitors can brush against it to release its scent.

Lavender (*Lavandula* spp.) is such a useful and versatile cottage garden plant that it's hard to know where to discuss it. Even if it did not have attractive gray-green foliage or long-lasting violet-colored flowers, we would grow lavender for scent alone. The varieties of lavender are far too numerous to name, so I will mention just a few that I especially enjoy. The old English selection *L. angustifolia* 'Hidcote' is reliable as rain (and that's saying a lot here in the maritime Northwest). It grows to 18 inches and has plenty of deep-violet flowers. *L. angustifolia* 'Twickel Purple' is a taller plant, with large violet spikes on long stalks well above the foliage. *L. x intermedia* 'Fred Boutin' grows up to 3 feet tall and has especially broad, bright silver foliage. Among the prettiest of all is the vigorous hybrid *L.* 'Goodwin Creek Gray'. This beauty grows up to 3 feet, with plenty of finely toothed gray foliage and violet flowers that appear from May to August.

One of the champions of summer fragrance in the Northwest cottage garden is the old-fashioned annual heliotrope, *Heliotropium arborensis*. Its sweet, pervasive scent is unmistakable, whether it blooms in purple, white, or lavender. Use it freely in container plantings, window boxes, or near patios—wherever you can relish its perfume. Another classic annual for summer scent is the old standby sweet alyssum *(Lobularia maritima)*. Once grown almost exclusively in white, *L. maritima* now shows up in shades of lilac, purple, and even pale apricot-pink. Scented sweet peas also thrive in Northwest cottage gardens, making a quick annual cover for a small trellis or a sunny fence. On horizontal surfaces the minuscule creeping Corsican mint, *Mentha requienii*, is a superb and startling source of fragrance. Grown between bricks or paving stones, it will release a strong dose of peppermint aroma whenever it is stepped on.

Fragrance in summer is plentiful in any well-stocked cottage garden; but it's on dreary Northwest winter days that scented plants can surprise and please us most of all. The modest-looking evergreen sweet box, *Sarcococca ruscifolia*, delights beyond compare in January's gloom, when clouds of honeyed perfume waft from its all-but-invisible cream flowers. I grow a clump of sarcococcas just outside my front door, where their fragrance is a special welcome for visitors who brave the rain to walk up to the stoop. By the time the sarcococca's scent has faded in the last days of February, the daffodils are opening and *Daphne odora* is again in bud, ready to usher in another fragrant cottage garden spring.

PLANTS FOR FORM

Every plant contributes form of one sort or another to the cottage garden. Some are just more dramatic and sculptural than others. Mounds of foliage are common among cottage garden plants, but plants with strong vertical profiles are less easily come by. Among the best vertical accent plants for Northwest cottage gardens are those with erect, swordlike foliage. The largest of these is the New Zealand flax (genus *Phormium*). Its leaves are arranged in broad fans, growing to 6 feet or more. The foliage is evergreen, and hybrids with leaves striped yellow, orange, pink, or burgundy are widely grown. Form, color, and size make phormiums imposing plants, so use them sparingly and place them with great care; set in too small a space or overused, they can easily overwhelm a modestly scaled cottage garden.

Smaller in scale, but still imposing, are the spuria irises. These underutilized beauties grow to 4 feet or 5 feet tall and form dense clumps of rigid, upright leaves. Their June flowers are both large and colorful, with patterns that blend yellow, white, blue, purple, and bronze—often in complex combinations. Among the most spectacular are the blue-and-yellow 'Clara Ellen', the bronze-and-lavender blend 'Betty Cooper', and 'Color Focus', with stripes of white on violet and strong yellow markings. All are tough and easy to grow, withstanding summer drought and increasing steadily from year to year.

Although it too provides a vertical accent, *Dierama pulcherrimum* (sometimes known as "angel's fishing rod") appears far more delicate than the irises. This plant's slender, grasslike foliage rises to 3 or 4 feet, topped in summer by curving, wiry stems, from which dangle bell-shaped blooms in shades of pink and lilac. *D. pulcherrimum* is slow to form clumps and demands fertile, moist, but very well drained soil in order to survive. Nevertheless, it has so much garden presence that it's well worth fussing over.

Bolder plants by far are the members of the genus *Yucca*, with their stiff, leathery leaves in spiky, angular rosettes. Their foliage makes quite an impact on its own, but when the long spikes of waxy white blossoms emerge from a mature plant in late summer, they take center stage. The most impressive of the yuccas are those with striped leaves, including *Y. filamentosa* 'Bright Edge' and *Y. flaccida* 'Golden Sword'. Yuccas like their soils warm and well drained, and flourish happily through Northwest summer droughts. Plant them in full sun with softer, mounding plants like purple heucheras or violet-flowered *Geranium* x *magnificum* to take advantage of their strongly sculptural form.

Dramatic upright form of a far different sort comes from the big flowering spurge *Euphorbia characias* subsp. *wulfenii*. This plant's big columnar masses of gray foliage and blunt clusters of bright lime-green bracts are familiar sights in Northwest rockeries in early spring. They can be just as effective in mixed plantings, where they contrast with the low, veined rosettes of *Eryngium variifolium* or the bright blue blooms of *Ceanothus* hybrids.

A columnar plant of more modest dimensions is gayfeather, *Liatris spicata*. The lilac-purple cultivar called 'Kobold' holds its fuzzy flowers on candlelike spikes that grow as tall as 2 feet. The slightly taller white form, 'Floristan White', makes an outstanding accent plant with crimson knautias or red shrub roses.

Phlomis russeliana, whose common name is Jerusalem sage, is unique in form among perennials. For most of the season its large, gray, felted leaves form a dense 8-inch mat along the ground. In late spring, though, 3-foot spikes emerge, supporting layered whorls of pastel yellow flowers at intervals along their lengths. These dignified flower stalks are as appealing with the warm, bright-orange blooms of annual nasturtiums as with blue-flowered aquilegias. *Acanthus mollis*, whose great scrolled leaves adorned the capitals of classical Corinthian columns, is another statuesque accent for cottage garden beds and borders. The enormous clumps of glossy foliage on this tough perennial would stand out in a crowd, even without their 5-foot spikes of hooded lilac flowers.

The flowers are the source of formal interest in the giant ornamental onion *Allium giganteum*. Each spring its bulbs send up 3-foot stalks supporting great big 6-inch balls of violet flowers guaranteed to stop all traffic in your Northwest

These marvelous lollipop blooms belong to a flowering onion (*Allium* spp.).

cottage garden. Later on, in June, the drumstick allium, *A. sphaerocephalum*, erects its 2-foot stalks ending in unique oval heads of wine-purple blooms.

Echinops ritro (globe thistle) tops its 3- to 4-foot stems of spiny gray-green foliage with perfect spheres of steely electric blue. These come in July and carry on for many weeks, making a perfect contrast to bright yellow daylilies and *Coreopsis*. Equally striking but totally different in its flower form is the rough-and-tumble gooseneck loosestrife, *Lysimachia clethroides*. Its leafy 2-foot stalks carry odd, curving S-shaped spikes of small white flowers that resemble no other plant in the garden. *L. clethroides* spreads aggressively in the moist, sunny locations that it favors, so be careful about planting it with more demure perennials.

Among woody plants, one of the best for interesting form is the much-ballyhooed doublefile viburnum, *V. plicatum* var. *tomentosum*. Every word of praise expended on this shrub is merited in spades. Its branches grow in what horticulturists refer to as "tabular" form, reaching out in neatly stacking horizontal layers. Every spring these wide-spreading branches are precisely outlined in flat, lacy clusters of pure white flowers, arranged in (what else?) double-file rows atop the leaves. In all the garden there is nothing like it! In good seasons the flowers give way to clusters of scarlet berries, though two plants of different clones may be required for fruit set.

In a class all of their own for form are the exotic calla lilies (genus *Zantedeschia*). The large white *Z. aethiopica* survives in old, neglected gardens all over the Northwest. Its big, tropical-looking foliage and long-lasting spathes look marvelous with light-textured plants like astilbes or striped Japanese sedges (*Carex morrowii* 'Expallida'), but newer hybrids offer even greater opportunities. Compact 18-inch cultivars with spathes in all shades of yellow, orange, pink, lilac, and red can now be found to complement any color scheme you could imagine. Some even have the added bonus of white-spotted foliage to prolong the plant's season of interest.

PLANTS FOR TEXTURE

Juxtaposing plants with different textures is an easy way to make your cottage garden plantings lively and engaging, no matter what your color scheme. Texture adds a new dimension to the cottage garden, bringing its own subtle contrast to each group of plants. There are plants with bold, coarse textures that leap right out of the border, and plants with fine or filmy textures that float like gauzy clouds among their neighbors. Well-thought-out cottage garden plantings will make use of both kinds, along with all the permutations in between.

BOLD TEXTURES

Big, brash plants with massive foliage and flowers blaze like clarions across the cottage garden. None trumpet louder than the cannas, whose foot-long paddle leaves and huge bright flowers rise above all other perennials wherever they are grown. Never subtle, cannas make an even greater impact when their foliage is flushed or striped in colors other than green. The leaves of *Canna* 'Pretoria' are boldly striped with yellow, in harmony with the copper-orange flowers. The hybrid 'Tropicana' blooms in the same color, but its foliage is striped in red and orange. The relatively compact (and I use the term with trepidation) clone 'Wyoming' carries orange flowers over 4-foot stalks with dark burgundy-purple leaves. These loud tropical giants please me most when they grow toward the rear of a dense cottage garden planting filled with warm-colored late-summer flowers like rudbeckias, *Monarda didyma*, and bright golden daylilies.

Nearly as large as cannas, but less ostentatious because of their more subdued coloration, are the cardoon and the artichoke. Both are members of the genus *Cynara*, and both produce great spiny silver leaves to more than 2 feet long. At 6 feet tall, the cardoon is the larger of the two, while artichokes usually top out at about 4 feet. Both require sun and well-drained soil, and will bear enormous lilac thistle flowers in midsummer. Neither overwinters too reliably in our region, but their growth is so rapid that they can be grown as giant annuals.

The ornamental rhubarb *Rheum palmatum* 'Atrosanguineum' takes much longer to display its virtues, but when it does, stand back! Its clumps of hand-shaped leaves, each as much as 3 feet wide, erupt after a few years' growth into a shocking 6-foot plume of tiny bright red blossoms. Plant this monster on moist soil in the sun and leave plenty of room for its expanding foliage.

For bold texture in shade, few plants are more reliable than the old standard *Fatsia japonica*. Though it is often planted in cramped spaces where its foot-wide leaves are out of scale, used wisely it provides strong texture where few other plants will grow. It looks splendid with the fine, gold-marked foliage of *Abelia* x *grandiflora* 'Francis Mason' or the spiny, white-edged leaves of *Osmanthus hetero-phyllus* 'Variegata'.

Hydrangea aspera villosa is another big-leafed plant for shade, with fuzzy leaves to 10 inches long and large heads of soft mauve-colored flowers. Unless pruned hard in its youth, it grows into an open 6- to 8-foot shrub with somewhat

151

twisted branches wrapped in exfoliating red-brown bark. Early pruning will encourage branching and yield a neater, if less picturesque, domed habit.

FINE TEXTURES

Coarse, heavy textures are dramatic, but if unrelieved their burden renders cottage garden plantings ponderous and earthbound. Fine-textured plants with fluffy, frothy foliage and flowers have the opposite effect. Their buoyancy can lift any planting to its feet, and fine texture in abundance is particularly essential to establish the lively and effusive spirit so characteristic of cottage garden plantings.

The great bronze fennel, *Foeniculum vulgare* 'Purpurascens', may be large, but it is also light as air. Its billowing foliage envelops its neighbors in a soft coppery-purple mist to heights of 5 or 6 feet. I especially enjoy it with the pale pink flowers of the old Bourbon rose 'Mme. Pierre Oger' and the big silver leaves of a cardoon.

For feathery texture on a smaller scale I often turn to *Coreopsis verticillata*, the threadleaf coreopsis, with its fluffy foot-tall mounds of finely cut leaves. The cultivar 'Zagreb' has perky 2-inch daisy flowers in bright golden yellow, while 'Moonbeam' blooms in pale lemon with a hint of green. Both flower from July until September if deadheaded, and will withstand dry soils and neglect once they are well established.

So small are the leaves on the oddball shrub *Corokia cotoneaster* 'Little Prince' that they seem hardly to exist. Instead, we see a loosely tangled mass of wiry branches, all dusted with a silver-lilac bloom. Each plant looks like a puff of pale purple smoke that has settled in the garden. *C. cotoneaster* 'Little Prince' is an outstanding fine-textured companion for bold purple heucheras or the broad gray-green foliage of *Phlomis russeliana*.

The fine texture of the meadow rues (genus *Thalictrum*) comes from both their leaves and flowers. *T. aquilegifolium* holds 4-foot-tall clouds of fluffy lilac flowers over gracefully divided foliage in late spring. *T. flavum* subsp. *glaucum* has flowers of soft pastel yellow and soft gray-blue leaves. Either makes a lovely picture grown on evenly moist soil in light shade. For sunny spots, Russian sage (*Perovskia atriplicifolia*) is just as airy in both flower and foliage. Its fine silvery leaves blend beautifully with the open spikes of violet flowers that emerge in mid-July. In winter the bare wispy branches bleach to a bright white that stands out starkly against dark mulch or soil.

Many common plant names seem to me confusing, inaccurate, or both, but in the case of "love-in-a-mist" I must admit somebody hit the mark. A mist of lacy foliage is exactly what surrounds the intriguingly complex flowers of *Nigella damascena*. Strains with flowers in blue, purple, pink, or white grow quickly and easily from seed. My favorite is the clear sky-blue selection 'Miss Jekyll'. *N. damascena* self-sows abundantly in Pacific Northwest gardens, but I have yet to see it plant itself anywhere I did not like it!

For fine texture at ground level at the front of cottage garden plantings, I like to use a range of tiny creeping plants with dainty foliage. *Sagina subulata*, known by the common name of Irish moss, makes little mats of truly mossy-looking leaves in clear, bright kelly green. *S. subulata* 'Aurea' is identical except for its electric gold-green color. The pancake-flat *Raoulia australis* has miniscule leaves of gleaming silver-gray that stand out splendidly along red brick or dark stone paving. *Cotula squalida* is only slightly taller, at 1 inch or so, but just as adorable, with deeply cut, fuzzy leaves like tiny fern fronds. I sometimes plant all four in combination for a mosaic of contrasting foliage.

Plants with upright forms can be fine-textured too, and nowhere is fine, vertical texture more elegant than on the tall, clump-forming grass *Miscanthus sinensis*. *Miscanthus* cultivars come in a range of sizes, from four-foot "dwarves" to stately seven-footers. Many are enhanced by striped or banded foliage that further highlights their light, airy texture. 'Strictus' and 'Zebrinus' have horizontal yellow bands across their blades, while 'Cabaret' has broad white central stripes running down each blade. All have pretty plumes of feather-duster flowers in late summer.

A grasslike plant with texture that's outright peculiar is the New Zealand hair sedge *Carex comans*. Here's another common name that says it all. *C. comans* forms a foot-tall, floppy mound of—well, hairlike foliage that is unlike any other plant I know. It may be odd, but it *does* look wonderful in front of boldly upright plants like crocosmias and spuria irises.

Unique in its own quiet way is *Alchemilla mollis*, or lady's mantle, an old-fashioned plant that's often used in English cottage gardens. Its round, pleated leaves are known for catching drops of water like pearls on their velvety surfaces. In June *A. mollis* sends up clouds of fluffy chartreuse flowers that are equally attractive with deep-violet salvias or bright orange floribunda roses.

CHAPTER SEVEN

Plants With a Purpose:
The Special Agents

S hade, dry soils, poorly-drained areas—none of these tricky conditions prevents establishing a suitably colorful and varied cottage garden planting. You simply have to call upon the "special agents," stalwart plants specifically adapted to such challenging garden niches. In this chapter I'll suggest a range of plants that will thrive under difficult growing conditions. I'll also talk about some plants that serve other special purposes in Northwest cottage gardens: plants for fall and winter interest, climbing plants, plants to attract wildlife, fast-growing plants to use as garden "fillers," edible plants, and plants for hedges.

PLANTS FOR FALL AND WINTER INTEREST

I said it before, and I'll say it again: Cottage gardens, especially here in the Pacific Northwest, are year-round gardens. With our accommodating climate and so many fascinating plants to choose from, there is no excuse for Northwest cottage gardens that go blank in fall and winter. The plants that make a cottage garden shine in fall and winter work their magic in all different ways—some with foliage, some with fragrance, some with their bare branches. Some even resort to that old standby, flowers. Whatever source of interest they tap, plants that extend the season of interest should appear in every part of the cottage garden.

FALL AND WINTER FLOWERS

Flowers may not come to mind when you imagine fall and winter gardens, but that doesn't mean that they have to be absent. Plenty of outstanding plants are available to provide fall and winter bloom in Northwest cottage gardens. For example, everybody seems to love the elegant Japanese anemone hybrids *(Anemone* x *hybrida)*. These adaptable plants grow well in sun or shade and bloom profusely from late August well into October. Popular selections include the single white

'Honorine Jobert', the single pink 'Prinz Heinrich', and the double-flowered 'Margarete', 'Queen Charlotte' (both pink), and 'Whirlwind' (white).

Another fine group of October flowers are the colchicums, which have short-stemmed chalice flowers, much like giant crocuses. Unlike crocuses, the toxic bulbs of Colchicum do not fall prey to rodents, and can be counted on for bloom year after year. Most bloom in shades of lavender or lilac, but there are white selections too. Alongside the colchicums appear the nodding flowers of the hardy cyclamens. These jewel-like miniature versions of the florist's plant come in a range of colors from deep pink to white, and most have boldly marked foliage to boot. Cyclamen hederifolium is my personal favorite. It grows from small tubers and forms slowly spreading colonies in the shade of deciduous azaleas or shrub roses. The hardy cyclamens have been over-collected in their native habitat, so try to purchase nursery-grown plants.

Perennial asters of all kinds display their daisy-shaped flowers from September until frost, bringing great mounds of color to the autumn garden. One of the loveliest and most reliable is *Aster* x *frikaartii* 'Mönch', which covers its 2-foot frame in hundreds of soft lavender flowers at a time. Altogether different is the *A. lateriflorus* selection 'Prince', which grows into an airy mound of dark purple, threadlike foliage studded with tiny pinkish white flowers. It makes a pretty autumn picture growing with the silver *Artemisia* 'Valerie Finnis'.

Witch hazel hybrids *(Hamamelis* x *intermedia)* are the aristocrats of the mid-winter cottage garden. These large shrubs outline their wide-spreading, horizontal-to-ascending branches with a fringe of deeply fragrant flowers that persist from January into early March. Their colors range from the soft yellows of *H.* x *intermedia* 'Pallida' and 'Arnold's Promise' through the copper-orange of 'Jelena' to the deep reddish bronze of 'Diane'. As if their winter display were not enough, most of them also flaunt a garb of gold and orange foliage in autumn.

H. x *intermedia* may rule the winter garden, but its court includes some other worthy flowering shrubs as well. Chief among these is the gloriously fragrant *Viburnum* x *bodnantense* 'Dawn', whose nodding clusters of pale pink flowers spill their perfume over the entire February garden. Hard on their heels emerge the flowers of the winter hazels (genus *Corylopsis*), dangling in the late-winter breeze like too many golden tassels. The open-growing *C. spicata* has some of the largest, most conspicuous blooms of all, with the bonus of a sweet and, at the same time, bracing fragrance.

At the very end of winter the peculiar shrub *Edgeworthia papyrifera* unfurls its scented clusters of yellow and white flowers, which sparkle seductively against a background of conifers or a dark colored wall. Even before it blooms, *Edgeworthia* adorns the winter garden with its slightly twisted branches clothed in attractively exfoliating bark.

Blooming beneath these winter shrubs, the hellebores display their waxy flowers for months, no matter how foul the weather. *Helleborus niger* shows its clear white flowers earliest of all, often in time for Christmas. *H. orientalis* is the most colorful member of the clan, with flowers in white, cream, pink, lavender, or deepest purple, frequently marked with darker speckles in elaborate patterns. *H. argutifolius* 'Pacific Frost'

Fragrant witch hazels bloom reliably from January until March, no matter how nasty the weather.

has white-marbled leaves and chartreuse flowers, while *H. lividus* has green flowers flushed with lilac-purple. All of the hellebores have handsome foliage that remains fresh throughout the spring and summer.

BARK AND BRANCHES

Decorative bark and branches are great contributors to winter plantings in the Northwest cottage garden. The maples (genus *Acer*) are the undisputed champions of ornamental bark. Everyone knows the coral bark Japanese maple, *A. palmatum* 'Sango Kaku', but it is only one of many stunning winter maples. The Asian species *A. davidii* and *A. capillipes* both have green bark bearing serpentine white markings that have earned them the name "snakebark maples."

Acer pensylvanicum is another pretty snakebark species from the eastern part of North America. Its clone 'White Tigress' has especially bold stripes, but the selection *A. pensylvanicum* 'Erythrocladum' is the most spectacular of all. The branches of this "candy cane maple" are bright scarlet with white stripes, truly reminiscent of peppermint sticks! Not to be outdone, the paperbark maple, *A. griseum*, sloughs off its cinnamon-red bark in long, translucent scrolls that glow when struck by the winter sun. All of these small maples raise the curtain on their winter performances with bright autumn foliage in shades of yellow, gold, orange, or red, depending on the species.

Stupendous as the maples are in winter, they don't hold a monopoly on decorative twigs and bark. Some of the dogwoods also perform well in this department. Most notable is probably the redtwig dogwood, *Cornus alba*. *C. alba* 'Sibirica' has deep blood-red branches in winter, while the selections 'Elegantissima' and 'Gouchaltii' have leaves edged in white and gold, respectively. The Northwest native *C. stolonifera* (red osier dogwood) comes in a red-twigged cultivar with bright green and yellow leaves, called 'Hedgerow's Gold', while its cousin *C. sanguinea* 'Midwinter Fire' has twigs that are red at their bases, blending up to yellow at their tips. All of these shrubby dogwoods give their best winter color if they are cut back very hard in spring before new growth emerges.

FRUITS AND BERRIES

Colorful fruits and berries help carry Northwest cottage gardens through the short, dark days of winter. Some of the most fascinating berries of all grow on *Leycesteria formosa*, a shrubby plant with long, arching branches that burst, fountainlike, to heights of 6 to 8 feet. From the tips of each branch dangle tapered clusters of deep purple berries sheltered by bright crimson bracts. These appear in the late summer and persist through fall.

Equally spectacular in fruit is the harlequin glorybower, *Clerodendrum trichotomum*. Its sweetly scented white summer flowers give way to electric blue berries that emerge from equally bright fuchsia calyces. In peak display during the autumn, this tall shrub is guaranteed to puzzle and enthrall all those who see it.

Most of us grow roses for their flowers, but some of the wild, or species, roses are worth having for their fruit alone. *Rosa glauca* is a twiggy, upright shrub whose fine, feathery foliage is flushed with shades of plum and dusted with a fine, gray, waxy bloom. Its small pink flowers can be hard to find, but the bright red, pea-sized fruits make quite a show in the fall garden. *R. villosa* has big, bristly fruits, an inch or more across, that glow orange-red when ripe in early autumn. *R. moyesii* 'Geranium' has bright red flowers that are pretty enough in summer, but the dangling, flask-shaped, scarlet fruits that follow in the fall are absolutely dazzling.

Just as vibrant are the shining berries of *Viburnum opulus*, which last well into October here in Pacific Northwest gardens. The berries of the common type are orange-red, but there are also clones whose berries are bright yellow. A dwarf form, *V. opulus* 'Compactum', grows more slowly than the species and is useful where garden space is limited.

Rosa glauca displays scads of bright red fruit in fall and early winter. The plummy foliage and dainty pink blooms are charming as well!

The fruit of *Callicarpa bodinieri* are an unusual shade of lavender, densely lining this sturdy shrub's branches in fall and winter like amethyst jewels. The cultivar 'Profusion' is especially generous in fruit production, while the related *C. japonica* 'Leucocarpa' has white berries (though I ask, "Why bother?"). For the best yield, plant callicarpas in full sun on fertile, well-drained soil.

PLANTS FOR TOUGH SOILS

I cannot count how many times I've read the words "loamy, well-drained soil" and cringed. In my gardening career I've had to deal with everything from gloppy clay to parched sand, but rarely have I had the luck to find that perfect mean, the archetypal loamy, well-drained soil. Most of us here in the maritime Northwest are forced to cope with less than ideal soils, at least in some portions of our gardens. Later on, in Chapter Eight, I'll share some suggestions for improving heavy clay or poor, dry sandy soils, but meanwhile I'll recommend some plants that thrive on soils that are challenging to garden.

DRY SOILS

No matter how much rain falls on our region between October and April, some of our soils are so full of sand that they are parched by May, and cannot be kept moist no matter how often we irrigate. No need to worry. These dry, nutrient-starved, sandy soils make the perfect home for some of the most striking Northwest cottage garden plants.

Take the shrub *Abutilon vitifolium* 'Veronica Tennant', for example. With its felted gray-green foliage and scads of big, pale lavender flowers, this is the kind of plant that makes gardeners drool. Don't drool anywhere near it, though, because the slightest hint of excess moisture will trigger instantaneous rot. I despaired of ever growing *A. vitifolium* 'Veronica Tennant' on the heavy clay soil in my garden, but became so obsessed with owning it that I finally set it out in its own container full of sand and packaged topsoil.

The so-called Matilija poppy, *Romneya coulteri*, is no less compelling. Its flowers do indeed look like enormous white poppies, with great bosses of yellow stamens in their centers. They appear in early summer on a 6-foot plant decked out in deeply lobed gray-blue foliage. Though considerably less fussy than *Abutilon*, *R. coulteri* still prefers a fairly dry, sandy soil.

The electric-blue spring flowers of the *Ceanothus* hybrids 'Dark Star', 'Concha', and 'Puget Blue' are eye-poppers too. These evergreen shrubs resent excess summer moisture and bloom magnificently on hot, dry soils. Among their best companions are the shrubby rock roses from the genus *Cistus*. All have grayish, hairy, sagelike leaves and dense, mounding habits. *C.* x *corbariensis* and *C. laurifolius* have white flowers, while those of *C. ladanifer* are marked with deep red blotches. *C. albidus* and the popular hybrid *C.* 'Sunset' bloom in bright lilac-pink.

Among herbaceous plants for poor, dry soils, some of the most spectacular are the foxtail lilies (*Eremurus* spp.). These send up narrow spikes to 6 feet tall, completely covered with small, furry-looking blossoms in a range of colors from white, pink, and yellow to bright orange. Their strap-shaped foliage goes dormant by midsummer, so consider pairing them with a late-blooming aster that will fill the vacant space.

On a very different scale, the low, trailing *Origanum rotundifolium* selections 'Kent Beauty' and 'Barbara Tingey' offer intriguing flowers and fine-textured foliage for dry containers or poor soils near the edges of pathways or paved patios. Both have rounded gray leaves and odd, dangling flower clusters wrapped in overlapping soft pink bracts. Odd, too, in its own way is *Parahebe perfoliata*, with round blue foliage arrayed on long, trailing stems that end in clusters of tubular blue flowers. It thrives on dry, gritty soils in bright sun.

The sedums as a group are tolerant of poor, dry soils, and they provide an array of colorful foliage and flowers for beds, borders, and containers. The tall *Sedum spectabile* selections 'Brilliant' and 'Meteor' become mounds of reddish pink in August and September, while the popular hybrid 'Autumn Joy' blooms in a softer pink. The trailing *S. sieboldii* has beautifully scalloped blue-green leaves with precise red edges and lovely soft pink flowers in the fall. The Northwest native *S. spathulifolium* 'Purpureum' carries clusters of bright yellow spring flowers over mats of gray-and-purple foliage. The selection 'Cape Blanco' has leaves dusted in soft silver. *S.* 'Vera Jameson' is a dramatic plant with dark purple foliage supporting bright magenta autumn flowers.

Whether called houseleeks or hens-and-chickens, the little succulents *Echeveria* and *Sempervivum* make charming, drought-tolerant plants for cottage garden containers, rockeries, and pavement edges. There are many cultivars available in each of these genera, with leaves in shades of gray, green, lilac, burgundy, and purple. They are lovely in mosaic plantings with woolly thyme *(Thymus pseudolanuginosus)*, *Raoulia australis*, or *Cotula squalida*.

Other fine cottage garden plants for droughty soils are the previously mentioned *Lavatera thuringiaca*, *Vitex agnus-castus*, *Eryngium*, *Coreopsis*, *Rudbeckia*, and *Yucca*. Many herbs, including thyme, rosemary, and sage, will also grow well on dry soils.

WET SOILS

Poorly drained soils can be even more challenging to cultivate than dry and gritty ones. While many plants will tolerate poor drainage while dormant, comparatively few can deal with wet feet right through the growing season. Luckily, among the ones that do are a few perennials with outstanding foliage and flowers. None of these is more brilliant than *Lobelia cardinalis*, an upright perennial with spikes of glowing scarlet flowers on 3-foot stems. The related hybrid *L.* x *gerardii* 'Ruby Queen' grows a bit taller and has deep burgundy-red foliage that complements the blazing blossoms. I grow it in a partly submerged pot along with the bright-yellow-leafed *Lysimachia nummularia* 'Aurea'.

Moist soils in part shade are perfect for the stunning candelabra primroses, including *Primula japonica, P. bulleyana, P. beesiana, P. prolifera,* and their many hybrids. These all have flowers arranged in tiers on upright stems to 2 feet tall, and bloom in all shades of red, pink, white, yellow, and orange. No less beautiful, but quite a bit more subtle, is *P. florindae,* which carries deeply scented, nodding, soft yellow flowers over rosettes of neat, bright green foliage.

The tall autumn-flowering sedums grow well in dry, sandy soils.

I have mentioned irises of one sort or another in the previous chapter, but it would be wrong of me not to include some of the best of them among the plants that thrive on wet soils. The much-admired cultivars of Japanese iris *(Iris ensata)* are often planted along ponds or streams, though they prefer even moisture to real flooding. On the other hand, the less familiar but equally impressive Louisiana iris hybrids are bog plants in nature. Louisiana irises are some of the most brilliant of all irises, with flowers in every imaginable shade of white, blue, purple, pink, orange, red, and yellow. Their flowers are large and flat, and they bloom on 3-foot stalks over bold, sword-shaped leaves. They prosper on wet, acid soils, where they rapidly form clumps up to 3 feet across. *I. pseudacorus* is another tall water-loving iris that bears bright yellow flowers on stalks up to 5 feet tall. *I. versicolor* is a shorter plant, with violet flowers held on 4-foot stems.

Astilboides tabularis (sometimes known as *Rodgersia tabularis*) is a bold perennial for sites with wet soil. Its lobed, circular leaves, which can be 2 feet across, are topped in summer by tall, feathery spikes of minuscule white flowers. Similar in scale and bloom is *Rodgersia aesculifolia*, with great, big divided leaves and shaggy brown stems. Both plants are at home along the edges of streams or next to standing water.

Sweet flag *(Acorus calamus)* is a grasslike bog plant whose striped cultivar 'Variegatus' makes a bold accent in moist borders or on the edges of a garden pool. On fertile ground it grows to an impressive 5 feet tall. *Filipendula ulmaria* (or meadowsweet) is also grown primarily for its colored foliage. The cultivar 'Variegata' has green compound leaves blotched in conspicuous pale yellow, while the leaves of 'Aurea' are a uniform bright yellow-green. Both grow happily on wet soils in partial shade.

PLANTS FOR HUMMINGBIRDS, BEES, AND BUTTERFLIES

Few things bring life to the Northwest cottage garden like the balletic play of bees, butterflies, and hummingbirds as they harvest nectar from the garden's many flowers. You can encourage these colorful visitors to favor your garden by planting a few of their favorite treats. Bees, butterflies, and hummingbirds alike enjoy the common butterfly bush, *Buddleia davidii*. The plain lavender types are common roadside weeds throughout most of our region, but there are a few exciting cultivars as well. *B. davidii* 'Black Knight' has jewel-like deep purple flowers that glow with a dark magic all their own. The leaves of 'Harlequin' are boldly painted cream, making it a lovely plant even without its bright wine-purple flowers. The hybrid *B.* 'Lochinch' has especially fragrant lavender flowers over handsome felted gray foliage. Another hybrid worth knowing is *B.* x *weyeriana* 'Sungold', which has flowers of bright apricot-yellow.

The evergreen cape fuchsias *(Phygelius* x *rectus)* are not fuchsias at all, but their nodding tubular flowers *are* a favorite stop for hummingbirds. 'Devil's Tears', 'Winchester Chimes', and 'African Queen' are all reddish orange, while 'Salmon Leap' blooms in coral pink and 'Moonraker' is soft, pale yellow. *P.* x *rectus* blooms on new wood and can be cut down hard during the winter to keep it tidy and compact. Other plants that hold appeal for bees and butterflies are *Eucryphia* x *nymansensis*, described in the previous chapter under "Flowering trees," and all of the hybrid *Ceanothus* cultivars, mentioned earlier in this chapter under "Dry soils."

163

Hummingbirds and butterflies both frequent the perennial bergamot, *Monarda didyma*. Unusually shaped flowers top this sprawling 3-foot plant from early July onward, appearing in succession provided the plants are deadheaded. Flower colors include the bright red of 'Cambridge Scarlet' and 'Adam', the lavender of 'Violet Queen', and the rosy pink of 'Marshall's Delight'. All have wonderfully fragrant foliage and thrive on moist, organic soils.

For fragrant foliage and plenty of pollinator action on drier sites, I recommend the anise hyssops, genus *Agastache*. These plants bear tall, narrow spikes of hooded blossoms in bright colors in the heat of summer. *A. foeniculum* bears dense spikes of violet or white flowers and grows to roughly 2 feet tall. *A. barberi* has loose spikes of larger blossoms in bright purplish pink. The hybrid *A.* 'Tutti Frutti' grows to 3 feet or more, with shocking fuchsia-pink flowers, while *A.* 'Apricot Sunrise' blooms in bright orange.

PLANTS FOR SHADE

Before European settlement, much of our region was home to vast and ancient forests, where sparse shafts of sunlight filtered through the shifting branches of gigantic evergreens. Though we now live in suburbs, cities, and small towns with domesticated lawns and gardens, the mystique of the forest still moves us, and its echoes still color the Northwest landscape. In our cottage gardens, shady areas call to mind the romance of the forest and give us a place to grow all of the charming woodland plants that would wither in harsh summer sun.

Mahonias (Oregon grape) are common denizens of Pacific Northwest forests. In fact, they are so familiar that we forget they are treasured landscape plants in other regions! Our native *Mahonia aquifolium* brings more than just fragrant yellow winter flowers and pretty blue fruits. It also instantly establishes a distinct Northwest flavor in any shady cottage garden planting. The Asian species *M. bealei* and the hybrid *M.* x *media* are more dramatic and exotic, with their great tropical-looking foliage and long sprays of flowers. Two other common Northwest woodland natives, the deer fern *(Blechnum spicant)* and the sword fern *(Polystichum munitum)*, are also cherished subjects for shade gardens elsewhere in the world. Like *Mahonia*, they contribute a strong sense of place to the Northwest cottage garden.

No shade-loving woody plants are more beloved—or more frustrating—in Pacific Northwest gardens than the hybrid camellias. They prosper on acid soils, and will bloom in full shade where few other shrubs will flower. Unfortunately, their exquisite blossoms turn into a foul brown mush at the very hint of rain. Since they bloom in March and April, spoiled blossoms are the rule unless you locate your camellias very carefully. A canopy of evergreens may offer enough shelter for the blossoms to survive early spring rains. Even better, take advantage of their adaptability to espaliered growth. Trained against a north-facing wall, fence, or building, camellias receive shade *and* protection from the rain, producing gratifying crops of waxy flowers.

As the camellia flowers fade in early spring, a parade of bulbs and perennials march in to provide color in shaded cottage garden plantings. In my garden, the dangling bells of *Fritillaria meleagris*, colored purple, or white, or checkered in both colors, hover above the long-spurred, clear blue flowers of *Corydalis flexuosa*, while the white flowers of shooting stars (*Dodecatheon* spp.) explode like fireworks nearby.

Ten great plants for shade

- *Astilbe* spp.
- Bleeding hearts (*Dicentra* spp.)
- *Brunnera macrophylla*
- *Epimedium* spp.
- *Geranium phaeum*
- Goatsbeard *(Aruncus dioicus)*
- *Kirengeshoma palmatum*
- Lungworts (*Pulmonaria* spp.)
- *Mahonia* spp.
- Sweet cicely *(Myrrhis odorata)*

The reliable display of the wood hyacinths (*Hyacinthoides hispanica*) begins at the same time, with spikes of dainty bells in white, pink, or blue, depending on which cultivar you choose. Fall-planted *H. hispanica* bulbs will spread into dense colonies under trees and shrubs in only a few seasons.

It would be hard to imagine a shaded cottage garden border in the spring without the pendent blossoms of the old-fashioned bleeding heart, *Dicentra spectabilis*, dangling from their slender stalks. The common pink form is lovely among spring bulbs and forget-me-nots, but the white-flowered *D. spectabilis* 'Alba' is especially impressive as it glows against dark, shaded foliage. Our own Northwest native bleeding heart, *Dicentra formosa*, has produced several fine hybrids and selections, including the deep pink cultivars 'Zestful' and 'Luxuriant'; 'Langtrees' is a white-flowered hybrid with outstanding blue-green foliage.

By far the most popular perennials for shade in Northwest gardens are the hostas, with cultivars available in countless sizes, foliage textures, and colors.

165

They are a favorite food for slugs as well, and need to be protected vigilantly against slimy marauders. Several other superb plants for foliage in shade offer a change from hostas, and are also far less appetizing to the slugs.

Brunnera macrophylla emerges as a foot-tall cloud of sky-blue flowers in the

spring. As its long-lasting flowers fade, the plant expands large, heart-shaped leaves that contribute bold texture at ground level. Several cultivars have colored leaves that are especially eye-catching in the shade. 'Langtrees' has leaves with rows of silver spots, while the foliage of 'Variegata' shows bold white margins. 'Hadspen Cream' resembles 'Variegata', but its markings are a soft, creamy yellow. The leaves of 'Jack Frost' are entirely suffused with white.

An even wider range of patterned foliage appears in the genus *Pulmonaria*, whose common name of lungwort may refer to the clear, round silver spots that decorate the leaves of some species. *P. saccharata* 'Janet Fisk', whose flowers open blue from clear pink buds, has leaves so densely spotted that they look almost completely silver.

The hybrid 'Roy Davidson' has similar flowers and narrow, silver-spotted foliage. *P. longifolia* 'Bertram Anderson' has narrow foliage as well, with flowers of a deeper blue. *P. saccharata* 'Sissinghurst White' is a useful white-flowered form with large

Bleeding hearts *(Dicentra spectabilis)* are perfect plants for shady cottage garden corners.

166

white spots on its leaves. The hybrids 'Spilled Milk' and 'Excalibur' have pink flowers that age to blue and silver leaves with clear green margins. One of the most dramatic pulmonarias of all is the *P. rubra* selection 'David Ward', with deep salmon-pink flowers and big, bold white-edged leaves.

For finer texture in the shade, try the variegated forms of *Lamium maculatum*. 'Pink Nancy' has pink, hooded flowers over green-edged white foliage, while 'White Nancy' is similar but with white flowers. 'Brocade' carries pink flowers over white-and-purple-speckled leaves, and 'Checkers' has white-striped leaves with purplish flowers. Most colorful of all is 'Golden Anniversary', with puckered leaves boldly striped in white and yellow. None of these lamiums grow more than 6 inches tall, and all spread politely to form shimmering mats of foliage in shade.

The cream-striped Japanese sedge *Carex morrowii* 'Expallida' is another fine-textured foliage plant for shade, with slender, grassy leaves that build into foot-wide, cascading mounds. It makes a fine partner for the shade-loving epimediums, whose heart-shaped leaves are topped in the spring by sprays of peculiar little short-spurred flowers. *Epimedium grandiflorum* 'Rose Queen' blooms in deep rosy lilac, while the hybrid *E.* x *perralchicum* 'Frohnleiten' has conspicuous bright yellow flowers. Lovely grown with either is the creeping woodland phlox, *Phlox stolonifera* 'Blue Ridge', with its flat clusters of starry lavender-blue flowers.

The versatile geraniums give us some fine perennials for sunny beds and borders, but several are great shade plants too. *Geranium nodosum* spreads by seed to form a foot-tall mat of glossy, bright green foliage. Its modest, lilac-pink flowers appear in waves throughout the summer, for long-lasting quiet color in the shade of shrubs and trees. The mounding *G. phaeum* is more conspicuous in flower, with dark purple-maroon blooms that stand out against light-colored neighbors like *Thalictrum flavum* subsp. *glaucum* or *Cornus alba* 'Elegantissima'. *G. phaeum* 'Lily Lovell' is a form with especially pretty deep-mauve flowers, while 'Album' has arresting pure white blooms.

Sweet cicely *(Myrrhis odorata)* is a graceful woodlander with ferny foliage that smells of licorice and new-mown hay when crushed. It forms an airy, 2-foot clump garnished in May with flat-topped clusters of lacy white flowers. Equally fine in texture are the blossoms of astilbes, whose colored plumes emerge to brighten shady plantings in the early summer. Most popular are the *Astilbe* x *arendsii* hybrids, including the white 'Bridal Veil' and 'White Gloria', the pinks 'Rheinland', 'Ostrich Plume', and 'Erica', and the blazing reds of 'Fanal' and 'Glut'. The shorter-growing *A. chinensis* 'Pumila' bears dense, bushy plumes of lilac-purple in late summer, while *A. taquetii* 'Superba' sends up 4-foot spikes of the same color.

In contrast to astilbes and sweet cicely, the unusual Asian campanula, *Campanula takesimana*, has big, bold-textured basal leaves above which dangle 2-inch bell-shaped blossoms of pale lilac-pink with many striking darker spots within. It is a quiet plant, but one that beguiles visitors with its subtle charms. Another group of woodland plants more subtle and curious than glamorous are the so-called toad lilies of the genus *Tricyrtis*. In the autumn these plants raise complex, oddly spotted flowers over their gracefully arched stems. *T. formosa*'s flowers open muted lavender, while *T. hirta* 'Miyazaki Gold' has pale lilac flowers densely spotted in dark purple above thinly yellow-margined leaves. *Kirengeshoma palmata* blooms at the same time as the *Tricyrtis* species, with loose spikes of soft yellow 2-inch bells above maplelike foliage. All three of these plants require fluffy, slightly moist, woodland soils with plenty of organic matter in order to grow and bloom successfully.

Tall perennials with conspicuous blooms bring drama to the shady cottage garden. The stately 5-foot spikes of the monkshood *(Aconitum napellus)* are seductive beauties when their blue flowers open in the shaded summer border, but the plant is toxic, so you may want to avoid it if your garden hosts pets or small children. Poisonous, too, is the common foxglove, *Digitalis purpurea*, whose lilac, pink, or white flowers light up dark places in so many Northwest gardens. Experienced gardeners know that this biennial seeds itself prolifically, with small plants popping up randomly in borders, beds, containers, and even cracks in the pavement. The soft yellow-flowered perennial foxglove *D. grandiflora* will stay where you plant it—an advantage for those cottage gardeners who prefer neatness and predictability.

Several members of the genus *Ligularia* offer bold-textured foliage and brash, hot-colored flowers for cottage garden plantings in the shade. The *L. dentata* selections 'Othello' and 'Desdemona' both have big, round leaves with deep purple undersides and 3- to 4-foot stalks with shocking orange-gold daisy flowers at midsummer. *L.* 'Gregynog Gold' is similar, but its bright yellow blooms are arranged more formally into 5-foot, or even 6-foot, spires. *L. przewalskii* 'The Rocket' has elegant, deeply cut leaves and narrow, 5-foot spikes of blazing yellow flowers that glow in the shade.

Just as remarkable in bloom is the great perennial goatsbeard, *Aruncus dioicus*. With feathery white flower spikes up to 6 feet tall or more over toothed, compound foliage, *A. dioicus* looks like an overgrown astilbe. A much smaller form with finely cut foliage, called 'Kneiffii', takes up less space, but at 2 or 3 feet it lacks the inherent drama of the parent plant. This is one case where more is, indeed, more.

Drama of another sort comes from the arisaemas, shade-loving forest plants whose bold foliage rises above peculiar, hooded jack-in-the-pulpit flowers. My favorite of these is *Arisaema sikokianum*, whose black-and-white-striped spathe enfolds a knobby spadix of pure, shimmering white. Arisaemas were once hard to find in gardens, but increased interest and advances in propagation have made them more common sights in local nurseries. Their mesmerizing blooms are guaranteed to enthrall garden visitors and spark plenty of conversation.

Arum italicum also sends up hooded spathes in springtime, but they are outclassed by the plant's shiny, white-veined foliage. The arrowhead leaves emerge in autumn and stay fresh during the winter, dying back after the flowers fade in early summer. Before the foliage reemerges, bright orange-red fruits ripen on short stalks for an excellent late-summer display.

CLIMBING PLANTS

Climbing plants have always been welcome in the cottage garden. Because they occupy vertical surfaces yet occupy very little ground, they contribute handsomely toward the efficient use of space. Their blooms and foliage clothe and soften harsh surfaces, reduce the apparent scale of large walls, fences, and buildings, and screen unsightly structures.

One of the most vigorous large climbers for the Northwest cottage garden is *Actinidia kolomikta*, a strapping cousin of the kiwi fruit. *A. kolomikta* grows to 15 or 20 feet, with twining stems and large, fuzzy leaves. In mature plants the end of each leaf is generously painted pink and white, so that the plant makes a great tapestry of pastel color in the garden.

The blue passion flower *(Passiflora caerulea)* is another large, aggressive climber, growing rapidly to smother any fence or trellis. *P. caerulea* clings to its support by tendrils and will climb almost indefinitely unless pruned. It earns its board by blooming through the summer, with large white-and-purple flowers that fascinate with their elaborate, complex structure.

The flowers of the trumpet vines (genus *Campsis*) are compelling in a very different way. *C. radicans* erupts every summer in clusters of big, bold orange trumpets that smolder and sizzle in the sunlight. *C. grandiflora* has larger flowers in a darker shade of orange-red, while the hybrid *C.* x *tagliabuana* 'Mme. Galen' bears big crops of scarlet-orange flowers. All grow rapidly to great heights if allowed, clinging to any surface with aerial rootlets.

Wisteria is a rambunctious climber, too, but the irresistible appeal of its great dangling clusters of bloom tempt many gardeners to plant it in tight spaces that cannot accommodate its rambling habit. Wisteria needs room! It also needs a sound support. The woody, twining stems exert enormous force and will slowly disassemble any structure too weak to resist. The glamour of wisteria in flower makes building special supports for it worth any effort, for no climber can quite duplicate the romantic impression that it makes. Of the two commonly grown species, *Wisteria floribunda* has the longer clusters, while *W. sinensis* is more fragrant. Light purple and lavender are the most common colors for both species, but *W. floribunda* also comes in a pink form, called 'Rosea', and white-flowered clones named 'Longissima Alba', 'Ivory Tower', and 'Issai Perfect'.

Much less rampant than these first four is the beautiful climbing hydrangea, *Hydrangea anomala* subsp. *petiolaris*. Clinging by adhesive holdfasts, it can scale any surface to great heights, but its slow growth makes it an easy plant to keep in check. Its glossy foliage and exfoliating reddish bark are both attractive, but the flat-topped white lacecap flowers in late spring are the real show. A new variety, going by the name 'Miranda', has broad yellow margins on its leaves and grows even more slowly than the species. Both forms are at their best in partial shade.

Schizophragma hydrangeoides looks remarkably like the climbing hydrangea, with similar flower heads and foliage. There is a pink-flowered form, *S. hydrangeoides* 'Roseum', and a variety called 'Moonlight', much sought after for its silver-flushed foliage. All of these establish slowly but can climb great distances over time.

170

There is nothing slow about the climbing honeysuckles (genus *Lonicera*), all of which will quickly occupy whatever space they are allotted. The Japanese honeysuckle *L. japonica* is a nasty weed, worth planting only its less aggressive, variegated form 'Aureo-reticulata'. On the other hand, several of the European and American species make rewarding, if sometimes intrusive, cottage garden

climbers. *L. sempervirens* is the most colorful of the whole clan, with tubular, bright orange flowers in loose clusters at the ends of its stems. A slightly softer yellow form *(L. sempervirens sulphurea)* is useful in less raucous cottage garden color schemes.

The fragrant *L. periclymenum* has probably graced English cottage gardens since their beginnings, and it adapts well to Pacific Northwest gardening conditions too. The form 'Belgica' bears pink and yellow flowers in late spring, while 'Serotina' repeat-blooms into autumn. 'Graham Thomas' is a very pretty variant with plentiful light yellow flowers. The hybrid *H.* x *heckrottii* has handsome grayish foliage and pink-to-purple flowers with yellow interiors, though without the fragrance of *L. periclymenum*. The climbing honeysuckles are all twining plants that can choke out their neighbors if not carefully contained by vigilant pruning.

The climbers that make up the huge genus *Clematis* are more polite by far, and most coexist comfortably with many cottage garden shrubs and perennials. The large-flowered hybrids make

Be sure your climbers' ultimate heights are in proportion with their supports!

superb companions for once-blooming old garden roses, and are just as comfortable growing up through spring-flowering shrubs like lilacs, *Carpenteria*, or *Weigela*. Their variety is too great to keep track of, but I can't help mention a few of my very favorites. The bright pink-and-violet-striped 'Dr. Ruppel' is superb behind deep-blue delphiniums and paler bearded irises, while 'The President', with superbly formed purple flowers, makes an outstanding replacement for the popular old *Clematis* x 'Jackmanii'. Its sport, called 'Multi-Blue' is semidouble, with a boss of odd, fluffy, silver-and-blue petaloids at the center of each bloom.

I like the soft mauve *C.* 'Silver Moon' with the pink flowers of *Geranium* x *oxonianum* in part shade, and the deep crimson 'Niobe' climbing among the white-edged leaves of *Cornus alba* 'Elegantissima'. 'Will Goodwin' has soft, light blue flowers with prettily scalloped edges. I love combining it with the wine-purple blossoms of the old rose 'Reine des Violettes'. 'Gillian Blades' is another cultivar with gently rippling flowers, this time in clear white. Grow it on a dark brown wall or fence, and its blooms will glow like headlights. 'Blue Ravine', bred in the Northwest at the University of British Columbia Botanical Garden, has lovely, large, pale lilac-blue flowers and especially strong growth.

Less well known than the large-flowered hybrids, but surely no less colorful, are the hybrids and selections of *C. viticella*. These all have dainty 2- to 3-inch upright or nodding flowers borne in great abundance from midsummer on. 'Mme. Julia Correvon' blooms in deep, rich crimson and is delightful grown among white climbing roses. 'Polish Spirit' has dark purple flowers with a velvet sheen that invites visitors to reach out and caress the petals. The larger flowers of *C. viticella* 'Venosa Violacea' are bright white with dense, complex purple veining over their entire surface, while the dainty 'Betty Corning' bears nodding, sky-blue bells late in the season.

More obscure still are the *C. texensis* clan, with their late-summer crop of small, gracefully curving, narrow blossoms. *C. texensis* 'Duchess of Albany' covers itself in 2-inch flowers striped with pale and dark pink, while 'Gravetye Beauty' blooms in smoldering deep ruby-red.

Long before any of these summer-blooming clematis come into flower, the springtime displays of *C. alpina* and *C. macropetala* are in full swing. Both species have compound foliage and small nodding flowers in shades of white, pink, and blue. The flowers of *C. macropetala* open a bit wider than those of *C. alpina* to reveal pale, fluffy centers. Both are popular with hummingbirds, who visit them for early spring snacks.

At the other end of the bloom season come the two pretty yellow-flowered species, *C. tangutica* and *C. orientalis*. Both bloom in September, both have 2-inch nodding, golden-yellow flowers, and the two are, quite frankly, hard for me to tell apart. 'Bill Mackenzie' is a form of one or the other (depending upon whom you ask) that has especially large flowers.

There are two popular clematis species that are just too large and vigorous to coexist with mild-mannered shrubs and perennials in a mixed planting in the cottage garden. One is the evergreen *C. armandii*, whose long, elegant leaves and orange-scented blossoms are such a common sight in Pacific Northwest gardens in early spring. With its dense, rapid growth, *C. armandii* really deserves a long fence or a pergola all to itself. Just as exuberant is *C. montana*, whose vanilla-scented 2-inch flowers open in April and May. The original *C. montana* blooms in white, but pink-flowered forms, including 'Tetrarose', 'Elizabeth', 'Mayleen', and 'Pink Perfection' are far more popular. Choose plants in bloom, if you can, to make sure that you like their color and fragrance. *C. montana* needs elbowroom as it clambers over its support, since it can choke out perennials and shrubs growing in its path.

Clematis montana rubens drapes a mantle of vanilla-scented blooms over trees, walls, or tall trellises.

PLANTS FOR QUICK RESULTS

Often a newly planted cottage garden will have many gaps in its beds and borders, places where woody plants and perennials have yet to reach mature dimensions. There are many plants with rapid growth that make fine fillers for

173

these empty spaces while their neighbors are maturing. Among woody plants, both buddleias and fuchsias build size rapidly and can add mass and color to a planting that looks thin. Most roses attain their full size quite quickly, too, for the same kind of quick cover.

The tall perennial *Verbena bonariensis* yields results that verge on instantaneous. Seed planted in spring produces flowering plants 6 feet tall by late summer. With its great stature, wispy texture, and pretty lilac-purple flowers, *V. bonariensis* would be well worth waiting for even if it grew slowly. As a fast-growing filler, it is indispensable.

Annual plants that gain size rapidly are the most easily managed filler plants for cottage gardens, since there is no need to worry about moving or removing them when their job is done. Sunflowers are champions of rapid growth, though the huge 8-footers will be out of scale in most cottage garden settings. Look instead for shorter, bushy cultivars, like the 4-foot tall, pale yellow 'Vanilla Ice' or the deep reddish 'Chianti'. Large as well, but much lighter in texture, is the annual *Cleome hassleriana*, which bears spidery heads of pink or white flowers on 4-foot stems over aromatic, lacy foliage.

On a much smaller scale, I like the annual herb borage *(Borago officinalis)*, whose bold, hairy leaves and nodding, clear blue flowers fit into so many cottage garden compositions. Annual nasturtiums *(Tropaeolum majus)* are great for filling up those pesky empty spaces too. Their large seeds are easy to plant in early spring, and by summer the bushy, trailing plants will bear their brightly colored blooms. The compact cultivars 'Peach Melba', with red-centered yellow blossoms, and the deep orange-red 'Empress of India' are two of my favorites.

Dismissed by many as a weed, the humble forget-me-not *(Myosotis sylvatica)* deserves much more respect. It may seed itself around the garden liberally, but there are few places where its sky-blue flowers will look out of place. Few plants can beat it for quick cover in dry, shady spaces.

Spring-planted bulbs and tubers that bloom during summer are another source of quick mass and color in the cottage garden. The startling Mexican shell flower, *Tigridia pavonia*, wastes no time producing 2-foot fans of long, pointed, strap-shaped leaves, topped at midsummer with large spotted flowers in shades of yellow, pink, or white. Each flower lasts only a day, but new blooms come in quick succession for a long period of bloom. The compact hybrid *Dahlia* 'Bishop of

Llandaff' carries bright red flowers on short, bushy plants that are less awkward than the giant exhibition dahlias, with their tall, leggy stalks. Even without bloom, its dark purple foliage is an attractive filler among slower-growing plants.

EDIBLE PLANTS

Much is made of the "new" trend of blending food crops into ornamental plantings, but cottage gardeners have been doing it for centuries. It has simply taken the rest of us a little longer to catch on! Edible plants of many kinds will always have a place in Northwest cottage gardens, especially when they have visual as well as gustatory appeal.

HERBS

While they bring flavor to the kitchen, culinary herbs also deliver fragrance, texture, form, and color to the Northwest cottage garden. Rosemary *(Rosmarinus officinalis)* offers the complete package: Its fine, grayish foliage is handsome all season long, and the sweet little blue flowers are a welcome sight on bleak February days. Upright cultivars like 'Arp' and 'Tuscan Blue' can be strong vertical accents in a mixed planting, while trailing forms, including 'Huntington Carpet' and 'Prostratus', drape languidly over retaining walls and rockeries. All forms are fine companions for deep-colored old garden roses.

The thymes (genus *Thymus*) are no less ornamental, with their variously colored and scented foliage and masses of tiny flowers. The smallest are the creeping thymes, *T. serpyllum*, with minuscule leaves beneath dense carpets of bloom in lilac, pink, or white. I like the sparkling white-margined leaves of the selection 'Hartington Silver', since they accentuate the plant's delicate texture. Woolly thyme, *T. pseudolanuginosus*, has its own unique texture, with fuzzy foliage that forms a velvet mat along the edges of a pathway or between stepping-stones. Common kitchen thyme, *T. vulgaris*, has its attractions, too, especially in its white-edged form 'Argenteus'. For a delicious scent and soft, warm color, plant the golden lemon thyme, *T.* x *citriodorus* 'Aureus'. Its yellow-edged leaves are a delight next to the gray-green foliage and violet flowers of *Salvia* x *sylvestris* 'Mainacht'.

The culinary sage *(Salvia officinalis)* so valuable for roasting game and poultry is lovely in the garden, too. The common form is pretty enough, with its gray

175

leaves and lavender-blue flowers, but the forms with colored foliage have even more to offer. The violet-flushed leaves of *S. officinalis* 'Purpurascens' stand out as well against the chartreuse leaves of *Geranium* 'Ann Folkard' as they do above the

silver *Sedum spathulifolium* 'Cape Blanco'. *Salvia officinalis* 'Icterina' rarely blooms, but makes up for its deficiency with broad gold margins on its leaves. The form 'Tricolor' blends soft pink through its creamy-edged leaves to make a mound of pastel confetti in the garden.

Like sage, oregano comes in several colored forms that combine well with perennial flowers and foliage in mixed plantings. My favorite is the bright golden oregano, *Origanum vulgare* 'Aureum'. I use it with *Geranium* 'Philippe Vapelle' to weave a tapestry of gold and purple at the front of a dry border. The white-edged *O. vulgare* 'Variegatum' is a useful, fine-textured creeper to plant in front of taller, dark-colored foliage.

Colored basils *(Ocimum basilicum)* are a palette unto themselves. The deep burgundy leaves of 'Red Rubin' are bound to turn heads when planted with golden lemon thyme or gold oregano, while 'Purple Ruffles' adds a fascinating baroque texture with its frilly leaves. 'African Blue' basil is a handsome and versatile garden plant, with leaves veined in violet and spikes of distinctive purple flowers. All of these adorn the garden with their sweet, seductive fragrance in the heat of the day.

Herbs add colored foliage, dainty blossoms, and delightful fragrances to sunny patches in the garden. Many are drought tolerant, to boot!

Chives *(Allium schoenoprasum)* combine vertical form with fine texture, and their clumps of grassy foliage offer relief between small mounding or horizontal plants. Their lilac globes of flowers are edible as well as decorative and make a colorful addition to green salads.

Parsley, chervil, and dill are just as pretty in the border as they are garnishing a plate. All form clumps of fine-textured foliage on a small scale that works well in the foreground of a cottage garden planting. Dill is especially nice when its lacy, yellow blooms open alongside the deep crimson *Persicaria microcephala* 'Red Dragon' or the silvered purple leaves of hybrid heucheras.

When planting aromatic herbs in your cottage garden, try to place them near paved areas that get a lot of traffic so that visitors can enjoy their scent. Thyme and oregano that trail onto a path deliver doses of delicious fragrance whenever visitors step on them. I like to grow rosemary and sage close to my cottage garden gate, which brushes against them to release their fragrance every time it opens.

FRUITS AND VEGETABLES

As symbols of abundance, fruits and vegetables fill the Northwest cottage garden with an air of generosity and comfort. What could be more inviting than bright red tomatoes ripening in clusters on a south-facing wall in August, or the big yellow flowers of a summer squash surrounded by enthusiastic bees? Strawberries glinting scarlet on the edges of a walk will delight any visitor, while a lush, cooling canopy of grape leaves can provide welcome cover for a rough-hewn pergola. The huge leaves and bright red stalks of rhubarb look divine with upright ornamental grasses in the spring border, and the brightly colored stems of rainbow chard sparkle like gems in container plantings.

Some vegetables are lovely to look at all on their own. Eggplants, for example, were grown strictly for ornament when they first appeared in European gardens! Their nodding purple flowers and large hairy leaves are fetching indeed, even without the shiny fruit. Novel varieties like the soft lavender 'Bride' and the densely speckled 'Purple Rain' are just as exciting on the bush as on the palate. Peppers are a great source of late summer color as well, especially the early-ripening hot chiles 'Marbles' and 'Riot'. Both cover themselves with small yellow, red, and orange fruits in August and September.

Mention kale as an ornamental plant, and the imagination lands at once on images of gas-station plantings and mall parking lots. Those lumpen pink-and-purple cabbages in front of every hardware store are far too clumsy for the cottage garden, but good old ruffled kale—the kind found in your supermarket produce aisle—is a perfectly fine plant for our purposes. The crinkled, *subtly purple tinted leaves* of 'Winter Red' and 'Redbor' are delightful in a border with *Artemisia* 'Powis Castle' and the deep violet Siberian iris 'Coronation Anthem'.

177

Edible crops have been part of the cottage garden tradition for centuries.

The narrow, bubbled, dark green leaves of the Italian kale *cavolo nero* stand out dramatically over silver thyme or white-marked lamiums. They also have a marvelous sweet flavor when harvested in early winter!

Earlier on I spoke of the ornamental kiwi vine, *Actinidia kolomikta*. The edible kiwi, *A. deliciosa*, is attractive in its own right. Its big fuzzy leaves look frankly tropical as it climbs through a sturdy trellis or an open fence. The fruits, which ripen in early autumn, start out as inconspicuous but highly fragrant flowers. You may need to grow both male and female plants in order to collect any fruit, and that *can* mean giving up a lot of garden real estate.

Fig trees also lend an air of exoticism to the Northwest cottage garden, and the heavy yields of sweet, fresh figs that they produce here in the Northwest are a welcome bonus. Just be sure to keep your figs well picked, because they overripen rapidly if left on the tree too long.

Peaches and apples are welcome in the Northwest cottage garden, both for their cheerful, if brief, floral display in spring and for their fruit. They also make fine hosts for *Clematis* and climbing roses, which add color while their fruit is ripening. To make the most of limited cottage garden space, look for dwarf or semidwarf varieties.

PLANTS FOR HEDGES

As I pointed out in Chapter Three, hedges are important structural components of the Northwest cottage garden. Their color, form, and texture depend upon the choice of their constituent plants. The range of plant material available for use in hedges in the Pacific Northwest is staggering, and includes deciduous plants, conifers, and broadleaf evergreens. Among deciduous plants, shrub roses are some of the most rewarding plants for informal hedges. They grow quickly into solid masses, and their thorns help make a secure barrier. *Ribes sanguineum* and *Hydrangea macrophyllum* make colorful informal hedges too, but in Pacific Northwest gardens broadleaf evergreens are far more popular as hedge plants.

BROADLEAF EVERGREENS

Like deciduous shrubs, broadleaf evergreens grow rapidly in comparison to conifers. Better yet, unlike deciduous shrubs they provide year-round privacy and greenery in the landscape. Their foliage may be coarse or fine textured, smooth or spiny. It may be dark green, or it may be striped, blotched, or spotted in white or gold. There are broadleaf evergreens that stay as low as 18 inches without trimming, and others that will grow to 20 feet or more. Many have colorful fruits, and some have fragrant and attractive blossoms.

I find it sad that with so many choices, Pacific Northwest gardeners rely almost entirely upon a narrow range of cherry laurels (genus *Prunus*) and photinias (genus *Photinia*) for their hedges. Overuse has robbed both plants of whatever glamour they once had, and both have large, coarse foliage that clashes with the intimate scale of the cottage garden. Most of the popular laurels and photinias grow much too large for the average home garden hedge, which means that they require constant topping and shearing. However, their large, glossy leaves are a sad sight when torn and tattered after shearing, and neither genus offers much by way of fruit or flower. Cottage gardens generally benefit from finer-textured hedges whose small foliage takes much more readily to clipping and shearing.

The shrubby honeysuckle *Lonicera pileata* is a fine-textured evergreen that holds its shiny foliage in neat rows on horizontal branches. It grows to 2 or 3 feet tall and nearly twice as wide, making it a fine subject for a low, unclipped hedge. *Leucothoe walteri* (*L. fontanesia*) also makes a nice, low informal hedge, especially on acid soils in the shade. Its languid, drooping habit is both relaxed and elegant, while its reddish emerging foliage adds a touch of color in spring. The cultivar 'Rainbow' has leaves splashed in cream and pink, making for a colorful hedge all year long.

Osmanthus delavayi is a tall-growing shrub whose fine-textured foliage takes well to clipping. In early spring it cloaks itself completely in small, bright white flowers with a lovely scent that travels far across the garden. *O. heterophyllus* has larger, spiny leaves that look a lot like those of holly, and it looks better as an informal hedge than when tightly clipped. The leaves of the form 'Variegatus' are edged in white, while 'Aureomarginatus' shows a similar pattern in bright yellow. The leaves of 'Purpureus' open deep blackish-purple, and 'Goshiki' has leaves speckled evenly in cream. *O. heterophyllus* bears white, scented flowers in October.

The evergreen barberries (genus *Berberis*) are decorative both in fruit and in flower, particularly when left unclipped. Allowed to grow naturally, *B. julianae* forms a 6-foot mound of arching branches, dusted in spring with bright yellow flowers and displaying deep-blue fruits in fall. Its forbidding spines make an impenetrable barrier against all intruders, human or otherwise. The much less vigorous *B. verruculosa* looks quite similar, but can be kept down to 3 feet with some light pruning.

Several plants in the genus *Escallonia* make good hedges for Pacific Northwest gardens, with fine twigs and small, glossy leaves that take well to shearing and clipping. Left to its own devices, *E. rubra* will grow 6 feet tall or more, covered in late summer and autumn with bright cherry-red flowers. The hybrid *E. x langleyensis* 'Pride of Donard' reaches 5 feet without pruning and bears flowers of a clear medium pink. *E. x langleyensis* 'Apple Blossom' is similar, with pale pinkish white flowers.

Abelia x *grandiflora* is another evergreen hedge plant that flowers in late summer. The fragrant blooms are small but numerous, and show up at a time when many other plants are winding down for autumn. The two variegated forms 'Sunrise' and 'Francis Mason' have leaves conspicuously edged in gold. Either makes a bright, sparkling hedge, but the patterns on their leaves can camouflage the flowers.

CONIFERS

Conifer hedges are invariably fine-textured, and coniferous plants are available in a tremendous range of forms and sizes. Conifers can be slow-growing compared to deciduous shrubs and broadleaf evergreens, and few contribute any color to the landscape from their fruiting bodies They do offer a dense barrier against noise, eyesores, and animal trespassers, and many are amenable to clipping and shearing. As with broadleaf evergreens, gardeners have been slow to take advantage of this range of options, and too many of the conifer hedges in our region consist of sheared 'Pfitzer' junipers or 'Emerald Green' arborvitae (*Thuja plicata* 'Emerald Green'). With so many conifers to choose from, it's a shame the local repertoire is so limited. Conifer selections with procumbent or weeping habits, such as the spreading plum yew, *Cephalotaxus harringtonia* 'Prostrata', make outstanding low, informal hedges. Pyramidal or columnar conifers like *Chamaecyparis pisifera* 'Boulevard' are superb as tall screens or windbreaks. Foliage colors range from the often-seen dark green to the blues and grays of Leyland cypress (x *Cupressocyparis leylandii* 'Haggerston Grey') and *Juniperus virginiana* 'Silver Spreader', through chartreuse or lime, as in *Chamaecyparis pisifera* 'Filifera Aurea'. These colored conifers offer alternatives to the dark greens of yews or arborvitaes. Their bright or cool colors can contrast nicely with cottage garden structures or with plantings that are set in front of them.

CHAPTER EIGHT

Maintaining Your Garden:
Preventive Medicine

The cottage garden is a relaxed and casual landscape, but that doesn't mean you can just "set it and forget it." Keeping your Northwest cottage garden lush and healthy won't require a squadron of landscapers, but it *will* take some involvement on your part. Seasonal precipitation cycles mean that Northwest cottage gardens will sometimes require supplemental water. The variable soils in our region often need improvement. A garden of any style faces challenges from weeds and pests, and the cottage garden is no exception. Still, maintaining a Northwest cottage garden in the face of these challenges becomes relatively easy if you concentrate your efforts on preparation and prevention. Carefully preparing your soil, watering judiciously, and taking a few steps to discourage garden pests will keep your plants healthy and vigorous. Seen to early on, these simple measures will help your Northwest cottage garden flourish season after season.

SOIL AND WATER

Somewhere between the redwood forests of Northern California and the coast of Southeast Alaska, I'm sure there is a patch of perfect soil. It is loose and loamy, well drained yet moisture retentive. It is nearly neutral in pH and naturally fertile. If that patch is on your property, consider yourself lucky. As for the rest of us, we have to deal with soils that are less than perfect. With all of the region's rainfall concentrated into a few months each year, even the best of Northwest soils tend to be soggy in winter and extremely dry by midsummer.

SOIL TEXTURE AND FERTILITY

During successive ice ages, the Pacific Northwest was buried deep underneath great sheets of glacial ice. When the glaciers retreated they left behind a hodgepodge of scraped bedrock, randomly strewn boulders, heaps of stone and gravel, and patches of sand and clay, some of which originated hundreds, even thousands of miles away. This irregular patchwork of glacial deposits makes it hard to generalize about the texture of the Northwest soils that have formed on top of them. Some Northwest soils are dense and heavy, full of sticky clay that becomes waterlogged in winter and dries into a hard, cracked mass in summer. Others are loose, sandy, and infertile, well drained even in winter, but dry and barren in the summertime. Most lie somewhere in between, but few are ideally balanced. The simple tests outlined in Chapter Two will tell you where your soil lies on the continuum between heavy clay and sand.

Heavy clay soils are often rich in nutrients, but poor aeration makes those nutrients hard for plants to use. The roots of many plants have trouble penetrating heavy soils, and may even rot if the clay remains waterlogged through spring and early summer. Sandy soils are well oxygenated, but usually poor in nutrients. They also tend to dry out quickly, no matter how much water you pour into them. Curiously, both types benefit from the same kind of initial preparation.

IMPROVING YOUR SOIL

Whether your soil is sandy or heavy to start with, proper soil preparation before planting will improve both its texture and its fertility. The two magic ingredients for soil preparation in your cottage garden are compost and elbow grease. Any soil benefits from having a layer of compost several inches deep worked into it. The technique is labor-intensive but simple, and will pay off handsomely in healthy plants and plentiful flowers.

To prepare the soil in a new bed or border, dig the soil to a depth of 12 to 18 inches. Turn it over as you go, and break up any big lumps or clods you may encounter. Now spread a 3- to 4-inch layer of compost on top, and turn this layer into the freshly dug soil. This work should be done in late spring or midautumn. If your soil is too wet from winter rains, it will turn to mud when you attempt to dig it, and you'll never be able to break up lumps and clods. You can work on sandy soils in summer, but try to dig dry clay, and your spade is liable to bounce right off it!

Adding compost helps sandy soils retain water and nutrients. When worked into clayey soils, compost adds fibrous texture that helps air and roots penetrate the soil. In both cases, compost encourages beneficial soil bacteria and earthworms, whose activities further enhance soil texture and nutrition. When your cottage garden plantings respond to these benefits, you'll thank yourself for all your effort.

pH

Much of the Pacific Northwest has spent the time since the last ice age as conifer forest. The soils under long-standing forests, especially conifer forests, tend to be acidic. Hence, acidic to neutral soils are far more common in our region than alkaline soils. The relative acidity, or pH, of a soil partially determines what will grow on it. Some plants, including rhododendrons and camellias, demand acidic soils, while others, such as delphiniums, prefer their soil to be somewhat alkaline. Luckily, most plants adapt to a wide range of pH, and will grow happily in your cottage garden as long as your soil is not too far out of balance. You can determine your own soil's pH with a home testing kit, or by bringing samples to your local agricultural extension office. (For hints on getting good samples, see the section "Soil" in Chapter Two.)

Whether it is acidic or alkaline, you can modify your soil's pH—*within limits*. Lime can neutralize overly acid soils, though the effect is usually temporary, and you're liable to need regular reapplications. Similarly, granular aluminum sulfate or ammonium sulfate can help correct soils that are very alkaline. But rather than

Soil preparation, careful watering, and consistent, routine maintenance keep this Northwest cottage garden healthy and productive.

pollute lakes and rivers with the runoff from these garden chemicals, I suggest you cope with your soil's pH by choosing plants that are naturally adapted to it. The chart of cultural notes in the Appendix will help you find plants that enjoy acidic or alkaline soils.

FEEDING

Modern gardeners thought they had invented something when they came up with "square foot" gardening, an intensive method of growing food crops close together in order to make the most efficient use of the available soil. Sound familiar? It should, since cottage gardeners have been doing it for centuries. The kind of intensive planting practiced in cottage gardens does, however, entail a certain risk: It depletes soil nutrients very rapidly. Applying a 2- to 3-inch layer of composted manure to beds and borders every year will supplement your soil's nitrogen supply *and* help to maintain good soil texture.

Naturally derived (as opposed to industrially processed) fertilizers that are high in potassium and phosphorus will encourage strong root growth and generous bloom in cottage garden plantings. These supplements alone will not replenish plant nutrients like iron, zinc, magnesium, and manganese, all of which are vital to healthy plant metabolism. For these elements, you will need a so-called complete fertilizer (those words will be printed somewhere on the label). The best complete plant foods for a healthy cottage garden are those relatively high in potassium and phosphorus. To determine a plant food's nitrogen, potassium, and phosphorus content, look for three numbers displayed on the bag or label. They may read something like 5-10-10 or 8-2-0. The first of these numbers represents the percentage content of nitrogen, the second phosphorus, and the third potassium. A fertilizer labeled "5-10-10" is 5 percent nitrogen, 10 percent phosphorus, and 10 percent potassium. Complete fertilizers may or may not be naturally derived. (Choose which you use according to your own priorities and inclinations.)

WATER

Where water is concerned it's always feast or famine—or should I say deluge or drought?—in the Pacific Northwest garden. Choosing plants that can adapt to our seasonal weather cycle will go a long way toward keeping your Northwest cottage garden green and blooming all year round. Even so, most cottage gardeners will want to undertake a little water management. The kind of soil preparation that I outlined a few pages back is by far the best way to cope with excess winter water. The next step, responsible irrigation, will help insulate your plantings from the impact of late summer drought.

Responsible irrigation means using no more of our region's water resources than necessary to sustain your plantings, in accordance with the cottage garden paradigm of thrift. One to two inches of water per week should be enough to keep most mixed cottage garden plantings growing and blooming through a dry July or August. *Where* and *how* you deliver those one to two inches of water makes all the difference between efficient watering and waste. Watering at night or in the early morning will ensure that most of the applied moisture stays on the ground, rather than evaporating. The more directly you deliver water to the roots, the better. Drip irrigation systems and soaker hoses, which put water on the soil surface and not on the foliage, are inherently more efficient than overhead sprinklers. Long, slow waterings at infrequent intervals soak the soil deeply, encouraging your plants to grow deep, healthy root systems. When you deliver such deep soakings, be sure not to water any faster than your soil can absorb the moisture; any excess that flows off is simply wasted.

MULCH

Conserving soil moisture is one of the best reasons for using mulch in Northwest cottage gardens. Two or three inches of loose, organic mulch cuts down on evaporation, moderates soil temperatures, and protects vulnerable surface roots from heat and drying. As a bonus, a good organic mulch will improve any soil texture as it decomposes. Annual mulching keeps down weeds as well, and even those that do sprout on a layer of mulch will be easy to pull.

WEEDS

One hidden advantage of dense, overstuffed cottage garden plantings is that weeds have little chance of taking hold. You'll be hard pressed to notice those that do, since they are liable to be buried under layer upon layer of foliage and flowers. Mulching and occasional pulling will suffice to keep down smaller weeds like pepper cress *(Cardamine oligosperma)* and willow herb *(Epilobium watsonii)*. The best way to deal with large, pernicious weeds like bindweed *(Convolvulus sepium)* and Himalayan blackberry *(Rubus procerus)* is to make sure they never gain a foothold. Blackberries often arrive as seeds deposited by passing birds; pull any seedlings as soon as you find them, before they start to send out their invasive rhizomes. Bindweed often gets its start from small pieces of stem or root that drop onto the soil during yard work or planting. Both bindweed and blackberries can also come into the garden with topsoil, compost, or fill, so if you purchase commercial topsoil or compost, make sure it's guaranteed weed free and sterile. Bindweed and blackberries are hard to eradicate once they become established, and you may need herbicides in order to be done with them. Systemic herbicides containing glyphosate are effective against both of these weeds. In order to avoid injury to desirable garden plants, paint the herbicide onto the weeds rather than spraying them.

Dense cottage garden plantings go a long way toward suppressing weeds.

SLUGS AND BUGS

Slugs are the bane of many Pacific Northwest gardens. They may move slowly, but their rasping mouthparts make quick work of shoots, leaves, and tender stems. Among their favorite foods are daylilies, irises, delphiniums, and especially hostas. You could avoid growing the plants slugs favor, but you would deny yourself some of the Northwest cottage garden's finest treasures. Conventional metaldehyde-based slug bait in dry or liquid form is very effective, but it's also highly toxic to pets and children. A new range of iron phosphate slug baits promise to eliminate the slimy pests without harming humans or domestic animals. Shallow dishes or jar lids filled with beer make effective traps for slugs and snails, though emptying them is unpleasant work!

Some of the common insect pests that invade Northwest cottage gardens include whiteflies, aphids, spider mites, and hoopworms. There are few effective treatments for spider mites during the growing season except for some highly toxic miticides, but aphids and whiteflies are easily controlled with relatively innocuous insecticidal soaps. The naturally derived insecticides pyrethrin and rotenone are also effective but can kill bees and butterflies on contact. Light aphid infestations can simply be washed away with jets of water from a hose.

Hoopworms are small caterpillars that chew holes in leaves and flower buds. They can be especially destructive to roses and other early-summer-flowering shrubs. Hoopworms and other caterpillars are susceptible to *Bacillus thuringiensis*, or Bt, a bacterium that disturbs their digestive systems. You can purchase Bt in liquid or powdered form at most nurseries and hardware stores. It is easy to apply and nontoxic to pets and humans. It also makes a safe and effective control for cabbage worms on broccoli, collards, kale, and other cole crops in the cottage garden.

Prevention is by far the most effective means of combating all of the common cottage garden pests. A single spraying of inert horticultural oil during winter dormancy will smother overwintering insect and mite eggs. Checking new plants for obvious insect infestations can stop the invasion before pests take over. Sanitation also helps to control insects and mites. As woody plants drop their leaves and annuals and perennials die back into dormancy, collect the waste for compost. Doing so cuts down on the number of places where insects, mites, and eggs can overwinter in your beds and borders. The high temperatures generated in a properly working compost heap will destroy any pests that linger on the dead stems and foliage. These simple preventive measures take some effort, but they will save you trouble during each growing season.

A FEW PARTING WORDS

It's true that a cottage garden asks for some care in cultivation, but its simple layouts and informal plantings are also endlessly forgiving. The cottage garden style is remarkably flexible, adapting to all kinds of home sites and to a wide range of Pacific Northwest architecture. Because cottage gardens are a part of folk tradition, they have no strict rules or encumbering formulae. Instead, they reward thrift and thrive on invention. A cottage garden can be made to suit almost any personal taste or style.

No other place in North America is more accommodating of the cottage garden style than our own Pacific Northwest. Cottage gardens call for diverse plantings, and our moderate, even temperatures and long growing season support a wealth of plant life. These same conditions guarantee that Northwest cottage gardens remain green and attractive all year long.

Northwest cottage gardens are easygoing gardens; they are casual and fun. They are also efficient and eventful. Above all, they are livable. A true cottage garden ought to be so full of charm and comfort that you'll want to spend time in it every day. You can count your own Northwest cottage garden a success as long as you, your family, and your friends enjoy it!

Cultural Notes for Northwest Cottage Garden Plants

T he following tables offer cultural guidelines for plants described throughout the book. Trees, shrubs, conifers, climbing plants, perennials, grasses, and annuals are each grouped together in alphabetical order by their Latin names.

The heights given for herbaceous perennials and annuals are for blooming plants and include flower stalks. When not in bloom, many of these plants may be significantly shorter. Heights of woody plants are for mature specimens. The size of any plant will vary with microclimate, soil, and other growing conditions.

Most plants in the table can adapt to a range of soil types and pH. Any special requirements are noted in the column labeled "Soil." I have also given preferred lighting conditions for each plant. Please note that many plants that prefer full sun can adapt to partial shade, though they may show more open, rangy growth and diminished bloom.

The maritime Pacific Northwest lowlands fall almost entirely within USDA Zone 8. Coastal areas in southern Oregon and northern California, along with sheltered environments elsewhere in the region, may fall into USDA Zone 9. The lower foothills of the Cascades, Coast Range, and Olympics fall mostly in Zones 6 and 7. Higher altitude locales may be as cold as USDA Zone 4, while most of the areas east of the Cascades are in USDA Zone 5. Hardiness Zones are not given for annuals, since they are not expected to overwinter.

Plants that require "average" water will need little supplemental water once established, except in cases of extreme drought. Plants requiring "even moisture" are likely to require supplemental water during the summer.

TREES

Name	Height	Soil	Light	Water	USDA Zone
Acer capillipes SNAKEBARK MAPLE	20'–30'	Neutral to acid	Part shade	Even moisture	5–8
Acer davidii SNAKEBARK MAPLE	20'–30'	Neutral to acid	Part shade	Even moisture	5–8
Acer griseum PAPERBARK MAPLE	20'–30'	Neutral to acid	Sun to part shade	Even moisture	4–8
Acer pensylvanicum 'Erythrocladum' CANDY CANE MAPLE	15'–20'	Neutral to acid	Part shade	Even moisture	3–8
Acer pensylvanicum 'White Tigress' 'WHITE TIGRESS' MAPLE	15'–30'	Neutral to acid	Part shade	Even moisture	3–8
Acer shirasawanum 'Aureum' GOLDEN FULLMOON MAPLE	20'	Neutral to acid	Part shade	Even moisture	5–8
Amelanchier alnifolia SERVICEBERRY	12'–20'	Neutral to acid	Sun to part shade	Average	4–9
Amelanchier x *grandiflora* SERVICEBERRY	12'–20'	Neutral to acid	Sun to part shade	Average	4–9
Amelanchier laevis SERVICEBERRY	12'–20'	Neutral to acid	Sun to part shade	Average	4–9
Cercis canadensis 'Forest Pansy' 'FOREST PANSY' REDBUD	20'–30'	Any well-drained	Sun to part shade	Average	4–9
Cornus alternifolia 'Argentea' WHITE-EDGED PAGODA DOGWOOD	15'	Acid to neutral	Part shade	Even moisture	3–8
Cornus kousa 'Wolf Eyes' 'WOLF EYES' DOGWOOD	20'–30'	Any well-drained	Sun to part shade	Average	4–9
Davidia involucrata DOVE TREE	20'–40'	Any well-drained	Sun to part shade	Even moisture	6–9

TREES CONT.

Name	Height	Soil	Light	Water	USDA Zone
Eucryphia x *nymansensis*	15'–30'	Any well-drained	Sun or shade	Average	8–10
Ficus carica FIG	10'–15'	Any well-drained	Sun	Average	8–10
Halesia carolina CAROLINA SILVERBELL	20'–30'	Acid to neutral	Sun to part shade	Average	4–8
Halesia monticola MOUNTAIN SILVERBELL	20'–60'	Acid to neutral	Sun to part shade	Average	5–8
Laburnum x *watereri* 'Vossii' GOLDENCHAIN TREE	12'–15'	Any well-drained	Sun or shade	Average	5–8
Magnolia x 'Elizabeth' 'ELIZABETH' MAGNOLIA	30'	Any well-drained	Sun	Average	4–9
Magnolia x *loebneri* LOEBNER MAGNOLIA	20'	Any well-drained	Sun	Average	4–9
Magnolia sieboldii OYAMA MAGNOLIA	10'–15'	Any well-drained	Part shade	Even moisture	6–9
Magnolia x *soulangiana* SAUCER MAGNOLIA	20'–30'	Any well-drained	Sun	Average	4–9
Magnolia stellata STAR MAGNOLIA	15'–20'	Any well-drained	Sun	Average	4–9
Parrotia persica	15'–30'	Any well-drained	Sun to part shade	Average	4–8
Pterostyrax hispida EPAULETTE TREE	20'–30'	Acid to neutral	Sun	Even moisture	4–8
Styrax japonicus JAPANESE SNOWBELL	20'–30'	Acid	Sun to part shade	Average	5–8
Styrax obassia FRAGRANT SNOWBELL	20'–30'	Acid to neutral	Sun to part shade	Even moisture	4–8

SHRUBS

Name	Height	Soil	Light	Water	USDA Zone
Abelia x *grandiflora* GLOSSY ABELIA	6'+	Any well-drained	Sun or shade	Average	6–9
Abutilon vitifolium 'VERONICA TENNANT'	6'+	Any well-drained	Sun	Avoid excess moisture	8–10
Berberis julianae WINTERGREEN BARBERRY	6'–10'	Any well-drained	Sun	Average	5–8
Berberis verruculosa WARTY BARBERRY	3'–6'	Any well-drained	Sun	Average	5–8
Buddleia davidii BUTTERFLY BUSH	6'+	Any well-drained	Sun	Drought tolerant	5–9
Buddleia x 'Lochinch'	6'+	Any well-drained	Sun	Drought tolerant	5–9
Buddleia x *weyeriana* 'Sungold'	6'+	Any well-drained	Sun	Drought tolerant	5–9
Callicarpa bodinieri BEAUTYBERRY	4'–6'	Any well-drained	Sun or part shade	Average	6–8
Camellia japonica JAPANESE CAMELLIA	6'–15'	Acid	Shade	Even moisture	7–9
Carpenteria californica BUSH ANEMONE	6'	Any well-drained	Sun	Drought tolerant	8–10
Caryopteris x *clandonensis* BLUEBEARD	2'	Any well-drained	Sun	Average	6–9
Ceanothus x 'Puget Blue', 'Dark Star', 'Concha' CALIFORNIA LILAC	6'–10'	Any well-drained	Sun	Drought tolerant	8–10
Cistus albidus WHITE-LEAVED ROCKROSE	4'–8'	Any well-drained	Sun	Drought tolerant	8–10
Cistus x *corbariensis* WHITE ROCKROSE	3'–4'	Any well-drained	Sun	Drought tolerant	8–10
Cistus ladanifer SPOTTED ROCKROSE	4'–6'	Any well-drained	Sun	Drought tolerant	8–10

SHRUBS CONT.

Name	Height	Soil	Light	Water	USDA Zone
Cistus laurifolius	4'–6'	Any well-drained	Sun	Drought tolerant	8–10
Clerodendron trichotomum HARLEQUIN GLORYBOWER	6'–15'	Any well-drained	Sun	Average	6–9
Cornus alba REDTWIG DOGWOOD	6'–10'	Any	Sun or part shade	Tolerates wet soils	2–8
Cornus stolonifera RED OSIER	6'–10'	Any	Sun or part shade	Tolerates wet soils	2–8
Corylopsis spicata SPIKE WINTER HAZEL	6'–8'	Acid	Sun or part shade	Even moisture	5–8
Cotinus coggygria PURPLE SMOKE BUSH	8'–15'	Any	Sun	Average	4–9
Daphne odora SCENTED DAPHNE	2'–4'	Neutral	Sun to part shade	Even moisture	7–9
Edgeworthia papyrifera	4'–6'	Any well-drained	Sun to part shade	Even moisture	7–10
Escallonia x *langleyensis*	5'	Any well-drained	Sun to part shade	Average	8–10
Escallonia rubra	6'+	Any well-drained	Sun to part shade	Average	8–10
Fatsia japonica	6'–10'	Any well-drained	Shade	Average	8–10
Fothergilla gardenii	3'	Acid, well-drained	Sun to part shade	Even moisture	5–9
Fothergilla major	6'–10'	Acid, well-drained	Sun to part shade	Even moisture	5–9
Hamamelis x *intermedia* WITCH HAZEL	10'–15'	Acid to neutral	Sun to part shade	Even moisture	5–8
Hydrangea macrophylla BIGLEAF HYDRANGEA	3'–8'	Any well-drained	Sun to part shade	Average	6–9
Hydrangea aspera villosa	6'–10'	Any well-drained	Part shade	Even moisture	6–9
Lavandula spp. LAVENDER	1'–3'	Any well-drained	Sun	Drought tolerant	6–10

SHRUBS CONT.

Name	Height	Soil	Light	Water	USDA Zone
Lavatera thuringiaca TREE MALLOW	6'+	Any well-drained	Sun	Average	5–9
Leucothoe walteri DROOPING LEUCOTHOE	3'–6'	Acid	Part shade	Even moisture	5–8
Lonicera pileata PRIVET HONEYSUCKLE	3'	Any well-drained	Part shade	Even moisture	6–8
Mahonia aquifolium OREGON GRAPE	6'+	Acid to neutral	Shade	Average	5–9
Mahonia bealei LEATHERLEAF MAHONIA	6'+	Acid to neutral	Shade	Average	7–9
Mahonia x *media*	8'–10'	Acid to neutral	Shade	Average	8–9
Osmanthus delavayii	6'–8'	Any well-drained	Sun to part shade	Average	8–10
Osmanthus heterophyllus	8'–10'	Any well-drained	Sun to part shade	Average	7–9
Paeonia hybrids TREE PEONIES	3'–6'	Any well-drained	Sun to part shade	Average	4–9
Rhododendron spp. RHODODENDRONS, AZALEAS	Varies	Acid	Part shade	Even moisture	Varies
Ribes sanguineum RED FLOWERING CURRANT	6'–10'	Any well-drained	Sun to part shade	Average	6–8
Rosa cultivars ROSES	Varies	Any well-drained	Sun	Even moisture	Varies
Rosmarinus officinalis ROSEMARY	2'–6'	Any well-drained	Sun	Drought tolerant	6–10
Sambucus nigra 'Madonna' 'MADONNA' ELDER	5'	Any well-drained	Part shade	Average	5–8
Sambucus nigra 'Pulverulenta' 'PULVERULENTA' ELDER	5'	Any well-drained	Part shade	Average	5–8
Sambucus racemosa 'Plumosa Aurea' GOLDEN FERNLEAF ELDER	8'	Any well-drained	Part shade	Average	5–8

SHRUBS CONT.

Name	Height	Soil	Light	Water	USDA Zone
Sarcococca ruscifolia SWEET BOX	3'	Any well-drained	Shade	Average	7–9
Spiraea japonica 'Magic Carpet' 'MAGIC CARPET' SPIRAEA	2'	Any well-drained	Sun	Average	6–9
Syringa patula 'Miss Kim' 'MISS KIM' DWARF LILAC	6'	Any well-drained	Sun	Average	3–8
Viburnum carlesii KOREAN SPICE VIBURNUM	4'–6'	Any well-drained	Sun	Average	4–8
Viburnum x *carlcephalum*	6'–10'	Any well-drained	Sun	Average	6–8
Viburnum opulus CRANBERRY BUSH	6'–12'	Any well-drained	Sun to part shade	Average	3–8
Viburnum plicatum var. *tomentosum* DOUBLEFILE VIBURNUM	6'–10'	Any well-drained	Sun	Average	5–8
Viburnum sargentii 'Onondaga' 'ONONDAGA' VIBURNUM	6'+	Any well-drained	Sun to part shade	Average	3–8
Vitex agnus-castus CHASTE TREE	6'+	Any well-drained	Sun	Average	7–9
Weigela florida 'Variegata' VARIEGATED WEIGELA	6'+	Any well-drained	Sun to part shade	Average	4–8

CONIFERS

Name	Height	Soil	Light	Water	USDA Zone
Cephalotaxus harringtonia PLUM YEW	5'–10'	Moist, well-drained	Shade to part shade	Average	5–9
Chamaeciparis pisifera JAPANESE FALSE CYPRESS	Varies	Moist, well-drained	Sun	Average	4–8
x *Cupressocyparis leylandii* LEYLAND CYPRESS	Varies	Any well-drained	Sun	Average	6–8
Juniperus virginiana EASTERN RED CEDAR	Varies	Any well-drained	Sun	Average	2–9

CLIMBERS

Name	Height	Soil	Light	Water	USDA Zone
Actinidia deliciosa KIWI VINE	15'+	Any well-drained	Sun	Average	7–10
Actinidia kolomikta	15'+	Any well-drained	Sun	Average	5–8
Campsis spp. TRUMPET VINES	15'+	Any well-drained	Sun	Average	5–9
Clematis spp.	Varies	Rich, loamy	Sun to part shade	Even moisture	5–9
Hydrangea anomala subsp. *petiolaris* CLIMBING HYDRANGEA	15'+	Rich, well-drained	Part shade	Average	5–8
Lonicera spp. HONEYSUCKLES	10'+	Any well-drained	Sun	Average	6–9
Passiflora caerulea PASSION FLOWER	15'+	Any well-drained	Sun to part shade	Average	8–10
Schizophragma hydrangeoides	15'+	Rich, well-drained	Partial shade	Average	6–9
Vitis spp. GRAPES	15'+	Rich, loamy	Sun to part shade	Average	5–9
Wisteria spp.	15'+	Any well-drained	Sun	Average	5–8

PERENNIALS

Name	Height	Soil	Light	Water	USDA Zone
Acanthus mollis BEAR'S BREECHES	4'	Any well-drained	Part shade	Average	7–10
Achillea x 'Moonshine' 'MOONSHINE' YARROW	2'	Any well-drained	Sun	Drought tolerant	4–8
Aconiutm napellus MONKSHOOD	3'–5'	Any well-drained	Part shade	Average	5–8
Acorus calamus 'Variegatus' VARIEGATED SWEET FLAG	5'	Moist	Sun to part shade	Bog plant	4–10
Agastache x 'Apricot Sunrise' 'APRICOT SUNRISE' HUMMINGBIRD MINT	3'	Any well-drained	Sun	Drought tolerant	7–10
Agastache barberi	3'	Any well-drained	Sun	Drought tolerant	7–10
Agastache foeniculum ANISE-HYSSOP	2'	Any well-drained	Sun	Drought tolerant	7–10
Agastache x 'Tutti Frutti' 'TUTTI FRUTTI' HUMMINGBIRD MINT	3'	Any well-drained	Sun	Drought tolerant	7–10
Alchemilla mollis LADY'S MANTLE	12"	Any	Sun to part shade	Average	4–8
Allium giganteum GIANT ALLIUM	3'	Any well-drained	Sun	Average	6–10
Allium schoenoprasum CHIVES	12"	Any well-drained	Sun	Average	3–9
Allium sphaerocephalum DRUMSTICK ALLIUM	2'	Any well-drained	Sun	Average	6–10
Anemone x *hybrida* JAPANESE ANEMONE	3'–4'	Any well-drained	Sun to part shade	Average	5–8
Aquilegia spp. COLUMBINES	12"–3'	Any well-drained	Sun to part shade	Average	3–9

PERENNIALS CONT.

Name	Height	Soil	Light	Water	USDA Zone
Arisaema sikokianum	18"	Loose, loamy	Shade to part shade	Even moisture	5–9
Artemisia abrotanum SOUTHERNWOOD	3'	Any well-drained	Sun	Average	5–8
Artemisia ludoviciana	3'	Any well-drained	Sun	Average	4–9
Artemisia x 'Powis Castle' 'POWIS CASTLE' ARTEMISIA	3'	Any well-drained	Sun	Average	5–8
Artemisia schmidtiana 'Silver Mound' 'SILVER MOUND' ARTEMISIA	8"	Any well-drained	Sun	Average	5–8
Arum italicum	12"	Any well-drained	Shade to part shade	Average	6–9
Aruncus dioicus GOATSBEARD	6'	Any well-drained	Sun to shade	Average	3–8
Aster x *frikartii* 'Mönch'	2'	Any well-drained	Sun	Average	5–8
Aster lateriflorus 'Prince'	4'	Any well-drained	Sun	Average	3–9
Astilbe x *arendsii*	18"–3'	Any moist soil	Sun or shade	Tolerates wet soils	4–8
Astilbe chinensis 'Pumila' DWARF ASTILBE	18"	Any moist soil	Sun or shade	Tolerates wet soils	4–8
Astilbe taquetii 'Superba'	4'	Any moist soil	Sun or shade	Tolerates wet soils	4–8
Astilboides tabularis	3'	Any moist soil	Part shade	Tolerates wet soils	5–8
Baptisia australis BLUE FALSE INDIGO	3'	Any well-drained	Sun	Drought tolerant	3–9
Brunnera macrophylla	18"	Any well-drained	Shade	Average	4–8
Camassia cusickii	3'	Any well-drained	Sun	Average	5–9
Camassia leichtlinii	3'	Any well-drained	Sun	Average	5–9
Camassia quamash	3'	Any well-drained	Sun	Average	5–9
Campanula lactiflora	4'	Any well-drained	Sun to part shade	Average	4–8
Campanula latiflora	4'	Any well-drained	Sun to part shade	Average	4–8

PERENNIALS CONT.

Name	Height	Soil	Light	Water	USDA Zone
Campanula persicifolia PEACH LEAF BELLFLOWER	2'	Any well-drained	Sun to part shade	Average	4–8
Campanula poscharskyana SERBIAN BELLFLOWER	12"	Any well-drained	Sun to part shade	Average	4–8
Campanula takesimana	2'	Any well-drained	Shade	Average	4–8
Canna hybrids CANNA	4'–8'	Any moist soil	Sun	Tolerates wet soils	8–10
Convallaria majalis LILY-OF-THE-VALLEY	8"	Any well-drained	Shade	Average	4–9
Coreopsis verticillata THREADLEAF COREOPSIS	18"	Any well-drained	Sun	Drought tolerant	4–9
Corydalis flexuosa	12"	Moist, well-drained	Part shade	Even moisture	5–9
Crocosmia x *crocosmiiflora* CROCOSMIA, MONTBRETIA	3'	Any well-drained	Sun	Average	5–9
Dahlia x 'Bishop of Llandaff'	2'–3'	Any well-drained	Sun	Average	8–10
Delphinium hybrids	4'–6'	Rich, neutral to alkaline	Sun	Even moisture	2–8
Dianthus spp. PINKS, CARNATIONS	6"–18"	Neutral to alkaline	Sun	Average	4–8
Diascia spp. TWINSPURS	12"	Any well-drained	Sun	Average	7–9
Dicentra formosa BLEEDING HEART	12"	Any well-drained	Part shade	Average	4–8
Dicentra spectabilis BLEEDING HEART	2'	Any well-drained	Part shade	Average	4–8
Dierama pulcherrimum ANGEL'S FISHING ROD	5'	Moist, well-drained	Sun	Even moisture	7–9
Digitalis grandiflora	2'	Any well-drained	Shade to part shade	Average	4–8
Dodecatheon hendersonii SHOOTING STAR	18"	Moist, well drained	Part shade	Average	5–8

PERENNIALS CONT.

Name	Height	Soil	Light	Water	USDA Zone
Echinops ritro	4'	Any well-drained	Sun	Average	3–9
Epimedium grandiflorum 'ROSE QUEEN'	12"	Any well-drained	Shade to part shade	Average	5–8
Epimedium x *perralchicum* 'FROHNLEITEN'	18"	Any well-drained	Shade to part shade	Average	5–9
Eremurus spp. FOXTAIL LILIES	6'+	Very well-drained	Sun	Drought tolerant	5–9
Eryngium alpinum BLUE SEA HOLLY	2'	Any well-drained	Sun	Drought tolerant	5–9
Eryngium bourgatii	18"	Any well-drained	Sun	Drought tolerant	5–9
Eryngium x *tripartitum*	3'	Any well-drained	Sun	Drought tolerant	5–9
Eryngium variifolium	12"	Any well-drained	Sun	Drought tolerant	5–9
Euphorbia characias subsp. *wulfenii*	4'	Any well-drained	Sun	Average	7–10
Filipendula ulmaria 'Aurea', 'Variegata'	3'	Moist soil	Sun to part shade	Tolerates wet soils	3–9
Foeniculum vulgare 'Purpurascens' BRONZE FENNEL	6'	Any well-drained	Sun	Average	4 9
Fritillaria meleagris CHECKERED LILY	18"	Any well-drained	Shade to part shade	Average	5–9
Fuchsia magellanica HARDY FUCHSIA	Up to 6'	Any well-drained	Part shade	Even moisture	8–10
Geranium x 'Ann Folkard'	18"+	Any well-drained	Sun	Average	5–8
Geranium himalayense	18"	Any well-drained	Sun to part shade	Average	4–8
Geranium macrorrhizum	18"	Any well-drained	Sun or shade	Average	4–8
Geranium x *magnificum*	2'–3'	Any well-dained	Sun to part shade	Average	4–8
Geranium nodosum	12"	Any well-drained	Shade to part shade	Average	5–8

202

PERENNIALS CONT.

Name	Height	Soil	Light	Water	USDA Zone
Geranium x *oxonianum*	2'–3'	Any well-drained	Sun or shade	Average	4–8
Geranium phaeum	2'	Any well-drained	Shade to part shade	Average	4–8
Geranium x 'Philippe Vapelle'	12"	Any well-drained	Sun	Average	4–8
Geranium pratense 'Victor Reiter'	2'–3'	Any well-drained	Sun to part shade	Average	4–8
Geranium psilostemon	3'–4'	Any well-drained	Sun or shade	Average	4–8
Geum chiloense	2'	Any well-drained	Sun	Average	5–9
Helleborus argutifolius CORSICAN HELLEBORE	2'–3'	Any well-drained	Shade to part shade	Average	5–8
Helleborus lividus	18"	Any well-drained	Shade to part shade	Average	8–10
Helleborus niger CHRISTMAS ROSE	18"	Any well-drained	Shade to part shade	Average	4–8
Helleborus orientalis LENTEN ROSE	2"	Any well-drained	Shade to part shade	Average	4–8
Hemerocallis hybrids DAYLILIES	16"–4'	Any well-drained	Sun to part shade	Drought tolerant	Varies
Heuchera hybrids CORAL BELLS	1'–2'	Any well-drained	Sun to part shade	Average	4–8
Hosta hybrids HOSTA	6"–4'	Any well-drained	Shade to part shade	Even moisture	4–9
Houttuynia cordata 'Chameleon'	18"	Any moist soil	Shade to part shade	Tolerates wet soils	5–9
Hyacinthoides hispanica WOOD HYACINTH	2'	Any well-drained	Sun or shade	Average	4–9
Iris x bearded hybrids BEARDED IRISES	8"–4'	Any well-drained	Sun	Average	4–9
Iris ensata JAPANESE IRISES	3'	Moist, acid soil	Sun	Tolerates wet soils	5–9
Iris x Louisiana hybrids LOUISIANA IRISES	3'	Moist, acid soil	Sun	Tolerates wet soils	5–9

PERENNIALS CONT.

Name	Height	Soil	Light	Water	USDA Zone
Iris x Pacific coast hybrids PACIFIC COAST IRISES	1'–2'	Well-drained, acid soil	Sun to part shade	Drought tolerant	7–10
Iris sibirica SIBERIAN IRIS	2'–3'	Any well-drained	Sun	Drought tolerant	4–9
Iris x spuria hybrids SPURIA IRISES	2'–5'	Any well-drained	Sun	Drought tolerant	5–9
Knautia macedonica	2'	Any well-drained	Sun	Average	5–9
Liatris spicata GAYFEATHER	2'–3'	Any well-drained	Sun	Average	4–9
Ligularia dentata	4'	Any moist soil	Part shade	Even moisture	4–8
Ligularia x 'Gregynog Gold'	6'	Any moist soil	Part shade	Even moisture	4–8
Ligularia przewalskii 'The Rocket'	5'	Any moist soil	Part shade	Even moisture	4–8
Lilium hybrids LILIES	2' – 6'+	Any well-drained	Sun to part shade	Average	5–9
Lobelia cardinalis CARDINAL FLOWER	3'	Any moist soil	Sun to part shade	Tolerates wet soils	3–9
Lysimachia ciliata 'Firecracker'	3'	Any moist soil	Sun to part shade	Tolerates wet soils	3–9
Lysimachia clethroides GOOSENECK LOOSESTRIFE	3'	Any moist soil	Sun to part shade	Tolerates wet soils	4–9
Lysimachia nummularia 'Aurea' GOLDEN CREEPING JENNY	1"	Any moist soil	Sun or shade	Tolerates wet soils	4–9
Lysimachia punctata 'Alexander'	2'	Any moist soil	Sun to part shade	Tolerates wet soils	4–9
Mentha requienii CORSICAN MINT	⅛"	Any well-drained	Sun to part shade	Average	6–10

PERENNIALS CONT.

Name	Height	Soil	Light	Water	USDA Zone
Monarda didyma BERGAMOT, BEE BALM	3'	Any moist soil	Sun	Even moisture	4–8
Myrrhis odorata SWEET CICELY	2'	Any well-drained	Shade to part shade	Average	4–8
Nepeta x *faassenii* CATMINT	18"	Any well-drained	Sun	Average	4–8
Nepeta govaniana YELLOW CATMINT	3'	Any well-drained	Sun to part shade	Even moisture	5–9
Nepeta x 'Six Hills Giant' 'SIX HILLS GIANT' CATMINT	3'	Any well-drained	Sun	Average	4–8
Origanum vulgare 'Aureum', 'Variegatum' OREGANO	12"	Any well-drained	Sun	Drought tolerant	4–8
Paeonia hybrids HERBACEOUS PEONIES	3'	Any well-drained	Sun	Average	3–8
Papaver orientale ORIENTAL POPPY	3'	Any well-drained	Sun	Drought tolerant	4–9
Parahebe perfoliata	2'	Any well-drained	Sun	Drought tolerant	8–10
Perovskia atriplicifolia RUSSIAN SAGE	4'	Neutral to alkaline	Sun	Drought tolerant	6–9
Persicaria microcephala 'Red Dragon'	3'	Any	Sun to part shade	Even moisture	5–8
Persicaria virginiana 'Painter's Palette'	3'	Any	Sun to part shade	Even moisture	5–8
Phlomis russeliana JERUSALEM SAGE	3'	Any well-drained	Sun	Drought tolerant	4–9
Phlox stolonifera 'Blue Ridge' 'BLUE RIDGE' CREEPING PHLOX	6"	Any well-drained	Part shade	Even moisture	6–9

PERENNIALS CONT.

Name	Height	Soil	Light	Water	USDA Zone
Phormium spp. NEW ZEALAND FLAX	6'+	Any well-drained	Sun to part shade	Even moisture	8–10
Phygelius x *rectus* CAPE FUCHSIA	3'+	Any well-drained	Sun to part shade	Average	8–10
Physostegia virginiana 'Variegata' VARIEGATED OBEDIENT PLANT	3'	Any well-drained	Sun to part shade	Average	4–8
Polemonium caeruleum 'Bris d'Anjou' 'BRIS D'ANJOU' JACOB'S LADDER	18"	Rich, loamy	Part shade	Even moisture	4–8
Primula beesiana	2'	Rich, moist	Part shade	Even moisture	5–8
Primula bulleyana	2'	Rich, moist	Part shade	Even moisture	5–8
Primula florindae	3'	Rich, moist	Part shade	Even moisture	5–8
Primula japonica	2'	Rich, moist	Part shade	Tolerates wet soils	5–8
Pulmonaria spp. LUNGWORTS	12"	Any well-drained	Shade to part shade	Average	5–8
Ranunculus ficaria BUTTERCUP	3"	Any well-drained	Part shade	Average	4–8
Raoulia australis	⅛"	Any well-drained	Sun	Average	4–10
Rheum palmatum 'Atrosanguineum'	6'+	Any moist soil	Part shade	Even moisture	5–9
Rodgersia aesculifolia	4'	Any moist soil	Sun to part shade	Tolerates wet soils	5–8
Romney coulteri MATILIJA POPPY	6'	Any well-drained	Sun	Drought tolerant	8–10
Rudbeckia fulgida 'Goldsturm' BLACK-EYED SUSAN	2'	Any well-drained	Sun	Drought tolerant	4–9

PERENNIALS CONT.

Name	Height	Soil	Light	Water	USDA Zone
Salvia nemerosa	2'	Any well-drained	Sun	Average	5–9
Salvia x *nemorosa*	2'	Any well-drained	Sun	Average	5–9
Salvia officinalis CULINARY SAGE	2'	Any well-drained	Sun	Average	5–9
Salvia verticillata 'Purple Rain'	3'	Any well-drained	Sun	Average	5–9
Scabiosa columbaria 'Butterfly Blue' 'BUTTERFLY BLUE' PINCUSHION FLOWER	12"	Any well-drained	Sun	Average	4–9
Scrophularia auriculata 'Variegata' VARIEGATED FIGWORT	3'	Any moist soil	Sun to part shade	Even moisture	5–9
Sedum sieboldii	12"	Any well-drained	Sun	Drought tolerant	6–10
Sedum spathulifolium	3"	Any well-drained	Sun	Drought tolerant	6–10
Sedum spectabile	2'	Any well-drained	Sun	Drought tolerant	4–9
Sedum x 'Vera Jameson'	12"	Any well-drained	Sun	Drought tolerant	4–9
Solidago spp. GOLDENRODS	18"–3'	Any well-drained	Sun	Drought tolerant	4–9
Stachys byzantina LAMB'S EARS	18"	Any well-drained	Sun	Average	4–9
Thalictrum aquilegiifolium MEADOW RUE	4'	Rich, loamy	Part shade	Even moisture	5–9
Thalictrum flavum subsp. *glaucum* YELLOW MEADOW RUE	4'	Rich, loamy	Part shade	Even moisture	5–9
Tigridia pavonia MEXICAN SHELLFLOWER	3'	Any well-drained	Sun	Average	8–10

PERENNIALS CONT.

Name	Height	Soil	Light	Water	USDA Zone
Tricyrtis spp. TOAD LILIES	3'	Rich, loamy	Shade to part shade	Even moisture	4–9
Tulipa spp. TULIPS	6"–12"	Any well-drained	Sun	Average	4–9
Verbena bonariensis	5'+	Any well-drained	Sun	Average	7–10
Viola labradorica LABRADOR VIOLET	3'	Any well-drained	Shade to part shade	Average	4–8
Yucca spp.	2'–6'	Any well-drained	Sun	Drought tolerant	5–10
Zantedeschia spp. CALLA LILIES	18"–3'	Rich, fertile	Sun	Tolerates wet soils	8–10

GRASSES AND SEDGES

Name	Height	Soil	Light	Water	USDA Zone
Carex buchananii NEW ZEALAND SEDGE	3'	Any well-drained	Sun to part shade	Average	7–9
Carex comans HAIR SEDGE	12"	Any well-drained	Sun to part shade	Average	7–9
Carex morrowii 'Expallida' STRIPED JAPANESE SEDGE	12"	Any well-drained	Part shade	Average	5–9
Festuca glauca BLUE SEDGE	12"	Any well-drained	Sun	Average	4–8
Helictotrichon sempervirens BLUE OAT GRASS	2'	Any well-drained	Sun	Average	4–9
Miscanthus sinensis MAIDEN GRASS	4'–8'	Any well-drained	Sun	Average	5–9

ANNUALS

Name	Height	Soil	Light	Water
Borago officinalis BORAGE	2'	Any well-drained	Sun	Average
Cerinthe major 'PURPURASCENS'	2'	Any well-drained	Sun	Average
Cleome hassleriana SPIDER FLOWER	4'–6'	Any well-drained	Sun	Average
Convolvulus tricilor 'Blue Ensign' DWARF MORNING GLORY	8"–12"	Any well-drained	Sun	Average
Helianthus annuus SUNFLOWER	12"–10'	Any well-drained	Sun	Average
Heliotropium arborescens HELIOTROPE	2'	Any well-drained	Sun	Average
Lathyrus odoratus SWEET PEA	5'	Rich, loamy	Sun	Even moisture
Lobelia erinus TRAILING LOBELIA	8"	Any well-drained	Sun to part shade	Average
Lobularia maritima SWEET ALYSSUM	4"	Any well-drained	Sun	Average
Myosotis sylvatica FORGET-ME-NOT	12"	Any well-drained	Sun or shade	Average
Nemophila menziesii BABY BLUE EYES	12"	Any well-drained	Sun to part shade	Even moisture
Nigella damascena LOVE-IN-A-MIST	2'	Any well-drained	Sun	Average
Phacelia campanularia	12"	Any well-drained	Sun	Average
Tropaeolum majus NASTURTIUM	18"–6'	Any well-drained	Sun to part shade	Even moisture

INDEX

A–C

Abelia x *grandiflora*, 151, 180
Abutilon vitifolium, 160
Acanthus mollis, 99, 102, 149
Acer: A. callilipes, 157; *A. davidii*, 157;
 A. griseum (Paperbark maple), 91,
 107, 158; *A. palmatum* (Japanese
 maple), 91, 157; *A. pensylvanicum*
 (Candy cane maple), 97, 158
Achillea, 124, 129
Acontium napellus (Monkshoods), 92,
 168
Acorus calamus (Sweet flag), 163
Actinidia kolomikta (Kiwi vine), 169
Agastache: A. barberi, 164; *A. foenicu-
 lum*, 164; Anise hyssops, 164
Age of exploration, 9
Aging, 109
Alba roses, 132
Alchemilla mollis, 153
Allium: A. giganteum (Onion), 149;
 A. schoenoprasum (Chives), 176;
 A. sphaerocephalum (Drumstick
 allium), 149
Amelanchier: A. laevis, 113; *A.* x *gran-
 diflora*, 113; Serviceberry, 112-13
Anemone x *hybrida* (Japanese anemone
 hybrids), 101, 155
Anise hyssops (*Agastache*), 164
Annuals, 209
Aquilegia spp. (Columbines), 123-24
Archways, 48-51
Arisaema sikokianum, 169
Artemisia, 91, 100, 177; *A. abrotanum*,
 146; *A. ludoviciana albula*, 142; *A.
 schmidtiana*, 142
Arum italicum, 169
Aruncus dioicus (Goatsbeard), 169
Asian campanula (*Campanula takesi-
 mana*), 168
Aster: A. lateriflorus, 108; *A.* x *frikartii*
 (Lavender), 84, 108
Astilbe: A. chinensis, 168; *A. taquetii*,
 168; *A.* x *arendsii*, 167-68
Astilboides tabularis, 162-63
Austin, David, 137-38
Autumn, 108-9

Baby blue-eyes (*Nemophila menziesii*),
 129
Baby's tears (*Soleirolia soleirolii*), 58
Bachelor's buttons (*Centaurea cyanus*),
 103
Bacillus thuringiensis, 189
Bark, 157-58
Barrel arch, 48
Basil (*Ocimum basilicum*), 176
Bees, 79-80, 163-64
Belgian block, 52
Berberis: B. julianae, 180; *B. thun-
 bergii*, 97; *B. verruculosa*, 180;
 Evergreen barberries, 180
Bergamot (*Monarda didyma*), 164
Berries, 158-59
Bigleaf hydrangea (*Hydrangea macro-
 phylla*), 115-16, 179
Bindweed (*Convolvulus sepium*, 187-
 88
Bird feeders, 79
Birdbaths, 75
Birdhouses, 79
Black-eyed susans (*Rudbeckia*), 129-30
Blechnum spicant (Deer fern), 105, 164
Bleeding heart: *Dicentra formosa*, 105,
 165; *Dicentra spectabilis*, 165-66
Blue fescue (*Festuca glauca*), 91, 142
Blue oat grass (*Helictotrichon semper-
 virens*), 85, 142, 144
Blue star creeper (*Pratia pedunculata*),
 58
Borage (*Borago officinalis*), 174
Borders: boundary uses of, 45-46;
 description of, 29
Boundaries: borders as, 45-46; fences.
 See Fences; forms of, 4; hedges,
 43-45; layout of, 26; masonry
 walls, 40-43; structures for, 36-46
Bourbon roses, 134-35
Branches, 157-58
Brick paving, 51-52
Brick walls, 41
Brightness, 85-86
Broadleaf evergreens, 179-80
Bronze fennel (*Foeniculum vulgare*),
 152
Brunnera macrophylla, 99, 108, 166

Buddleia davidii: Butterfly bush, 163;
 Lavender, 84
Bugs, 188-89
Bush anemone (*Carpenteria califor-
 nica*), 116-17
Butterflies, 79-80, 163-64
Butterfly bush (*Buddleia davidii*), 163

Caenothus, 160
Callicarpa, 91; *C. bodinieri*, 159;
 C. japonica, 159
Camas *Camassia quamash*, 120
Campanulas (*Campanula*): *C. lacti-
 flora*, 95, 127; *C. latifolia*, 127;
 C. persicifolia, 127-28; *C.
 poscharskyana*, 127-28; *C. takesi-
 mana* (Asian campanula), 168
Campsis (Trumpet vine): *C. grandi-
 flora*, 170; *C. radicans*, 86; *C.* x
 tagliabuana, 170
Candelabra primroses, 162
Candy cane maple (*Acer pensylvan-
 icum*), 97
Canna, 151
Cape fuchias (*Phygelius* spp.), 85
Cardamine oligosperma (Pepper cress),
 187
Carex: C. buchananii (New Zealand
 sedges), 91, 99, 143; *C. comans*
 (New Zealand hair sedge), 153;
 C. morrowii (Japanese sedge), 92,
 167
Carnations (*Dianthus*): *D. deltoides*,
 125; *D. gratianopolitanus*, 125;
 D. plumarius, 125-26
Carpenteria californica (Bush
 anemone), 88, 116-17, 171
Caryopteris x *clandonensis*, 141
Catnip (*Nepeta*), 125
Cavolo nero (Italian kale), 178
Ceanothus, 163
Cedrus libani (Lebanon cedar), 100
Centaurea cyanus (Bachelor's buttons),
 103
Centifolia roses, 132
Cephalotaxus harringtonia, 181
Cercis canadensis (Eastern redbud),
 139
Cerinthe major, 129

Chamaecyparis pisifera, 181
Chameleon plant *(Houttuynia cordata)*, 143-44
Chaste tree *(Vitex agnus-castus)*, 117, 161
Cherry laurel *(Prunus)*, 179
China roses, 133-34
Chives *(Allium schoenoprasum)*, 176
Circulation, 24-25
Cistus: C. albidus, 160; *C. ladanifer*, 160; *C. laurifolius*, 160; *C. x corbariensis*, 160
Clematis, 171; *C. alpina*, 172; *C. armandii*, 173; *C. macropetala*, 172; *C. montana*, 173; *C. orientalis*, 172-73; *C. tangutica*, 172; *C. texensis*, 133, 172; *C. viticella*, 133, 172; *C. x jackmanii* (Violet), 84, 172
Clerodendrum trichotomum (Harlequin glorybower), 158
Climbing plants: on archways, 50; description of, 50, 97-98; supports for, 73-74; types of, 169-73, 198
Clipped hedges, 43-44
Colchicums, 156
Color: accent palette of, 89-91; adjusting of, 90; arranging of, 93-94; balancing of, 86-87; blue, 127-29; brightness of, 85-86; contrast of, 83-84, 86, 93; cool, 84-85; diluting of, 86; green, 93; harmony of, 83-84; hot, 129-30; light, 106; palette of, 86-89; principal palette, 87-89; quirks of, 91-93; rhythm created by, 101; saturation of, 85-87; seasonal variations in, 109; sources of, 91; symmetry of, 94; variations in, 109; warm, 84-85
Color wheel, 84
Columbines *(Aquilegia* spp.), 123-24
Compost, 184-85
Concrete paving, 52-54
Concrete walls, 42-43
Condominiums, 35
Conifers, 180-81, 198
Containers, 72-73
Convallaria majalis (Lily-of-the-valley), 145
Convolvulus: C. sepium (Bindweed), 187-88; Morning glory, 23, 129
Cool colors, 84-85

Coreopsis verticillata, 121, 150, 152, 161
Cornus (Dogwood): *C. alba*, 91, 158, 167, 172; *C. alternifolia*, 140; *C. florida*, 140; *C. kousa*, 140; *C. nuttallii*, 140; *C. sanguinea*, 158; *C. stolonifera*, 158
Corokia cotoneaster (Oddball shrub), 152
Corsican mint *(Mentha requienii)*, 58, 147
Corydalis flexuosa, 165
Corylopsis spicata (Winter hazels), 156-57
Cosmos, 103
Cotinus coggygria (Purple smoke bush), 91, 100, 140-41
Cottage garden: aging of, 109; boundaries of. *See* Boundaries; components of, 4-6; designing of, 1; early types of, 7-8; hallmarks of, 4; increased interest in, 12; layout of. *See* Layout; origins of. *See* Origins; scale of, 2; structures in. *See* Structures
Cotula squalida, 99, 153, 161
Crocosmia, 129
Crocus *(Crocus tommasinianus)*, 120
Cupressocyparis leylandii (Leyland cypress), 181
Cynara, 151

D–F

Daffodils: *Geranium pratense*, 108; *Narcissus*, 119
Dahlia, 174-75
Damask roses, 131-32
Daphne *(Daphne odora)*, 103-04, 145, 147
Davidia involucrata, 114-15
Daylilies *(Hemerocallis)*, 124
Decking, 55
Decor, 6
Decorative ornaments. *See* Ornaments
Deer fern *(Blechnum spicant)*, 105, 164
Dianthus (Carnations): *D. deltoides*, 125; *D. gratianopolitanus*, 125; *D. plumarius*, 125-26
Diascias *(Diascia): D. barberae*, 126; *D. rigescens*, 126

Dicentra: D. formosa (Bleeding hearts), 105, 165; *D. spectabilis*, 165-66
Dictamnus albus (Gas plant), 103
Dierama pulcherrimum, 148
Digitalis spp. (Foxglove), 96; *D. grandiflora*, 168; *D. purpurea*, 168
Dill, 177
Dodecatheon spp. (Shooting stars), 165
Dogwood *(Cornus): C. alba*, 158; *C. alternifolia*, 140; *C. florida*, 140; *C. kousa*, 140; *C. nuttallii*, 140; *C. sanguinea*, 158; *C. stolonifera*, 158
Drumstick allium *(Allium sphaerocephalum)*, 149
Dry soil, 160-61

Earthworms, 21
Eastern redbud *(Cercis canadensis)*, 139
Echeveria, 161
Echinops ritro (Globe thistle), 149-50
Ecology, 12
Edges: grass pathway, 57; walkways, 57-58
Edgeworthia papyrifera, 157
Edible plants, 175-78
Eggplants, 177
Eglantine *(Rosa eglanteria)*, 104
Electricity, 23
England, 16-17
Entrances, 4
Entry structures: archways, 48-51; description of, 46; gaps as, 50-51; gates, 46-47; location of, 46; simplicity of, 46
Epaulette tree *(Pterostyrax hispida)*, 114
Epilobium watsonii (Willow herb), 187
Epimedium: E. grandiflorum, 167; *E. x perralchicum*, 167
Eremurus spp. (Foxtail lilies), 102, 108, 160
Eryngium, 161; *E. variifolium*, 143, 149
Escallonia: E. rubra, 180; *E. x langleyensis*, 180
Espaliers, 98
Eucryphia x nymansensis (Evergreen tree), 114, 163
Euphorbia characias subsp. *wulfenii*, 148-49

European elderberry (*Sambucus nigra*), 141
Evergreen barberries (*Berberis*), 180
Evergreen cape fuchsias (*Phygelius* x *rectus*), 147
Evergreen sweet box (*Sarcococca ruscifolia*), 147
Evergreen tree (*Eucryphia* x *nymansensis*), 114, 163
Evergreens, broadleaf, 179-80
Expansion joints, 54

Fall flowers, 155-57
Farmhouse, 32
Fatsia japonica, 151
Fences: dark-colored, 37; height of, 37; maintenance of, 38, 40; metal, 40; open, 36-37; painting of, 37; panel, 39; picket, 38-39; post-and-rail, 39; wooden, 37-40
Fertilizer, 186
Festuca glauca (Blue fescue), 91, 142
Filipendula ulmaria (Meadowsweet), 163
Fine-textured plants, 152-53
Flat-topped portal, 49
Floribundas, 138-39
Flower(s): fall, 155-57; rhododendrons, 118-19; roses. See Roses; winter, 155-57
Flowering plants: blue, 127-29; hot colors, 129-30; perennials, 121-27, 199-208; rhododendrons, 118-19; roses. See Roses; shrubs, 115-17; spring bulbs, 119-21; trees, 112-15
Flowering tobacco (*Nicotiana*), 104
Foeniculum vulgare, 152
Foliage: herbaceous plants, 141-44; shrubs for, 140-41; woody plants for, 139-41
Forget-me-nots (*Myosotis sylvatica*), 92, 174
Form: climbing plants for, 97-98; description of, 94-95; espaliers, 98; finding of, 95-96; mixing of, 96-97; plants for, 97-98, 147-50; sculpting plants for, 97; variety of, 96
Fothergilla: F. gardenii, 145; *F. major*, 145
Fountains, 74-76
Foxglove (*Digitalis* spp.), 96, 168

Foxtail lilies (*Eremurus* spp.), 102, 108, 160
Fragrant plants: roses, 131-32; types of, 103-04, 144-47
Fritillaria meleagris, 165
Fruits, 8, 158-59, 177-78
Fuchsia magellanica, 89, 116
Furniture: arranging of, 69-70; description of, 6, 67-68; location for, 69-70; materials for, 69; scale of, 69; style vs. comfort, 68

G-I

Gallica roses, 131
Gaps, 50-51
Garden activities, 25-26
Garden edging, 57
Garden spaces, 28
Gardening, 12
Gas plant (*Dictamnus albus*), 103
Gates, 46-47
Gayfeather (*Liatris spicata*), 149
Gazebos, 64-65
Geraniums (*Geranium*): *G. himalayense*, 121; *G. macrorrhizum*, 121-22; *G. nodosum*, 167; *G. phaeum*, 167; *G. pratense*, 108, 121; *G. psilostemon*, 122; *G.* x *magnificum*, 101, 121, 148; *G.* x *oxonianum*, 121, 172
Geum chiloense, 130, 143
Globe thistle (*Echinops ritro*), 149-50
Goatsbeard (*Aruncus dioicus*), 169
Goldenchain tree (*Laburnum* x *watereri*), 113-14
Goldenrods (*Solidago* spp.), 85, 130
Gooseneck loosestrife (*Lysimachia clethroides*), 150
Grape hyacinths (*Muscari* spp.), 101, 120
Grass walkways, 57
Grasses, 208
Gravel paving, 56
Green, 93
Greenhouses, 64
Ground plan, 2

Halesia spp. (Silverbells), 113
Hamamelis x *intermedia* (Witch hazel), 104, 156
Hardware, 47
Harlequin glorybower (*Clerodendrum trichotomum*), 158

Hedges: clipped, 43-44; conifer, 180-81, 198; description of, 43; plants for, 179-81; unclipped, 44-45; watering of, 45
Helictotrichon sempervirens (Blue oat grass), 85, 142, 144
Heliotrope (*Heliotropium arborensis*), 147
Helloborus: H. argutifolius, 157; *H. lividus*, 157; *H. niger*, 157; *H. orientalis*, 157
Hemerocallis (Daylilies), 124
Herbaceous foliage plants, 141-44
Herbs, 58, 175-77
Heuchera, 144
Himalayan blackberry (*Rubus procerus*), 188
Home: condominiums, 35; farmhouse, 32; Italian Renaissance Revival, 32-33; newest types of, 34-35; postwar construction of, 33-34; Queen Anne, 32; "ramblers," 33-34; Spanish Colonial, 33; townhouses, 35; traditional, 31-33; traditional styles of, 14, 31-32
Honeysuckle (*Lonicera*): *L. japonica*, 171; *L. periclymenum*, 171; *L. pileata*, 179; *L. sempervirens*, 171; *L. sempervirens sulphurea*, 171
Hoopworms, 189
Hostas, 165-66
Houttuynia cordata (Chameleon plant), 143-44
Hummingbirds, 79-80, 163 64
Hyacinthoides hispanica (Wood hyacinths), 165
Hyacinthus orientalis, 145
Hybrid musk roses, 137
Hybrid perpetual roses, 136
Hydrangea: H. anomala, 170; *H. aspera villosa*, 151-52; *H. macrophylla* (Bigleaf hydrangea), 115-16, 179

Industrial Revolution, 9-10
Irises (*Iris*): *I. pseudacorus*, 162; *I. versicolor*, 162; Japanese iris (*Iris ensata*), 162; Louisiana, 162; types of, 122-23, 148, 162
Irish moss (*Sagina subulata*), 58
Irrigation, 186-87
Island beds, 29

Italian Renaissance Revival home, 32-33

J–M

Japanese anemone hybrids (*Anemone* x *hybrida*), 155
Japanese iris (*Iris ensata*), 162
Japanese maple (*Acer palmatum*), 140, 157
Japanese sedge (*Carex morrowii*), 150, 167
Japanese snowbell tree: *Styrax japonicus*, 114-15; *Styrax obassia*, 114
Jekyll, Gertrude, 10-11
Jerusaleum sage (*Phlomis russeliana*), 85, 129, 149, 152
Juniperus virginiana, 181

Kale, 177-78
Kirengeshoma palmata, 168
Kiwi vine (*Actinidia kolomikta*), 169, 178
Knautia macedonica, 86, 124
Korean lilac (*Syringa patula*), 146
Korean spice viburnum (*Viburnum carlesii*), 145

Laburnum x *watereri* (Goldenchain tree), 113-14
Lamb's ears (*Stachys byzantina*), 142
Lamium maculatum, 167
Land: assessment of, 20-21; circulation of, 24-25; inventory of, 20-21
Lavandula spp. (Lavender): *L. angustifolia*, 146-47; *L.* x *intermedia*, 147
Lavatera thuringiaca (Tree mallow), 86, 117, 161
Lavender: *Aster* x *frikartii*, 84, 108; *Buddleia davidii*, 84; *Lavandula* spp., 146-47
Lavender cotton (*Santolina chamaecyparissus*), 142
Lawn: cottage garden vs., 11; historical views of, 11
Layout: boundaries, 26; elements of, 19; garden activity considerations, 25-26; needs-based assessment, 23-26; overview of, 2-4, 19-20; planted areas, 29; sample, 27; site analysis. *See* Site analysis; walk way, 26-27
Lebanon cedar (*Cedrus libani*), 100

Leucothoe walteri, 179
Leycesteria formosa, 158
Leyland cypress (*Cupressocyparis leylandii*), 181
Liatris spicata (Gayfeather), 149
Light: for highlighting, 78; natural, 22-23; ornamental, 76-78; plantings to enhance, 105-06; site analysis of, 22-23
Ligulari: *L. dentata*, 168; *L. przewalskii*, 95, 169
Lilies: *Lilium*, 126-27; *Zantedeschia*, 150
Lily-of-the-valley (*Convallaria majalis*), 145
Lime, 185
Lobelia: *Lobelia cardinalis*, 161-62; *Lobelia erinus*, 129
Lobularia maritima (Sweet alyssum), 147
Loebner magnolias (*Magnolia* x *loebneri*), 112
Lonicera (Honeysuckle): *L. japonica*, 171; *L. periclymenum*, 171; *L. sempervirens*, 171; *L. sempervirens sulphurea*, 171
Louisiana irises, 162
Lysimachia: *L. ciliata*, 144; *L. clethroides* (Gooseneck loosestrife), 150; *L. nummularia*, 90, 144, 162; *L. punctata*, 144

Magnolia: *M. sieboldii*, 112; *M. stellata* (Star magnolias), 112; *M.* x *loebneri* (Loebner magnolias), 112; *M.* x *soulangiana* (Pink saucer magnolia), 112
Mahonia aquifolium: *M. bealei*, 164; *M.* x *media*, 164; Oregon grape, 164
Maiden grass (*Miscanthus sinensis*), 94
Main walkway, 26-28
Maple trees: *Acer callilipes*, 157; *Acer davidii*, 157; *Acer pensylvanicum*, 158; Candy cane maple (*Acer pensylvanicum*), 97; Japanese maple (*Acer palmatum*), 140; Paperbark maple (*Acer griseum*), 91, 107, 158
Masonry walls. *See* Walls
Massing of plantings, 101-03
Matilija poppy (*Romneya coulteri*), 160

Meadow rue (*Thalictrum* spp.), 100, 152, 167
Meadowsweet (*Filipendula ulmaria*), 163
Mentha requienii (Corsican mint), 58, 147
Metal arch, 49
Metal fences, 40
Metal gate, 47
Metal pillars, 74
Mexican bamboo (*Polygonum cuspidatum*), 23
Mexican shell flower (*Tigridia pavonia*), 174
Microclimates, 15, 20-21
Monarda didyma (Bergamot), 144, 151, 164
Monkshoods (*Acontium napellus*), 92, 168
Monthretia, 129
Morning glory (*Convolvulus* spp.), 23
Morning glory (*Convolvulus tricolor*), 129
Mulch, 187
Muscari spp. (Grape hyacinths), 101, 120
Myosotis sylvatica (Forget-me-nots), 92, 174
Myrrhis odorata (Sweet cicely), 167

N–P

Narcissus (Daffodils), 119
Nasturtiums (*Tropaeolum majus*), 174
Needs assessment: circulation of property, 23-25; garden activities, 25-26
Nemophila menziesii (Baby blue-eyes), 129
Nepeta spp.: *N. govaniana*, 125, 129; *N.* x *faassenii*, 125
New Zealand flax (*Phormium* spp.), 95, 148
New Zealand hair sedge (*Carex comans*), 153
New Zealand sedges (*Carex buchananii*), 91, 99, 143
Nicotiana (Flowering tobacco), 104
Nigella, 103; *N. damascena*, 153
Night-time walks, 22
Noisette roses, 136-37
Nuisances, 23

Ocimum basilicum (Basil), 176
Oddball shrub *(Corokia cotoneaster)*, 152
Old garden roses, 131-33
Onion *(Allium giganteum)*, 149
Opaque shades, 78
Open spaces, 4-5
Oregano *(Origanum vulgare)*, 176
Oregon grape *(Mahonia aquifolium)*, 164
Oriental poppy *(Papaver orientale)*, 122
Origanum: O. rotundifolium, 161; *O. vulgare* (Oregano), 176
Origins: age of exploration, 9; in America, 11-13; early cottage gardens, 7-8; nineteenth century, 9-10; overview of, 6-7; twentieth century, 9-10
Ornaments: containers, 72-73; description of, 70-71; found objects, 80-81; lights, 76-78; placement of, 81; plantings placed next to, 101; sights and sounds, 71-72; supports, 73-74; water features, 74-76; wildlife, 79-80
Osmanthus: O. delavayi, 179; *O. heterophyllus*, 151, 179-80
Outbuildings: design of, 62-63; gazebos, 64-65; greenhouses, 64; playhouses, 64; sheds, 63-64; size of, 63
Outdoor lighting, 76-77
"Overstuffed" appearance, 102-03

Pacific Northwest: climate of, 14-16; coastal lowland sites, 16; construction styles, 14, 31; cottage gardens in, 13-14; England vs., 16-17; geology of, 17; growing conditions in, 14-16; homes of. *See* Home; microclimates of, 15-16; rainfall in, 14-15; regional descriptions, 13; summer season in, 15; winter in, 15; zones of, 191
Panel fences, 39
Papaver: P. orientale (Oriental poppy), 122; Poppies, 122
Paperbark maple *(Acer griseum)*, 91, 107, 158
Parrotia, 108
Passion flower *(Passiflora caerulea)*, 170

Pathways. *See also* Walkways: existing, 24-25; intersection of, 59; lighting of, 77-78; width of, 59
Pavers and paving: brick, 51-52; concrete, 52-54; gravel, 56; plantings between, 57-58; stone, 52; wooden, 55
Peaked arch, 48-49
Pelargonium, 121
Pepper cress *(Cardamine oligosperma)*, 187
Perennials, 121-27, 199-208
Perovskia atriplicifolia (Russian sage), 152
Persicaria: P. microcephala, 144, 177; *P. virginiana*, 144
Pests, 188-89
pH of soil, 21-22, 185-86
Phacelia campanularia, 129
Philadelphus: P. coronaria, 146; *P.* x *lemoinei*, 146
Phlomis russeliana (Jerusaleum sage), 85, 129, 149, 152
Phlox stolonifera, 167
Phormium spp. (New Zealand flax), 95, 148
Photinias, 179
Phygelius spp. (Cape fuchias), 85
Physostegia virginiana, 143
Picket fences, 38-39
Pink saucer magnolia *(Magnolia* x *soulangiana)*, 112
Plant(s): annuals, 209; arrangement of, 5; for bees, 163-64; berries, 158-59; for butterflies, 163-64; climbing. *See* Climbing plants; containers for, 72-73; description of, 111; edible, 175-78; feeding of, 186; fine-textured, 152-53; flowering. *See* Flowering plants; form use of, 147-50; fragrant, 103-04, 144-47; fruit, 8, 158-59; for hedges, 179-81; for hummingbirds, 163-64; light-colored, 106; malodorous, 104; quick growing, 173-75; roses. *See* Roses; sculpting, 97; shade, 164-69; site analysis of, 23; texture, 150-53; for tough soils, 159-63; woody, 139-41
Planted areas: design of, 2-3, 5; layout of, 29

Plantings: bark, 157-58; branches, 157-58; color of. *See* Color; darkness-based designs, 105-06; description of, 83; foliage color, 139-44; form of. *See* Form; fragrance of, 103-04, 144-47; light-based designs, 105-06; massing, 101-03; "overstuffed" appearance of, 102-03; rhythm of, 100-101; scale of, 99-100; seasonal considerations, 107-09; sharing of space, 107-08; texture of, 99-100; time considerations, 107-09
Playhouses, 64
Polemonium caeruleum, 143
Polyanthas, 138
Polygonum cuspidatum (Mexican bamboo), 23
Polystichum munitum (Sword fern), 164
Poppies *(Papaver)*, 122
Portland roses, 134
Post-and-rail fences, 39
Pratia pedunculata (Blue star creeper), 58
Primula: P. beesiana, 162; *P. bulleyana*, 162; *P. florindae*, 162; *P. japonica*, 162; *P. prolifera*, 162
Property: access points, 24; circulation of, 24-25
Pterostyrax hispida (Epaulette tree), 114
Pulmonaria: P. longifolia, 166; *P. rubra*, 167; *P. saccharata*, 166
Purple smoke bush *(Cotinus cogygria)*, 91, 100, 140-41

Q-S

Queen Anne home, 32

Railings, 60
"Ramblers," 33-34
Ranunculus ficaria, 108
Raoulia australis, 161
Rear garden, 3-4
Red flowering currant *(Ribes sanguineum)*, 115, 179
Reflecting pool, 76
Repeat-blooming roses, 133-39
Retaining walls, 61-62
Rheum palmatum (Rhubarb), 151
Rhododendrons, 118-19; *Rhododendron* x *mollis*, 103

Rhubarb *(Rheum palmatum)*, 151
Ribes sanguineum (Red flowering currant), 115, 179
Rodgersia: R. aesculifolia, 163; *R. tabularis*, 162-63
Romneya coulteri (Matilija poppy), 101, 160
Rosa: R. chinensis, 133; *R. eglanteria* (Eglantine), 104; *R. gallica officinalis*, 131; *R. gallica versicolor*, 131; *R. glauca*, 158-59; *R. moschata*, 136; *R. villosa*, 159; *R. x centifolia*, 132
Rosemary *(Rosmarinus officinalis)*, 175
Roses: alba, 132; Austin's, 137-38; Bourbon, 134-35; care of, 132-33; centifolia, 132; China, 133-34; damask, 131-32; description of, 130-31; favorite types of, 133; floribundas, 138-39; fruit-bearing, 158-59; hybrid musks, 137; hybrid perpetual, 136; Noisette, 136-37; old garden, 131-33; pegging down of, 134-35; polyanthas, 138; Portland, 134; repeat-blooming, 133-39; shrub, 137-38; tea, 135-36; thornless, 136; training of, 134-35
Rubus procerus (Himalayan blackberry), 188
Rudbeckia, 151, 161; Black-eyed susans, 129-30
Russian sage *(Perovskia atriplicifolia)*, 152

Sage *(Salvia officinalis)*, 175-76
Sagina subulata (Irish moss), 58, 153
Salvia: S. nemorosa, 90, 124-25, 125; *S. officinalis* (Sage), 175-76; *S. verticillata*, 101, 125; *S. x sylvestris*, 124-25, 137
Sambucus nigra (European elderberry), 141
Sandy soil, 184
Santolina chamaecyparissus (Lavender cotton), 142
Sarcococca, 103, 109; *S. ruscifolia* (Evergreen sweet box), 147
Saturated color, 85-87
Scabiosa columbaria, 128
Scale: of furniture, 69; of garden, 2; of plantings, 99-100

Schizophragma hydrangeoides, 170
Scilla sibirica, 101
Scrophularia auriculata, 142-43
Sculpting plants, 97
Sea hollies *(Eryngium). E. alpinum*, 128; *E. bourgatii*, 128; *E. x tripartitum*, 128
Seasons, 107-09
Secondary walkways, 28, 56
Sedges: Japanese sedge *(Carex morrowii)*, 150, 167; New Zealand hair sedge *(Carex comans)*, 153; New Zealand sedges *(Carex buchananii)*, 91, 99, 143; types of, 208
Sedums *(Sedum): S. sieboldii*, 161; *S. spathulifolium*, 161, 176; *S. spectabile*, 161
Sempervirum, 161
Sequoia sempervirens, 100
Sequoiadendron giganteum, 100
Serbian bellflower *(Campanula poscharskyana)*, 128
Serviceberry *(Amelanchier)*, 112-13
Shade plants, 164-69
Sheds, 63-64
Shooting stars *(Dodecatheon* spp.), 165
Shrubs: flowering, 115-17; foliage use of, 140-41; types of, 194-97; winter, 157
Siberian irises, 123
Silverbells *(Halesia* spp.), 113
Site analysis: inventory of site, 20-21; light, 22-23; nuisances, 23; plants, 23; soil, 21-22; view, 23; water, 21
Slugs, 188-89
Snowberries *(Symphoricarpos albus)*, 91
Soil: analysis of, 21-22; dry, 160-61; earthworms in, 21; fertility of, 183-84; improving of, 184-85; pH of, 21-22, 185-86; sandy, 184; testing of, 22; texture of, 183-84; wet, 161-63
Soleirolia soleirolii (Baby's tears), 58
Solidago spp. (Goldenrod), 85, 130
Spanish Colonial home, 33
Spiraea japonica, 141
Spring bulbs, 119-21
Spurge *(Euphorbia characias* subsp. *wulfenii)*
Spuria irises, 148

Stachys byzantina (Lamb's ears), 142
Stairways: description of, 60; lighting of, 77-78
Star magnolias *(Magnolia stellata)*, 112
Steps, 60-61
Stone paving, 52
Stone walls, 41-42
Structures: boundary. *See* Boundaries; description of, 6; entry. *See* Entry structures; home. *See* Home; outbuildings. *See* Outbuildings; retaining walls, 61-62; steps, 60-61; walkways. *See* Walkways
Style: furniture, 68; home, 14, 31
Styrax: S. japonicus (Japanese snowbell tree), 114-15; *S. obassia* (Japanese snowbell tree), 114
Supports, for climbing plants, 73-74
Sweet alyssum *(Lobularia maritima)*, 147
Sweet cicely *(Myrrhis odorata)*, 167
Sweet flag *(Acorus calamus)*, 163
Sword fern *(Polystichum munitum)*, 164
Symphoricarpos albus (Snowberries), 91
Syringa patula (Korean lilac), 146

T-V

Tea roses, 135-36
Texture, 99-100, 150-53
Thalictrum spp. (Meadow rue), 100; *T. aquilegifolium*, 152; *T. flavum* subsp. *glaucum*, 152, 167
Thornless roses, 136
Thuja plicata, 181
Thyme *(Thymus): T. pseudolanuginosus*, 175; *T. serpyllum*, 175; *T. vulgaris*, 175; *T. x citriodorus*, 175
Thymus pseudolanuginosus (Wooly thyme), 58, 161
Tigridia pavonia (Mexican shell flower), 174
Townhouses, 35
Tree(s): flowering, 112-15; types of, 192-93
Tree mallow *(Lavatera thuringiaca)*, 86, 117, 161
Tree peonies *(Paeonia)*, 115
Tricyrtis: T. formosa, 168; *T. hirta*, 168

Tropaeolum majus (Nasturtiums), 174
Trumpet vine *(Campsis): C. grandi-
flora*, 170; *C. radicans*, 86; *C.* x
tagliabuana, 170
Tulips *(Tulipa): T. bakeri*, 120;
T. clusiana, 120; *T. humilis*, 120;
T. tarda, 120

Unclipped hedges, 44-45
United States, 11-13

Vegetables, 177-78
Verbena bonariensis, 103, 174
Viburnum: *Viburnum carlesii* (Korean
spice viburnum), 145; *Viburnum
opulus*, 159; *Viburnum plicatum* var.
tomentosum, 97, 150; *Viburnum
sargentii*, 141; *Viburnum* x *bodnantense*, 97, 156
View: furniture placement for, 70;
site analysis, 23
Viola labradorica, 90
Violet *(Clematis* x *jackmanii)*, 84
Vitex agnus-castus (Chaste tree), 117,
161

W–Z
Walkways: brick paving, 51-52; concrete paving, 52-54; design of, 2-5,
58-59; edgings for, 57-58; existing,
24-25; grass, 57; gravel paving, 56;
layout of, 24, 26-27, 58; main, 26-
28; pavement of, 27; plantings for,
57-58; secondary, 28, 56; stone
paving, 52; subsidiary, 3; surfaces
of, 4, 51; width of, 46, 59; wooden,
55
Wall(s): brick, 41; concrete, 42-43;
drainage for, 61-62; retaining, 61-
62; stone, 41-42
Warm colors, 84-85
Water: irrigation uses, 186-87; ornamental features involving, 74-76;
site analysis, 21
Weeds, 56, 187-88
Weigela florida, 141, 171
Wet soil, 161-63
White bush anemones *(Carpenteria
californica)*, 88
Wildlife, 79-80
Willow herb *(Epilobium watsonii)*, 187
Window boxes, 73

Winter: description of, 15, 108-9;
flowers for, 155-57
Winter hazels *(Corylopsis spicata)*,
156-57
Wisteria floribunda, 170
Witch hazel *(Hamamelis* x *interme-
dia)*, 104, 156
Wood hyacinths *(Hyacinthoides his-
panica)*, 165
Wooden arch, 48
Wooden decking, 55
Wooden fences: description of, 37-
38; maintenance of, 38; panel
fence, 39; picket fence, 39; post-
and-rail fence, 39; setting of, 38,
40; styles of, 38-39
Wooden gate, 47
Wooden walkways, 55
Woody plants, 139-41
Wooly thyme *(Thymus pseudolanugi-
nosus)*, 58, 161

Yucca: Y. filamentosa, 102, 148; *Y. flaccida*, 148

Zantedeschia (Lilies), 150

ABOUT THE AUTHOR

An avid gardener since childhood, Andrew Schulman studied both landscape architecture and landscape history
before beginning design practice in the Pacific Northwest.
He writes for many garden periodicals and is a regular con-
tributor to *Fine Gardening* magazine. Andrew tends his own
cottage garden in Seattle with his wife, his daughter, and one
great big dog.